Community Organization
and
Social Planning

Community Organization
and
Social Planning

Robert Perlman
and
Arnold Gurin

Published jointly by
John Wiley & Sons, Inc.
New York • London • Sydney • Toronto
and
The Council for Social Work Education,
New York, N.Y.

To Bernice and Helen

Preface

This textbook,* along with several other publications, is the product of a comprehensive study of the community organization curriculum in graduate social work education sponsored by the Council on Social Work Education.

This volume reviews and examines community organization and social planning and the problems inherent in its practice. In compiling the information necessary for this examination, the staff of the Community Organization Curriculum Development Project conducted interviews with practitioners and made field visits to a number of programs in different areas of the country, including projects in both voluntary and governmental agencies at national, state, and local levels. This textbook reflects these studies as well as the project staff's review of the literature in the field. Included in that review is a thorough consideration of the attempts that have been made to date to develop a conceptual framework for community-organization practice.

The key purpose of the textbook is to provide faculty and students with current, relevant, and useful information and insights for use in schools of social work and other disciplines concerned with preparing

* This textbook draws on its companion volume, *Community Organizers and Social Planners*, by Joan Levin Ecklein and Armand Lauffer (Wiley, 1972) for illustrative material. The complete contents of the Ecklein and Lauffer book are included here as an appendix with the kind permission of the authors. An asterisk in the reproduced contents indicates all chapters and cases in the companion volume which have been quoted here.

people for practice in this area. It will also be of value for agency in-service training and continuing-education programs. This textbook can be used independently, but its effectiveness will be enhanced when used in conjunction with the companion casebook, *Community Organizers and Social Planners: A Casebook*, by Joan Ecklein and Armand Lauffer, also copublished by CSWE and John Wiley & Sons.

Other publications resulting from the community organization curriculum study are an overview of the project, *Community Organization Curriculum in Graduate Social Work Education: Report and Recommendations* by Arnold Gurin (published by CSWE); a guide for faculty, *A New Look at Field Instruction: Education for Application of Practice Skills in Community Organization and Social Planning* by Jack Rothman and Wyatt Jones (co-published by CSWE and Association Press); and *Students in Schools of Social Work: A Study of Characteristics and Factors Affecting Career Choice and Practice Concentration* by Deborah Golden, Arnulf M. Pins, and Wyatt Jones (published by CSWE).

Publication of this textbook and the other materials of the project occurs at a significant time in the history of our society and social work education. The many social problems facing our nation today underscore the need for personnel with competence in community organization and social planning; the textbook and the material produced by this project can assist in the preparation of needed qualified staff.

The Council on Social Work Education and the field of community organization and social planning owe a debt of gratitude to Dr. Robert Perlman and Dr. Arnold Gurin for preparing this volume; Dr. Gurin for his effective leadership of the total project; and the total project staff and the advisory committee for their many contributions. Thanks are expressed to the Office of Juvenile Delinquency and Youth Development, Social and Rehabilitation Service, Department of Health, Education, and Welfare, whose grant made this project possible.

Arnulf M. Pins
Executive Director
Council on Social Work Education

New York, N.Y.
June 1971

Acknowledgments

We are grateful for the assistance and the interest of a number of people who contributed to the production of this book. Its foundations were built during the Community Organization Curriculum Development Project and we are indebted to our colleagues in that project— Wyatt C. Jones, Joan Ecklein, Armand Lauffer, and Jack Rothman—for the thinking that we did together.

We also thank Violet Sieder, who drafted material on the community work of service agencies that appears in Chapter 7. David Jones, O.B.E., Vice Principal of the National Institute for Social Work Training in London, contributed substantially through his co-authorship of "Neighborhood Service Centers," which was published by the Department of Health, Education, and Welfare and which we drew upon extensively in Chapters 5 and 6. Gunnar Dybwad and Thomas P. Holland were generous in helping with the illustrative material on mental retardation in Chapter 8.

We appreciate the thoughtful comments we received from David M. Austin, who read the manuscript, and we thank Ruth Berger, Ione Vargus, and Ronald Walters for reviewing specific parts of the book. We are particularly grateful for the loyal and tireless work of Ruth Daniels, Marianne Muscato, and Betty Akberian in preparing more drafts of these chapters than we care to remember. Its final version is entirely our responsibility.

Robert Perlman
Arnold Gurin

Contents

CHAPTER 1

An Emerging Discipline

Compassion for victims of misfortune, anger at injustice, and fear of unrest have impelled people throughout this country's history to turn their thoughts and energies to our social problems. Whether compassion, anger, or fear predominated has depended on the state of knowledge and beliefs concerning social problems and on the interests and ideologies of those who sought to resolve the problems.

One can, for instance, define poverty, which is the most general and persistent of our social problems, as the misfortune of the individual or as an injustice for a group or class of people. Either definition will profoundly affect the actions taken to deal with poverty. A program based on the concept of misfortune and animated by compassion will stress the provision of help to the victim. Centuries of charitable activities have taken this approach, often based on the religious obligations of the more fortunate to help the less fortunate—an approach that usually validated the existing social institutions and arrangements.

On the other hand, if social injustice in the form of systematic deprivation is seen as the root of problems, the emphasis shifts to finding ways of altering something within the arrangements of society. In actuality, however, it is difficult to make so sharp a distinction. Efforts to deal with individual misfortune develop into programs for organizational or institutional change when it is perceived that individualized solutions are not adequate. Conversely, broad programs of social change require implementation at the level of individuals and groups to assure that their potential benefits will be realized.

1

Philanthropy and social reform are two organized approaches to dealing with social problems. As we indicate in a brief historical review in the following chapter, American philanthropic and reform movements have been closely interrelated, particularly around the turn of the century when many of today's institutional forms originated. The efforts of philanthropists, reformers, and a wide assortment of voluntary groups resulted in the creation of new governmental and voluntary agencies to provide financial aid and social services to people in distress and also in legislation designed to protect vulnerable individuals and groups against economic exploitation, to assure individual rights and, at least in intent, to distribute social benefits more equitably.

Contemporary agencies and institutions in the human services (health, welfare, education, housing, work training, corrections, rehabilitation, and others) incorporate many different responses to human needs. Some of their programs rest on the view of these as a matter of individual difficulty, deficit, or misfortune; others look on them as defects in the way society and its institutions function; many programs incorporate both approaches. Still others are weighted heavily in the direction of social control and are based primarily on fear of the deviant and the desire to contain him. Increasingly services are being provided as a matter of right and are based on the assumption of collective responsibility for meeting the normal needs of people in an industrial, urban society.

Human services today are provided through a complex network of formal organizations differentiated by functions, auspices, and domains. Over the decades specialization and bureaucratization have developed in the human services as they have in all aspects of modern industrial society. They have also taken the form of professionalism. Agencies and programs are subject to the hazards of all bureaucracies in their tendencies toward rigidity and toward concern with maintenance of the organization sometimes at the expense of meeting the needs they were designed to serve.

The growing complexities in these fields have given rise to new kinds of tasks that are concerned not with rendering services directly but rather with the development of policies and programs and with the direction of organizations. There has been a parallel evolution of specialized tasks in the service of citizens' groups, consumers' organizations, and voluntary associations concerned with social problems. It is with these tasks and with the practitioners responsible for them that this book is concerned.

It is our contention that increasingly the professionals who carry out organizing and planning functions in the human services represent an emerging discipline, one that cuts across such fields as education and social welfare, health, and urban planning. More and more, this new breed of practitioner is coming to utilize similar methods and techniques. But something more fundamental provides a common base for their efforts. Social needs and problems are so inextricably interrelated and intermingled that traditional boundaries between fields and disciplines are being everywhere breached. Clearly, the issues involved in poverty, racism, and population growth and movement demand interventions that knit together the best knowledge and skills from many sources.

Today's search for more effective methods of organizing and planning and for more comprehensive approaches to human needs and services resembles efforts made 60 and 70 years ago. At that time reformers and philanthropists, with a mixture of motivations, were developing new institutions and techniques. Typical of their efforts were the charity organization societies dedicated to uplifting and reforming the poor. These societies soon embraced specialization and professionalism. Social work emerged as the profession of caseworkers and friendly home visitors. But the demand for economies in fund-raising and the need for coordination of services gave rise to a further specialization. Community chests and councils of social agencies were organized, and by the mid-1920's their professional leaders, most of them social workers, were calling their work "community organization."

The early efforts at community organization were directed almost entirely to middle- and upper-class philanthropists and volunteers, one of whose motivations was to find more efficient ways of dispensing charitable funds. In other quarters there was an uneasiness about the decline of the small American community with its face-to-face contacts and its "grass-roots democracy." Some social philosophers were proposing to develop community organization as a means of countering both the centralization and the professionalization of decision-making in American life. Simultaneously with these two developments, another group, concerned with guiding the physical growth of cities, was emerging as the new profession of city planning. Their emphasis was on "bricks and mortar" and on the most productive use of land. Some were deeply interested in social considerations and some were trying to develop a technology for planning.

America's search for efficiency and its headlong growth after World War I were rudely shaken by an economic depression of critical proportions in the 1930's. The social programs that had been devised at the turn of the century to deal with the worst excrescences of the Industrial Revolution were overwhelmed. Neither private philanthropy nor state-supported agencies could deal with the widespread unemployment and deprivation. Changes came rapidly in Roosevelt's New Deal— an elaborate system of public assistance and social insurance, public housing, and Federal laws protecting labor's right to organize. These were the fruits of a coalition of urban politicians, liberals, and trade unions who were convinced that only Federal intervention on a massive scale could match the economic and social dislocations of that period.

The programs they fashioned also proved unequal to new demands. The pressures that built up after World War II broke, in the 1960's like a pounding sea upon America's institutions. Deprived and disadvantaged people, led by black Americans, vowed that through their own efforts they would overcome their poverty, their ostracism in slums, and their exclusion from America's affluence. In an uneasy partnership with liberals in Washington and in city halls, the "war on poverty" was to be waged through "community action," which was adopted as a main strategy of social change by groups acting under the aegis of "community-action agencies" supported by the Federal government and localities. It was employed by black, Puerto Rican, Chicano and other groups acting independently of those agencies.

The strategy of community action had two prongs. The poor were to be organized as a political force to influence specific decisions concerning the allocation of resources. Perhaps more important, their political "muscle" would be strong enough to place representatives of the poor in the important decision-making centers of the community so that spokesmen for the disadvantaged would make schools, hospitals, the public housing authority, and the welfare system more responsive to their needs.

The other prong of community action involved the establishment of new mechanisms for the delivery of social services. These new agencies would be located in the neighborhoods of the poor, would be controlled by them, and would offer a range of services more relevant to their problems—skill training and aggressive employment placement that would overcome racial discrimination; legal aid for dealing with landlords, creditors, and foot-dragging welfare departments; credit unions and buying cooperatives; and health services that would be closer to people in need than the impersonal out-patient clinics of city hospitals. Some of these services were to help the ghetto residents as a group or community; others were to assist individuals to "make it up and out" of the urban and rural slums.

These were the expectations. In many respects they had their counterpart in the community development movement in Asian, African, and Latin American countries, where the United Nations and other agencies were stressing self-help projects and village-level decision-making. By most accounts, both community action in this country and community development in the developing nations accomplished only a few of their objectives and failed to reach their most significant goals.

Among the positive achievements of community action was the articulation of problems and needs as perceived by the poor themselves. Their living conditions and their frustration and anger were brought closer to the consciousness of the majority of Americans, although it is difficult to know how much of this was accomplished by the violence that broke out in many cities during this period. Clearly, the organizing of many people who had not participated before in collective action helped to train a cadre of indigenous leaders better equipped for the demands and opportunities of the 1970's. Much the same can be said of thousands of paraprofessional workers who got training and jobs in the social services.

It is still too early to assess the long-range effects of the negotiations and confrontations between organized residents and consumers and some of the established service systems, such as public education and public welfare. Certainly the principle of participation in policy-making by those affected has become more generally accepted. The history of urban renewal (nicknamed "Negro removal" in the 1950's) was dismal from the point of view of residents of slum areas and no doubt contributed to this acceptance, as did the increasing strength of the minority groups who were insisting on having more than a token voice in decisions. In any case, the policy of including "community representatives" had by the end of 1970 become an accepted part of the planning of mental health programs, Model Cities projects, the administration of public housing, the operation of health services, and many other programs.

But if the success of community action is to be measured by its impact on poverty in America, it did not succeed. In part it failed because the organizations of the poor did not amass sufficient influence on their own or through alliances to make lasting changes in the social structures they were trying to affect. In part, their frustrations and failures stemmed from the misplaced hope that small-scale, locally based activities could substitute for jobs and adequate income and housing, which depend on national policies and national resources. The wish that self-help activities and "participation" *per se* could take the place of these indispensable provisions proved self-defeating in terms of the main goal of the "war on poverty."

There was still another basic reason for the inability of community action to achieve its primary goal. Neither the "grass-roots" organizers nor the professional planners and experts had clear notions of what policies and programs would be most effective in dealing with the complexities of poverty. Rhetoric about "basic institutional change" did not specify with sufficient clarity the ends to be achieved and the means to be used. Militancy and radicalism reflected a style of action—undoubtedly necessary in many circumstances—but did not project a well-defined program and strategy.

By the same token, community organization as practiced since the 1920's in councils of social agencies, composed mostly of the socio-economic elite, had had no appreciable impact on major social problems. In part, the limited scope of the health and welfare councils, focused on coordination of services among voluntary agencies, hobbled their effectiveness. In part, community organization among middle-class-dominated agencies, like community action among the poor, stressed the process of bringing people together for joint activity, but it also lacked a policy foundation for meaningful social change. Nevertheless, practice in the community welfare councils had been the principal source of conceptualization for the teaching of community organization that by 1960 was being offered in social work schools across the country.

In the last few years there has been a quickening interest in the analysis and formulation of policies that can inform action. This interest in "social policy" or "social planning" extends well beyond the traditional confines of the field of social welfare. Moreover, it stresses planning and action not only at the community level but also at the state and national levels—and it is concerned with the flow of authority and resources among these levels.

By accretion, then, there has developed a practice with many facets. It is addressed to change and improvement in the human services. It encompasses voluntary groups who organize to press for changes as well as the institutions and agencies that are the target of their efforts. Its practitioners function as organizers and consultants to these citizen groups that operate outside of the established agencies and as policy and program planners within the agencies.

One of the difficulties in a field of activity as young and fluid as this has to do with semantics. The terms "community organization" and "social planning" are subject to many interpretations. Some writers and practitioners have used the former to refer to organizing population groups to act on goals of their own choosing. "Planning" has often been applied to the work of policy development within agencies and to coordination among organizations. Neither term is, in our view, adequate to describe what is now evolving. Rather than invent a new terminology prematurely, we have resorted to an awkward phrase—community organization and social planning—in the hope that the accumulated meanings of these terms, taken together, will convey the essence of this practice. In Chapter 4 we discuss the elements of practice as we see them and present a working definition of community organization and social planning.

What are the boundaries and the foundations of this emerging discipline? With what professions is it, or should it be, affiliated—social work, urban and regional planning, public administration? And with what fields of activity—education, housing, health, economic development, social welfare services? The answers to all these questions are fluid and unclear. We take the position in this book that there is no single profession that today encompasses all the facets of the practice of community organization and social planning, and that by its nature, this practice is an aspect of many fields, each with its own area of responsibility.

The market demand for practitioners in this field in the United States and in other countries is growing. The people who perform these functions are known by various names and come from different professional backgrounds, some without formal training. They operate in many fields and settings. A few illustrations will suffice.

Educators are increasingly concerned about establishing effective relationships between school and community in order to resolve problems in the functioning of the educational system. Other professionals have been involved for decades in the organization of people and services to improve health conditions in the community. More recently, psychiatrists and other mental health personnel have been trying to organize a more "therapeutic" community in which social relationships and service networks will mitigate or prevent mental illness. Physical planners, who in the past tended to be concerned with land use, economic development, and spatial arrangements, are now focusing their attention more on social policies and relationships. And increasingly, there is a counterpoint to all these activities in the work of organizers and advocates of consumers of these very services.

In the welter of unresolved questions about this evolving practice, one thing at least appears clear. The major unsolved problems of our times call for comprehensive approaches that cut across fields and professions and demand close collaboration by a wide range of social sciences and applied disciplines. It would be unwise, assuming that it were even possible, to propose tight definitions of the boundaries and content of this new discipline at this time. We prefer in this text to focus on the practitioner and on the tasks and problems with which he must grapple in his environment. Many of those tasks can be identified within several different program fields.

The role of practitioner has developed to assist organizations to identify and measure social problems, to understand their causation, to devise new approaches to their resolution, and, not the least important, to gain support for the actions chosen to deal with them. The practitioner is necessarily an adjunct of an organized group that is engaged in these processes. Unlike a writer, for example, who is a social critic (and may contribute much to the identification of social problems), the practitioner is not independent; he serves a group interest.

The practitioner is necessarily a specialist or an expert. If he were not, there would be no reason for employing him. But there are alternative bases for his expertness. In some instances it derives from nothing more than the fact that he spends his full time at a task rather than working at it in a limited way as most volunteers must. In this case his contribution rests not on superiority of talent or training but simply on the marginal increase in knowledge and facility that comes with additional investments of time.

On the other hand, the practitioner's expertise may derive from very substantial components of knowledge, talent, and skill, based on considerable training. In fact, there are various levels or kinds of practice, and one of the major unanswered questions in this field is whether there is any "glue"—conceptually or empirically—that holds so diverse a set of activities and tasks together. How much similarity in responsibilities is there, for example, between the neighborhood organizer and the policy planner in a service bureaucracy?

The concepts of this field that are reviewed in Chapter 3 reflect differing views on this issue. It would be more accurate to say that the writers whose approaches are summarized in that chapter were responding to the requirements of different periods in the development of this field, each emphasizing what seemed to him to be the core of practice.

We argue in Chapter 4 that it is useful to think in terms of a common framework that embraces all aspects of the practice of community organization and social planning. The key to comprehending this view lies in an understanding of the *organizational contexts* in which practice takes place. As we have pointed out, the exercise of organizing and planning functions is not the responsibility of an individual change agent but the expression of an organized effort that has sponsorship, legitimation, purpose, and resources. The tasks that the individual organizer and planner must perform are set by the organizational functions to which his efforts are committed.

This perspective, based on observations in the field, suggests that *the characteristics of organizations will significantly determine the tasks of the practitioner and that these tasks will vary according to the purpose, composition, power position, and structure of the organization.* Instead of dealing with countless variations along these dimensions, our framework proposes that practice can be productively analysed in three organizational contexts, each with its typical issues and tasks facing the practitioner. Chapters 5 to 9 deal with these three arenas of community organization and social planning.

We first survey practice with the *voluntary association,* composed of a membership that is developed around common interests, status, or residence. In Chapters 5 and 6 we review lower-class and middle-class organizations, their development, and their tendencies to change over time in certain predictable ways, all of which have direct implications for the practitioner. In Chapter 7, the *agencies that provide services* directly to consumers or clients are examined in order to understand the work of specialists responsible for their community work and for program planning and development. Whether it is a school or a welfare department, a housing project or a health center, the organization that offers services must continually adapt to a changing environment at the same time that it must maintain itself as a going concern. These requirements are usually handled by administrator-planners.

Finally, in Chapters 8 and 9, we look at *planning organizations.* Here the ability to decide on policies and implement programs is affected by the strength of the central council or commission in relation to the autonomy of the participating organizations. Decision-making powers are problematical in these settings and this colors the work of the practitioner.

In all these settings the practitioner must relate to many groups and individuals in their roles as citizens, consumers, policy makers, or victims of circumstances that they want to alter. We shall view this entire field of activity—politicians, citizens, movements, and agencies—from the point of view of the practitioner. He must think and act in the interest of the organization he is serving and must take into account its relationship to other groups. This calls for deliberate, planful behavior on his part that is qualitatively different from what is expected of a voluntary participant in a social change enterprise. It is this behavior that we call "practice."

It is not likely that practitioners or students will be equally identified with each of the types of intervention this broad field includes. Some will specialize in the organizational work with voluntary associations. Others will be specialists in the community work responsibilities of service agencies, and still others will function for the most part in interorganizational planning settings. While they are engaged in very different and oftentimes conflicting purposes and responsibilities, several elements tie them together: (1) a body of theoretical understanding concerning institutions and organizations in general; (2) concrete knowledge about particular systems, such as the health or social welfare or education network; (3) a problem-solving approach to the solution of social problems; (4) analytic competence; and (5) skills in communication and in interaction with other people.

Our decision to write a textbook on this subject would imply that these activities constitute a field of practice with principles and methods that can be transmitted to students and practitioners. The reality is quite otherwise. The field that this book attempts to describe is ill-defined. The body of knowledge on which it should rest is spotty and unsystematic, and there are few reliable guides or proven methods that can be transmitted.

What is available is a loose collection of ideological orientations, assumptions as to what are effective strategies for social change, and a welter of experiences only partially recorded and analyzed. On what basis, then, do we have the temerity to undertake the writing of a textbook on "community organization and social planning"? For all the ambiguities involved in the meaning of those terms, our answer is that they point nevertheless to tasks that are real, vital, and of growing importance. And for all the uncertainties, there is at least an emerging body of practice that can be described.

We approach our task with a sense of urgency and a feeling of caution. The turbulent social problems of our times—poverty, racism, imbalances in the distribution of power, and the disaffection of many young people —account for our feeling of urgency. But the gravity of these problems and the hunger for solutions make us cautious and compel us to clarify what we intend to do.

This is not a text on social problems as such nor on social policies. It does not undertake, for example, to recommend an effective program for income maintenance, specific forms of citizen participation, or designs for "ideal" communities. It is concerned with how people engaged in an emerging field of practice can effectively analyze and act on issues such as these. These people have a share of the responsibility for intervening in a period of social change whose nature and magnitude are difficult to comprehend. Surrounded by uncertainty, they must nevertheless respond to the urgent need for decisions and action.

This is the background and motivation for this textbook, which is intended for students in professional schools and for practitioners in many settings. Its purpose is to contribute to a greater understanding, on the part of all who are engaged in community organization and planning, of the problems involved in practice, of the ways in which those problems are being addressed, and of the growing body of knowledge that can hopefully contribute to more effective solutions in the future.

CHAPTER 2

The Roots of Practice

CAUSES AND REFORMERS

America has been prodigal in its production of social problems and prodigious in its efforts to cope with them. The costs of its remarkable development have fallen heavily and unevenly among the economic, racial, ethnic, and regional groups who farmed its lands, manned its machines, and built its cities. But always—in the face of hunger and disease, slavery and slums, exploitation and injustice—there have been people who protested, organized, and planned.

Observers have frequently remarked on the tendency of Americans to form associations of all kinds. De Tocqueville wrote:

"As soon as several of the inhabitants of the United States have taken up an opinion or a feeling which they wish to promote in the world, they look out for mutual assistance; and as soon as they have found one another out, they combine. From that moment they are no longer isolated men, but a power seen from afar, whose actions serve for an example and whose language is listened to."[1]

The practice that is the subject of this book stems from the rich history that these men and women made, working through a variety of organiza-

---

[1] Alexis de Tocqueville, *Democracy in America*, pp. 117–118, "Of the Use Which the Americans Make of Public Associations in Civil Life," Vol. II, New York: Vintage Books, 1960. (The Henry Reeve Text, rev. by Francis Bowen and further edited by Phillips Bradley).

tional forms. These different types of organizations, which continue today to constitute the arena in which community organization and social planning are practiced, included self-help groups, special-interest associations, single-purpose or "cause" organizations, broad social and political movements, and agencies established to provide services and later to coordinate the work of the providers.

This chapter takes a brief backward glance at such organized efforts and at their place in the development of social action in this country. First, however, we shall present some general comments on the nature of social action and social change and on the groups that labor to bring them about. We shall begin with the issue of identifying social problems.

The decision to do something about a need or problem—indeed, the very recognition that one exists—rests on a value judgment. It reflects a desire to change social arrangements in order to bring them closer to what some group considers a better state of affairs. The value positions of such groups are not abstractions; they are the anguish and bitterness of victims, the outrage of humanitarians, the fear of men threatened by rising discontent, or the response to "deviant" behavior that a majority cannot accept and therefore tries to control.

One task of the specialized practioner—and he is the focal point of this textbook—involves this process of identifying social needs and problems. Along with others, he "produces" social problems by calling attention to deprivations. He helps to place them on the agenda for action by stimulating awareness about them, as crusaders for causes have done over the years. But as those men and women knew, more than rhetoric is required. The practitioner must document the nature and extent of a problem, describe and measure its impact on people's lives, and help find solutions.

But everyone does not agree on the agenda for action. Groups in society differ in their values and interests and therefore perceive problems and their causation in different ways. For example, it is still widely believed in some quarters that poverty is an individual affliction subject to solution, if at all, only by changing the attitudes and behavior of the individuals affected. Another view, which considers social intervention and individual freedom incompatible, accepts poverty as socially determined but looks on it as the necessary price to be paid for economic progress.

Depending on a group's interests and its ideology, the same condition can be considered perfectly satisfactory or a burning injustice. Differences in values and goals often become political conflicts between groups, with some promoting particular changes and others resisting them. What is singularly important in this competition is that groups also differ in the amount of power they can muster. This suggests another of the practitioner's functions—the analysis of power resources and relationships and the mobilization of influence to achieve certain ends. But what ends?

Some resources are addressed to *individuals* who are problems to themselves or to others, in order to help them cope more effectively with their environment. This is the case with a mother's mental illness, a young man's lack of employable skills, or the law-violating behavior of a juvenile. Programs of training, education, therapy, and correction fall into this category. There can be no doubt that these supportive, remedial, and rehabilitative services will continue to be necessary for people who are culturally, mentally, or physically handicapped.

But increasingly in our highly complex society, attention is being given to the *institutions* and structural arrangements that generate social problems and that thwart the satisfaction of people's needs. Basic criticisms are being made of the deficiencies in society that result in deprivation and degradation of human beings, the contamination of man's physical environment, and the type of deviant behavior that is destructive to the self and to others. Moreover, the ways in which established agencies deliver educational and therapeutic services are under fire. Those responsible for the management of these agencies are being pressed to examine their assumptions and modes of operation in order to counteract existing inadequacies and achieve more positive results than are now evident.

The authors of this text subscribe to the view that the practice of community organization and social planning would have no *raison d'être* if it did not rest on the assumptions that many human problems are social in their causation, that there is a societal obligation to do something about them, and that they can be reduced or resolved if appropriate means can be found. In our view this practice is part of a new world view that treats the utopian visions of earlier times as realistic aspirations for the immediate future and rejects many aspects of human misery as no longer necessary or tolerable.

Thus, practitioners of community organization and social planning ought not to be essentially reactive but should actively search out interventions that anticipate and forestall social hardships and dislocations. This has been the stance of countless groups and organizations at every stage in this country's development. We turn now to some observations about the nature of these change-oriented groups.

There is a tendency for the structure, the style, and even the purpose of these groups to change with the passage of time. Thus, for example, a movement led by a crusader and his disciples often turns into a formal organization, taking on the original "cause" as its permanent responsibility or function. By the same token, informal groups that originally came together to do what seemed necessary for themselves or helpful for their neighbors were frequently transformed into voluntary associations; some of their functions later became institutionalized in the form of governmental agencies whose systematized operations might not be recognized by their founding fathers.

All these types of social action must be seen, then, as fluid and dynamic in both form and function. The general tendency, though by no means a universal one, is the movement over time from informal to more institutionalized structures and functions. We briefly note here the main forms of organized social action.

Reliance on the assistance of family, friends, and neighbors has always been an important way of meeting life's exigencies in America, especially in the days of frontier settlements. *Self-help activities* provided important supports in times of emergency. Some never developed beyond informal arrangements; others provided the base for more sustained programs. A few self-help groups, spurred by innovative ideas of communal living, went off to form utopian communities and "capsule ventures in socialism."[2] Others tried to cope with the precarious life of urban wage-earners by organizing sick benefits, life insurance, burial facilities, and loan funds—self-protective measures that were sometimes combined by immigrant groups with cultural and recreational programs. Under the sponsorship of the Catholic Church, the Jewish community, and Protestant denominations, some of these self-help enterprises developed in time into what are today substantial networks of health and social services.

Special interest groups of industrial workers, farmers, manufacturers, retailers, consumers, and racial, ethnic, and other minorities have always been a potent force for social change in this country. Since the earliest days of the colonies along the Eastern seaboard, by mobilizing and concentrating their influence and activity, they have advanced the interests of their members in the rough and competitive marketplaces of America. Economic interest and a shared socioeconomic status have been the cement that has held together associations of miners, bankers, druggists, grape pickers, physicians, plumbers, and veterans. These groupings have

[2] Arthur M. Schlesinger, *The American as Reformer*, Cambridge: Harvard University Press, 1951, p. 46.

existed at every class level in American society, with organizations of the poor among the latest to emerge.

The struggles of these groups to protect their members' position have ranged from long-term educational programs to sharp and violent confrontations. In general, interest groups representing middle- and upper-class people have tended to rely on legislative lobbying, public education, and legal action. Organizations that speak for workers, small farmers, and the economically disadvantaged have depended to a greater extent on overt pressure, strikes, and public demonstrations.

A body of techniques has been forged out of the experience of interest groups. Their use of voting strength, picketing, sit-ins, and other methods has been passed along to an army of indigenous leaders and paid officials serving a variety of special causes. The same can be said of another type of social action in the American tradition—the *radical movements* dedicated to fundamental social and economic change. Although their leaders came from all social classes, their appeal has been primarily to working-class men and the economically dispossessed. Some, like Henry George's Single Tax Movement, were conceived entirely in American terms: others were influenced by Marxist thinking, advocating control of the means of production by the working class.

That Americans showed a "national preference for evolution over revolution"[3] and never mustered a majority for these radical movements should not conceal the fact that many of their policies (such as regulation of monopolies and guarantees of the right to organize) were taken over by the established political parties and eventually enacted into law. Another avenue included the "third party" efforts of the Populists, the "bull moose" Progressives, and others. The organizers and agitators of these dissident political movements were often effective in influencing attitudes and sometimes events, but their work has never taken shape as a generalizeable method for achieving change.

As a means of grappling with social problems, the two-party system of politics has been more congenial to America's essentially pragmatic ideology, better suited perhaps to the balancing of strong pluralistic interests, ethnic differences, and regional loyalties than separate radical political parties. The major parties have served as broad organizations within which negotiation and bargaining have resulted in piecemeal commitments to limited social and economic changes.

The highly pluralistic pattern of American social and political life reflected the great heterogeneity of its population. This heterogeneity,

[3] Schlesinger, *op. cit.*, p. 10.

among other factors, has fostered voluntary groups and activity. In other industrialized countries with more homogeneous populations, there has been a stronger tendency to turn to the government for social programs and provisions.

In colonial times friendly societies "organized along national, occupational, or religious lines" dispensed material aid and helped to establish colleges and other institutions.[4] A most delightful story is told by Benjamin Franklin of his part in founding the Pennsylvania Hospital, when he talked the provincial assembly into matching pound for pound what he raised from private contributions. Franklin closes the account with the observation that "I do not remember any of my political manoeuvers, the success of which gave me at the time more pleasure."[5]

The shape of things to come was clear well before the Civil War. In 1840 Ralph Waldo Emerson attended a congress in Boston called by the "Friends of Universal Reform."[6] Only four years before this an unsympathetic critic had described the pattern of the reformers in this way:

". . . the first step was to choose an 'imposing' designation for the organization; the second, to obtain 'a list of respectable names' as 'members and patrons'; the next, to hire 'a secretary and an adequate corps of assistants'; then a 'band of popular lecturers must be commissioned, and sent forth as agents on the wide public' and the press be 'put in operation'; finally, 'subsidiary societies' must be 'multiplied over the length and breadth of the land.'"[7]

The abolitionist movement was one of the most significant reform efforts in American history. Negroes, both free and enslaved, and middle-class whites played an important part in it. People divided on strategies. Men like Emerson and Channing believed that "all reform must begin with the individual, that you must remake souls before you remake institutions," while men like Garrison tried "to arouse a mass demand for immediate and total emancipation. He beat his breast; he spoke and

[4] Robert H. Bremner, *American Philanthropy,* Chicago: University of Chicago Press, 1960, p. 25.

[5] Ralph E. Pumphrey and Muriel W. Pumphrey, Eds., *The Heritage of American Social Work,* New York: Columbia University Press, 1961, pp. 40–42, reprinted from John Bigelow, Ed., *The Life of Benjamin Franklin, Written by Himself,* Philadelphia: Lippincott, 1876, Vol. I, pp. 6–7.

[6] Stewart H. Holbrook, *Dreamers of the American Dream,* Garden City, New York: Doubleday and Company, 1957, p. 36.

[7] Schlesinger, *op. cit.,* p. 52 quoting *Protestant Jesuitism,* New York: 1836, pp. 53–54, written anonymously by Calvin Colton, "Who regarded such bodies disapprovingly."

wrote; he defied mobs; he formed organizations." Others conducted the Underground Railroad, "an extensive secret movement to advance human rights by illegal means." Schlesinger notes that the "Civil War was America's greatest failure to attain a reform peaceably."[8]

Negroes initiated actions to improve their situation well before the end of the 18th century. A group of slaves petitioned the provincial legislature in Massachusetts for freedom in 1773, pointing out that the Revolutionary leaders were throwing off English enslavement. There were scores of slave revolts before 1861.[9] And there were the beginnings of an organized self-help movement among free blacks through such organizations as the African Methodist Episcopal Church (1799),[10] the Baptist Church (1779),[11] and nonreligious groups like the Free African Society (1787)[12] and the Boston African Society (1796).[13] The black abolitionist movement was coexistent with the Negro Convention Movement from 1830 to 1861.[14]

After the Civil War, leaders like Frederick Douglass and organizations like the National Negro Convention in 1874 insisted on the right of the black man to vote. Plans were advanced for aiding the freed slaves. "Northern Negroes were active in these freedmen's aid societies to provide relief for the homeless ex-slaves, and they were active in setting up schools and teaching freedmen, both in the North and South."[15]

As with other American social movements, the strategies of black movements have been varied. Their basic survival issues have been approached through both economic and political strategies. Booker T. Washington stressed self-help and training for jobs and businesses through which Negroes could become economically independent. W.E.B. DuBois called for the use of militant political agitation led by an intellectual elite.[16] Both men wanted to further the integration of the Negro

8 Schlesinger, *op. cit.*, pp. 32–44.

9 Joanne Grant, Ed., *Black Protest*, Greenwich, Connecticut: Fawcett Publications, Inc., 1968, pp. 28–29 and 35–45.

10 John Hope Franklin, *From Slavery to Freedom*, New York: Knopf, 1967, Third Edition, p. 162.

11 *Ibid.*

12 Herbert Aptheker, Ed., *A Documentary History of the Negro People in the United States*, New York: The Citadel Press, Fourth Edition, 1967, p. 17.

13 *Ibid*, p. 38.

14 Benjamin Quarles, *The Black Abolitionists*, New York: Oxford, 1969. Also, Leon Litwack, "The Black Abolitionists," *Black History*, Melvin Drimmer, Ed., Garden City, New York: Doubleday, 1968. Also, Ronald Walters, "Political Strategies of the Reconstruction," *Current History*, September, 1969.

15 Grant, *op. cit.*, p. 106.

16 August Meier, *Negro Thought in America 1880–1915*, Ann Arbor: The University of Michigan Press, 1963.

into American society with full equality. The ideological currents that ran through Negro communities under the leadership of Washington, DuBois, Marcus Garvey, and others were responses to the end of the Civil War, the failure of Reconstruction, rapid and socially disorganizing urbanization and black migration, and the racism of Social Darwinism. While these forces had predominantly negative effects on blacks, they also produced the black cultural movement known as the Harlem or "Negro" Renaissance.[17]

The discernible beginnings of a self-conscious practice of community organization and social planning are to be found in the outpouring of middle-class reform activity that was a response to rapid industrialization, urbanization, and immigration toward the end of the last century. The incredible growth of cities and slums provided the soil in which reform movements proliferated on a corresponding scale during the Progressive Era. Agricultural America was being transformed, and the cities and factories drew in farmers from their own hinterland as well as millions of peasants and artisans from Europe. While the power loom and the Bessemer furnace poured forth their products, the country produced the social conditions described in these words:

"The Industrial Revolution had made the United States the greatest of manufacturing nations but the process had depressed a large element of society and had been accompanied by monstrous perversions in the employment of women and children and in the treatment of the aged, the incompetent and the infirm. Unemployment and child labor went hand in hand; machinery was marvelously efficient, but no other industrial nation confessed so many industrial accidents. The nation was fabulously rich but its wealth was gravitating rapidly into the hands of a very small portion of the population and the power of wealth had already undermined the political integrity of the Republic. In a land of plenty there was never enough food, clothing, and shelter for the underprivileged, and the cyclical depressions, apparently unavoidable, plunged millions into actual want. In the great cities the slums grew apace, and from the slums spread corrupting disease, crime and vice. Science told how to control many of the diseases that plagued mankind but poverty interposed between science and health, and tuberculosis, hookworm, malaria, syphilis, and other diseases of poverty and ignorance took an annual toll that ran into millions."[18]

---

[17] John Hope Franklin, *op. cit.*, Chapters 23–25, pp. 433–498.

[18] S. E. Morison and H. S. Commager, *The Growth of the American Republic*, New York: Oxford University Press, 1930, pp. 355–56, quoted by Nathan E. Cohen, *Social Work in the American Tradition*, New York: The Dryden Press, 1958, p. 52.

Standing between the rich and the poor in this society, Pease writes, was a significant and lively middle class, possessed of political power, economic skill, education, and "an interest in assuring a minimum of well-being among all classes which shared a stake in the efficient functioning of the whole interlocking system" of the economy, the government, and health, education, and welfare services. Pease continues:

". . . their professions placed them in a strategic position in society, and in consequence their influence grew all out of proportion to their numbers. Most were graduates of the small rigorous Protestant colleges . . . were widely read in the classics and in the great tradition of social and philosophic speculation that formed the staple fare of the well trained nineteenth century mind. Most of them on graduation became lawyers, journalists, politicians, administrators, economists, or teachers: a striking number were women who became the pioneer social workers of the new century. Their distinguishing feature was a passion for writing. . . . [They were] continually in touch with the currents of social thought sweeping the Western world. They studied the history of British labor and factory reform and the reports of municipal socialism emanating from New Zealand and from Bismarck's Germany . . . . [They went] to see for themselves how the East End Settlement Houses were run [in London] . . . . they returned to confront the poverty of their own cities with a new confidence."[19]

The activities of these people filled hundreds of pages in "The New Encyclopedia of Social Reform" published in 1908 near the peak of the Progressive period. The overt and the unspoken purposes of their activities were a mixture of self-interest and humanitarianism—of conviction about the necessity for changing institutions and strong desires to uplift and reform the fallen and wayward one by one. There were the muckrakers whose exposure of corruption in the cities inspired campaigns for "clean government," although Lincoln Steffens and others argued that political corruption was due to basic defects in the economic system and not solely to the city political machines.

There were the humanitarians, outraged at the squalor and degradation in which people lived. And there were philanthropists, some of whom bought insurance against potential excesses of the "depressed and dangerous classes" by supporting charitable work. Some of this was "in large measure, an instrument for urban social control for the conservative

[19] Otis Pease, Ed., *The Progressive Years*, New York: George Braziller, 1962, pp. 6–7.

middle classes."[20] But whatever the mixture of purposes and motives, the reformers attacked on a broad front what they considered to be wrong in housing, education, public health, factory working conditions, child labor, women's rights, poor nutrition, inadequate recreation, lack of "community" and a thousand other evils of the city.

The stereotype of the unrealistic, muddled "do-gooders" would not fit many reformers who were technically competent, politically wily, and clear and strong in their objectives. They were pragmatic and skeptical of dogma; they believed with William James that "the world resists some lines of attack on our part and opens herself to others, so that we must go with the grain of her willingness."[21] Armed with such sentiments, the reformers were equipped to negotiate with men like the politician of the day who remarked, "Let me make the deals and I care not who makes the ideals."[22]

The work of the reformers took various forms, often shifting, as pointed out earlier, from one kind of structure and strategy to another. Three main types of activity can be identified: the single-purpose "cause" or crusade; the broad educational or developmental movement; and the organization whose function is to deliver specific services. We shall deal with service agencies in the next chapter and will comment here briefly on the cause-oriented organization and the more general organizing effort, usually concentrated in the neighborhood of a city.

The number of crusades to deal with specific social problems was legion. Under banners of indignation, the reformers battled *against* sweatshop conditions, unjust courts, disregard of the consumer's rights, and prostitution—and *for* temperance, workmen's compensation, free milk, and, perhaps most urgently, government control of concentrated economic power. We have selected one of these for a few observations that will illustrate the course of social reform.

"Of all the great social problems of modern times, incident to the growth of cities," Robert W. DeForest and Lawrence Veiller wrote in 1903 in *The Tenement House Problem*, "none is claiming public attention in greater degree than that of the housing of the working people."[23]

[20] Roy Lubove, *The Professional Altruist*, Cambridge: Harvard University Press, 1965, p. 5. For a discussion of the social control aspects of philanthropy, see also Oscar Handlin, "The Social System," *Daedalus, Journal of the American Academy of Arts and Sciences*, Winter, 1961, p. 27.

[21] Pease, *op. cit.*, p. 9.

[22] Schlesinger, *op. cit.*, p. 53.

[23] Robert W. DeForest and Lawrence Veiller, Eds., *The Tenement House Problem*, New York: The Macmillan Company, 1903, p. 3.

Housing could not be built fast enough to shelter the thousands who poured into the cities. Land values and building costs were so high that the result was large, airless, sunless tenement houses, utterly lacking in family privacy and sanitary provisions, although not in handsome financial returns to their owners.

These conditions had been exposed in the writings of Jacob Riis and others. In 1900, Veiller put on display in New York City a cardboard model of "the famous Canal Street slum (in which 2781 residents shared 264 toilets and not a single bathtub)." One of the shocked viewers was Governor Theodore Roosevelt, who backed Veiller and DeForest in their successful efforts to obtain state legislation governing the construction and maintenance of tenement houses.[24]

In housing, as in many other fields of the reformers' endeavors, the results led in several directions. Permanent voluntary organizations, such as Housing Associations, came into being as watchdogs and sources of pressure. Limited dividend corporations were formed to build and operate low-cost housing. But the target for much of the reformers' energy was the government; they fought for governmental regulation of housing conditions, as in the case of the New York State Tenement Law, and for public services, such as housing inspection. By the turn of the century, as Pease observes, "state legislation provided the first cutting edge for progressivism."[25]

Reform, however, was becoming more than a municipal or even a state matter. Dorothea Dix, successful in Massachusetts in her crusade for proper care for the mentally ill, had appealed to Congress for Federal aid to the "indigent insane," but had been stopped by President Pierce's veto in 1854 on the grounds that this would make the Federal government vulnerable to demands that it assume responsibility for all the poor in all the states. As Cohen points out, "it was well into the 20th century before this stance on the part of the Federal Government was changed."[26] By the end of the 19th century, nevertheless, the Progressive reformers were aware that the country was becoming more of a single economic unit and they were "compelled to shift their attention upward from city and state to the nation; one keynote of the progressive years is the nationalizing of the reform efforts hitherto confined to local problems."[27]

The men and women who worked in the social services supported by

[24] Pease, *op. cit.*, p. 99.
[25] *Ibid.*, p. 14.
[26] Cohen, *op. cit.*, pp. 35–36.
[27] Pease, *op. cit.*, p. 3.

state governments, in response to the unemployment and suffering that accompanied the financial panic of 1873, held a national conference the following year. It is interesting to note that the conference was held under the sponsorship of the American Social Science Association, which had been founded in 1865 to study society and to promote human welfare through the dissemination of social-science knowledge. When the state groups withdrew from this Association and in 1874 formed the National Conference of Charities and Correction, they were satisfying their primary interest in the planning and administration of services as distinct from scientific inquiry.[28] This separation between social scientists on the one hand and practitioners and administrators of services on the other has persisted for decades, with some efforts now being made to establish two-way communication and collaboration between the groups.

We turn now from the crusades concerned with specific social problems to the broader attempts of reformers to organize and educate people, primarily at the neighborhood level, to take a hand in shaping their environments. The settlements, an outstanding expression of this goal, developed rapidly in this country after the opening of Toynbee Hall in London in 1884. They fulfilled a number of functions. "The resident workers were not merely reporting to the rest of society as they had originally intended," Lorene Pacey wrote, "but they were stimulating their neighborhoods to cooperate in the battle to secure equal privilege for the economically dispossessed, the educationally deprived, the physically handicapped, and those discriminated against because of race, foreign birth, nationality, or religion."[29]

The settlement movement was an integral part of the reform movement. It was not revolutionary. On the contrary, the central ethos of the settlement movement was integration rather than class conflict.

"Concerned about the schisms that were dividing America in the latter years of the nineteenth century, the settlement pioneers sought to reconcile class to class, race to race, religion to religion."[30]

The settlements sought to engage the people of the neighborhoods, most of them immigrants, as well as middle-class volunteers in "making democracy work."

[28] Frank J. Bruno, *Trends in Social Work, 1874–1956,* New York: Columbia University Press, 1957, pp. 4–7.

[29] Lorene M. Pacey, Ed., *Readings in the Development of Settlement Work,* New York: Association Press, 1950, pp. 2–3.

[30] Clarke A. Chambers, *Seedtime of Reform: American Social Service and Social Action 1918–33,* Minneapolis: University of Minnesota Press, 1963, p. 14.

But there were other manifestations of this interest in citizen organization at the grass-roots level. In their reaction against the impersonal and alienated quality of urban life, reformers gave great importance to the "community." There was, for example, the interesting social-unit experiment in which a middle-class area of about 15,000 people in Cincinnati was organized to define its own needs and work with specialists to produce new programs and services, particularly in the public health sphere. Lubove notes that the experiment failed because it did not have the capacity "to survive the shock of sharp political and economic controversy on radical, religious and cultural differences."[31]

The heavy emphasis that we shall be placing on the urban scene should not obscure the fact that parallel and significant developments were taking place in rural America. There is a long history of indigenous organization among farm people in the United States through agrarian and populist parties, the Grange, farmers' cooperatives, and farmers' unions. Government resources were also employed. The agricultural extension movement was an "effort to put the vital information of the agricultural scientist, whether he be a physical or social scientist, at the disposal of the farmer and his wife."[32] County agents lived among the people and were supervised by the state agricultural colleges. Throughout there was a stress on education and a concern for enlisting farmers, their wives, teachers, ministers, businessmen, and others in "helping to carry the message. . . of the better way of farming, homemaking, and community life to their neighbors."

Our backward glance at the age of reform at the turn of the century has shown an outburst of activity from which emerged voluntary associations and pressure groups, governmental and private social agencies, and new forms of neighborhood organization and grass-roots democracy. For the most part the energy that went into producing these new instrumentalities came from citizen volunteers. There were of course paid officials who administered the public and private services, but the impetus for improving social conditions came from charismatic crusaders and columns of citizens marching under an unbelievable array of banners and slogans. These people did not think of themselves as professionals, nor with few exceptions were they conscious of the methods they were using. People like Veiller and Dorothea Dix probably thought of themselves as active promoters of change in housing and mental illness; other reformers may have looked on themselves as social scientists or social

[31] Lubove, *op. cit.*, p. 179.
[32] Edmund deSchweinitz Brunner, Irwin T. Sanders, and Douglas Ensminger, Eds., *Farmers of the World,* New York: Columbia University Press, 1945, pp. 182 ff.

philosophers. But few of them spoke specifically about techniques of social reform.

ORGANIZATIONS AND PROFESSIONALS

There is a paradox about social reform. It usually springs from passionate indignation but has a way of setting, like plaster, into institutional molds. The end result, if the crusader is successful, may well be an efficiently operating bureaucracy engaged in doing what the reformer had worked so hard to bring into existence, but the outcome often seems alien to the reformer who started the process. The program that emerges becomes either flaccid or rigid, and a new cycle of discontent and reform is generated.

This institutionalization of reform was at work at the turn of the century. Lubove describes this process in the field of social work.

"Believing that social problems were subject to rational analysis and control, but also that their scope and complexity were too vast to be handled by the impulse of benevolent individuals, reformers in the late nineteenth and early twentieth centuries created an immense network of welfare organizations to care for the deprived and maladjusted. Among the consequences for remedial, preventive and constructive philanthropy were function instead of cause; administrative instead of charismatic leaders; rational organization and centralized machinery of control instead of individual impulse and village neighborliness."[33]

These trends ran against the grain of some perceptive reformers, who foresaw quite clearly that organization meant the formalization of policies, deliberation by committees, and limits on their freedom. In a statement that anticipated issues concerning the role of the community organizer in the 1960's, Wendell Phillips, a Boston abolitionist and later an advocate of women's rights and labor unions, wrote that "the agitator must stand outside of organizations, with no bread to earn, no candidate to elect, no party to save, no object but truth."[34]

Nevertheless, the hallmark of the agitator's success is the establishment of some new entity—an organization, a program, a new piece of legislation. The typical outcome of the energies of the turn-of-the-century reformers was an expanding network of service programs. It was also the emergence of new professional functions that began to institu-

[33] Lubove, *op. cit.*, p. 157.
[34] Arthur M. Schlesinger, *op. cit.*, p. 35.

tionalize some of the activities of the reformers themselves. The forces of specialization and of professionalization were at work, and we now look, again only briefly, at their unfolding.

From the earliest days in America's colonial period, the government had attempted to deal with poverty and dependency, however grudging and punitive was the poor relief system set up in New England on the English model. By the middle of the 19th century, the states were operating institutions "for the dependent, defective, and delinquent." The first local health departments had been established decades before, and health departments on the state level were functioning before the Civil War.

Beginning in Massachusetts in 1863, state boards of charities were formed to administer correctional institutions and hospitals and to supervise private institutions receiving public funds. Gradually, these boards developed standards for voluntary hospitals, orphanages, homes for the aged, nursing homes, and other agencies. Planning at the state level for a wide range of institutional and noninstitutional services is the outgrowth of those early efforts at supervision and standard-setting.

Reformers and philanthropists also produced a forest of voluntary agencies dedicated to serving individuals and families in want and need of help. Of particular interest was the Charity Organization Society (C.O.S.), also patterned on the English model. The C.O.S. had, as one of its original purposes, teaching small voluntary societies how to give relief so as to avoid "pauperizing" people while at the same time providing them with proper friendly, spiritual help. The paid workers engaged to demonstrate new methods proved so effective that the voluntary societies began to relinquish their relief-giving functions to the C.O.S. By 1892 there were C.O.S. agencies in 92 cities in North America.

As the C.O.S. groups expanded, they took on additional functions. They maintained a central registration bureau of charitable agencies in order to avoid duplication of services to individuals. They tried to organize assistance for their clients from relatives, churches, employers, and other private sources in the community. Moreover, although their work was on a case basis, the C.O.S. was able to identify the problems and needs of categories of people. The volunteer leaders of the C.O.S. agencies engaged in some social and legislative action on these problems, although Kidneigh points out that their efforts were restricted for decades by their opposition in principle to governmental involvement in social services.[35]

---

[35] John M. Kidneigh, "History of Social Work," in Harry L. Lurie, Ed., *Ency-*

Unlike radical social movements sponsored by disadvantaged groups, the C.O.S. was clearly dominated by the privileged members of society, whose motivations were a mixture of humanitarianism and attempts to maintain social control. There was no thought in this movement of changes in the distribution of community power. Its object was to change the behavior and conditions of life of the underprivileged through provisions made by the privileged.

These efforts had lasting institutional results. The C.O.S. agencies established patterns for bringing groups together into a framework calling for joint consideration of needs and coordination of activities. They thus provided a foundation for the *planning of service programs* that is reflected in the work of their successor organizations, the councils of social agencies and health and welfare councils.

Parallel with the C.O.S. development, the settlement houses were pursuing new forms and methods of organizing people and helping them to work on the problems of their neighborhoods. "Starting from these beginings in the settlement movement," Grace Coyle wrote,

"the new concepts of community organization on a neighborhood level have made their way increasingly into other related organizations. The development of area and community councils, the opening of public schools as community centers, the decentralized programs of YMCA's and YWCA's and the Jewish centers, the development of community activities as a part of public housing, the provision for community organization in such artificial communities as the camps for migratory workers—all these are extensions of the concept of neighborhood-making into new situations."[36]

While they were learning and teaching others how to participate in practical ways in the shaping of their urban environment, the settlements like the C.O.S. were also service agencies. Their approach, described below, bears a striking resemblance to the neighborhood-based programs that appeared in community action agencies in the 1960's:

"When specific needs seemed too pressing to be ignored, settlements tried to meet them temporarily in a local, neighborhood way, meanwhile seeking a wider, more adequate, permanent solution. Often they treated symptoms while seeking causes. Frequently they had to lead a

clopedia of Social Work, New York: National Association of Social Workers, 1965, pp. 3–18.

[36] Grace Longwell Coyle, *Group Work with American Youth,* New York: Harper & Brothers, 1948, pp. 9–10.

fight against authorities before they could demonstrate what could be done. Educational opportunity for working men, trade union organization, garbage inspection, boys' clubs, nursing care, housing standards, industrial and homemaking workshops, libraries, playgrounds, kindergartens, health clinics, training for charity workers as well as settlement staff, shelter for the homeless, emergency relief, child protection, legal aid, immigrant protection, consumer education, social legislation, decent working conditions, milk pasteurization, nursery schools and child care education, vocational guidance, behavior clinics, recreation for the handicapped and the aged—at some time or other some settlement has sponsored them all."[37]

From the C.O.S. and the settlement experience, the studies of social scientists, the day-by-day work of architects and lawyers, and the increasing expertness of social reformers themselves, there began to germinate in the first decade of the 20th century a recognition of the usefulness of principles and methods to guide efforts at community improvement. This was one evidence of a growing professionalism that was expressed in meetings, conferences, permanent organizations, journals, training, and ultimately university-based education. These developments can be seen in the establishment of the American Public Health Association in 1872 and the National Conference of Charities and Correction in 1874, and the sprouting of the adult-education movement in the 1870's and 1880's.[38]

The two fields that have contributed most to the concepts and methods of planned change are city planning and community organization in social work.[39] Both fields began with a commitment by their early leaders to social ideals during the age of reform, and both moved during the period of "normalcy" in the 1920's toward a concern with rationality, efficiency, and professional technology.

The notion of planning the physical growth of cities represented a coalition of various interests. Civic leaders and architects had become deeply interested in the esthetics of the modern city, inspired by the Chicago World Fair of 1893, which was constructed as a symbol of "the City Beautiful." They joined with other Americans who were enamored with the idea of the Garden City proclaimed by Ebenezer Howard in England and with those who were "reaching out for status and symbols

---

[37] Lorene M. Pacey, Ed., *op. cit.*, p. 3.

[38] Coyle, *op. cit.*, p. 8.

[39] Robert Perlman, "Social Welfare Planning and Physical Planning," unpublished doctoral dissertation, Waltham, Massachusetts: Brandeis University, 1961.

of achievement on the part of rich and powerful individuals and groups
. . . through the creation of urban 'monuments' and parks."[40]

But the men who called the first city planning conference in 1909
were concerned with housing, economic conditions, parks, and health.
Housing reformers, Lubove observed, grasped the planning movement

"as a young but powerful ally—city planning became a new ingredient
in the philosophy and methods of housing reformers, who now realized
that the maximum effectiveness of their own work depended upon its
coordination with other elements of urban life. Along with conservation,
the city planning movement symbolized the Progressive infatuation with
efficient social organization."[41]

In its second phase city planning became deeply immersed in
technical problems of transportation, zoning, and legal and administrative procedures and in drawing up master plans for "the City Practical."
The engineer became as important in city planning as the architect.
Recently city planning has become involved in coordinating all governmental activities that bear on community growth, "especially those that
influence or regulate private development of all kinds, so that they all
work in the direction of perceived comprehensive objectives."[42]

Perloff summarizes the evolution of city planning in these stages.

"From (1) an early stress on planning as concerned chiefly with esthetics,
planning came to be conceived also in terms of (2) the efficient functioning of the city—in both the engineering and the economic sense;
then (3) as a means of controlling the uses of land as a technique for
developing a sound land-use pattern; then (4) as a key element in
efficient governmental procedures; later (5) as involving welfare considerations and stressing the human element; and, more recently (6)
planning has come to be viewed as encompassing many socio-economic
and political, as well as physical, elements that help to guide the functioning and development of the urban community."[43]

Our interest, however, is not only in the subject matter and the sub-

[40] Harvey S. Perloff, *Education for Planning: City, State, and Regional,* Baltimore:
The Johns Hopkins Press, 1957, p. 9.
[41] Roy Lubove, *The Progressives and the Slums,* Pittsburgh: The University of
Pittsburgh Press, 1962, p. 215.
[42] John T. Howard, "City Planning as a Social Movement, A Governmental Function, and a Technical Profession," in Harvey S. Perloff, Ed., *Planning and the Urban
Community,* Pittsburgh: University of Pittsburgh Press, 1961, p. 155.
[43] Perloff, *Education for Planning,* p. 12.

stantive concerns of city planning, but also in its methods and in the tasks of its practitioners. In view of the emergence of policy analysis and planning as a discipline that cuts across several fields, it is important to take note here of Howard's description of the functions of the planner or the planning agency. He writes that these involve

"analysis of problems, which includes making projections of what is likely to happen; goal formulation, the determination of the objectives, limited by the analysis, to realizable objectives; the design aspect, that is, the preparation of the plan to achieve these objectives; and finally, the implementation of these plans . . . city planning is like all other operations of government in having social and economic objectives and political methods of application."[44]

In the field of social welfare, planning and community organization developed along several different lines. We have seen that the early charity organization societies had a double function. One was to render direct assistance to families. That function became professionalized as social casework and was carried forward by family service agencies that eventually shed most of their relief-giving functions in favor of more intensive counseling of individuals and families.

The other prong of the C.O.S. is reflected in the *"organization"* part of its title. Its early purpose was to bring order out of the activities of the many independent relief societies that functioned in that period, to eliminate duplication of relief grants, and to coordinate the separate efforts. This line of activity led over a period of time to the establishment of a new type of organization composed of representatives of "social agencies that want to unite in a common project of establishing and improving standards."[45] Councils of social agencies, welfare councils, and community chests were the organizational forms that developed. The concept of a community planning function in relation to social services thus began to emerge, paralleling the physical planning functions that were being articulated in the field of city planning.

Early antecedents of social welfare planning were not confined to the local community. Some of the major developments took the form of organized programs at the state level to deal with the needs of special groups suffering from particular handicaps. Frequently institutional care was the pattern of provision made available for such groups as dependent and neglected children, the indigent aged, and the mentally

[44] Howard, *op. cit.*, p. 164.
[45] Lubove, *The Professional Altruist*, p. 172.

ill. A major thrust toward the organization and rationalization of social services in these areas came about through the development of specialized institutions and ancillary programs. We noted earlier that this was done under the aegis of the state boards of charities that represented an early form of planning in the social welfare field.

In social work, the period of the 1920's was one of developing professionalization centered in the casework method of dealing with problems of individuals and families. Its community organization aspects came to be identified primarily with the financing and coordination of voluntary social agencies and with their efficient management.

As major social problems affecting the total society came to the fore again with the Depression of the 1930's, social work was reminded forcefully of its earlier identification with social reform and of its larger responsibilities to the community and society. One historian observes that the responsibility was undertaken in some measure, although there was now a difference in role.

"The role of direct agitation was often left largely to voluntary reform associations, to politicians, to labor leaders. . . ; social workers were more often found now working in and through government, on the staffs of numerous commissions, committees, bureaus, and agencies, than as voices crying in the wilderness."[46]

Another historian, taking a less complimentary view, says that "community organization had barely emerged as a cause before it had become a function absorbed into the administrative structure of social work.[47]

However one evaluates these observations, the concern of social work with its duality as "cause" and "function" has been a major theme of the profession's history.[48] It is an issue that is posed with particular sharpness when the pressures of social problems demand greater commitment to the "cause" of social change. The 1930's were such a period, as were the 1960's. During the 1930's the issues were primarily economic. Today they are both economic and more broadly social.

In its search for a proper response to contemporary conditions, social work is turning back to its origins and early experiences in social reform. Out of those experiences came the professionalization of community organization and planning functions in social welfare. As more people

---

[46] Clarke A. Chambers, "Social Service and Social Reform: A History Essay," *Social Service Review,* **XXXVII**, No. 1, March 1963, p. 82.

[47] Lubove, *The Professional Altruist,* p. 180.

[48] Porter L. Lee, *Social Work as Cause and Function and Other Papers,* New York: Columbia University Press, 1937, pp. 3–24.

became engaged in these activities on a full-time career basis, it was natural for them to seek to conceptualize what they were doing, to learn from their experiences, and to strive for greater effectiveness in their performance. This was the beginning of professional thinking. Over a period of time, more or less systematic conceptualizations of practice have developed and have provided a basis for theorizing, teaching, and research. The next chapter reviews these alternative conceptualizations of practice.

CHAPTER 3

Concepts of Practice

STRENGTHENING THE COMMUNITY THROUGH PARTICIPATION

The first writings on community organization as a distinctive field appeared early in the 1920's with the publication of books that sought to establish common principles and methods. Two main themes were prominent in these early efforts to conceptualize a field of practice. These stemmed from different ways of defining social problems and led to correspondingly different approaches to intervening in them.

One approach stressed the *improvement of social provisions and services,* and the other concentrated on *changing social relationships.* The former emphasized the determination of needs and the development of services to meet them effectively. The latter focused on groups in the community and on improving their capacity to deal with each other, most often by encouraging cooperation among them.

In the 1920's the concern with improving social relationships was strongly linked to a desire to preserve the values of the small community in a changing society. The key to its methodology was the strengthening of democratic participation. Lindeman and other spokesmen for this point of view believed that

"the future of democracy depended upon the ordinary citizen's ability to regain control of his own destiny through intensive civic association. Only in a creative group life could he realize his own potential as a human being and citizen and find the strength to resist the external manipulating forces which relegated him to the role of passive observer."[1]

In *The Community*, Lindeman described community organization as "a conscious effort on the part of a community to control its affairs democratically, and to secure the highest services from its specialists, organizations, agencies and institutions by means of recognized interrelations."[2] He was deeply concerned about the threats to democracy that seemed to be coming from the institutionalization of social functions and particularly from specialization and bureaucratization.

The loss of the small community and the changes brought about by rapid urbanization dominated much of sociology of the period, finding its classic expression in Louis Wirth's essay on "Urbanism as a Way of Life." Lindeman and Pettit, both teachers, were in the sociological tradition of their time.[3] Lindeman's book on the community was written within a few years of the classic sociological work of the period on the same subject by Robert MacIver, who put the issue as follows:

"But there is one universal problem which presents itself wherever localities—villages, cities, counties or greater areas—form part of a larger community. For the unity which the larger community attains is not the unity which the smaller community had previously attained. The former pays a price for its greater universality and efficiency. If needs essentially universal find their purer form in the large community, there are more intimate needs, needs more deeply rooted in the emotional nature, which it cannot satisfy. It cannot take the place of the near community, but can only supplement it. Insofar as it becomes a substitute for the near community, men have but found one good at the cost of another."[4]

Much of the early writing both assumed and urged collaborative re-

---

[1] Roy Lubove, *The Professional Altruist*, p. 173.

[2] Eduard C. Lindeman, *The Community*, New York: Association Press, 1921, pp. 139, 173. (Quoted in Ernest B. Harper and Arthur Dunham, *Community Organization in Action: Basic Reader and Critical Comments*, New York: Association Press, 1959, p. 55.)

[3] Walter W. Pettit, "Some Prognostications in the Field of Community Work," *Proceedings of the National Conference of Social Work*, Denver, 1925, Chicago: University of Chicago Press, 1925.

[4] Quoted in Roland L. Warren, Ed., *Perspectives on the American Community*, Chicago: Rand McNally and Co., 1966, p. 26. Taken from Robert M. MacIver, *Community: A Sociological Study*, Macmillan Company, printed in Great Britain in 1917 and in the United States in 1928.

lationships among community groups. A somewhat different premise was voiced by Steiner, who wrote in his textbook in 1930 that

"society is made up of elements more or less antagonistic to each other, which must through a process of accommodation develop a working arrangement that will resolve the conflicts and make consistent progress possible."[5]

But a concern with services and provisions was also reflected in early formulations. Edward T. Devine wrote that "the educational and preventive social movements of the present century have a common method consisting of research, publicity, and propaganda, which . . . is fairly distinctive." One aspect of this was described as having "for its object the coordination and harmonizing of existing agencies, the organization of resources of the community . . . and planning for future development of a community's social work."[6]

There appeared to be a choice between focusing attention on services or on the relationships among the groups needing and supporting the services. To state the issue in this way is to reveal that the two concerns, far from being mutually exclusive, are intimately related. On the one hand, agencies and services are directed toward consumers; on the other hand, one of the purposes of group interaction is the mobilization of resources and the development of services for people.

That there is a strong relationship between these two approaches has been clear in most of the conceptual development that followed Lindeman, Steiner, and the other pioneers. The Lane Report of 1939, an important landmark in the history of community organization concepts, represented a synthesis of earlier views, although it tended to come down more on the side of services and coordination than on direct work with groups. The "Lane Report" grew out of the responsibilities of practitioners and administrators of social welfare programs, particularly in voluntary agencies. That orientation was reflected in its key recommendation that the general aim of community organization is to "bring about and maintain a progressively more effective adjustment between social welfare resources and social welfare needs."[7]

[5] Jesse F. Steiner, *Community Organization,* rev. edition 1930, The Century Co. (Quoted in Harper and Dunham, *op. cit.,* p. 56.)

[6] Edward T. Devine, *Social Work,* New York: The Macmillan Company, 1922, pp. 67–68. (Quoted in Harper and Dunham, *op. cit.,* p. 56.)

[7] Robert P. Lane, "The Field of Community Organization," *National Conference of Social Work Proceedings,* New York, National Conference of Social Work, 1939, pp. 495–511.

The Lane Report was concerned with defining the professional character of community organization work and particularly with defining the place of community organization within the social work profession. The Report argued that community organization should be considered an integral part of the social work profession, together with casework and group work. That view did not attain immediate acceptance. There was a continuing debate for some years afterwards as to how the professional components of community organization work were to be defined. It was not until 1962 that community organization was accorded equal status with case work and group work as a legitimate area of concentration within social work education.[8]

The position of community organization as one of the primary methods of social work was reviewed in the late 1950's as part of a general Curriculum Study sponsored by the Council on Social Work Education. Lurie, who edited the volume on community organization, acknowledged the existence of different concepts and approaches to the subject and did not attempt to resolve them. He confronted the issue pragmatically and noted that the distinguishing feature of community organization professionals "is that they are primarily concerned with maintaining and developing the programs and standards of welfare agencies and services rather than directly helping individuals and groups."[9]

Thinking in the field shifted a few years later to more of a middle position between the two emphases: services or social relationships. The same year in which Lurie's volume appeared, a committee of the National Association of Social Workers undertook to develop a working definition of community organization practice. Their report, published in 1962, speaks of the purpose of practice as "intervening in the community process with a problem-solving approach . . . to achieve a viable interaction pattern of relationships and of selected social goals . . ."[10] This meant, in other words, both strengthening the community's capacities and improving social conditions, policies, and services. The statement goes on to say that community organization should offer opportunities to citizens, social agencies, and social workers to meet their communal responsibilities.

[8] Council on Social Work Education, "Curriculum Policy Statement," New York: CSWE, 1962.

[9] Harry L. Lurie, Ed., *The Community Organization Method in Social Work Education*, Vol. IV, A Project Report of the *Social Work Curriculum Study*, New York: Council on Social Work Education, 1959.

[10] National Association of Social Workers, *Defining Community Organization Practice*, NASW, New York: 1962.

In the theoretical work that has been done in the three decades since the Lane Report there has been some tendency to focus on one or another of the two poles—strengthening provisions or strengthening people's relationships and capacities. Some writers have defined community organization almost entirely in terms of involving people in self-help organizing efforts. Others have identified it with the coordination of institutional resources. In most writings, however, some consideration is given to the connections between the two and to their interdependence.

In order to illustrate these variations in approach and emphasis that have contributed to the conceptualization of practice, we have selected four representative writers of the post-World War II period. Each has a distinctive point of view that reflects important orientations in the field. This survey will help to identify the dimensions that must be considered in a comprehensive approach to practice. The four views of practice are summarized first according to the dominant purposes they ascribe to community organization and planning. They were written at different times and to a considerable extent represent responses to changing demands and circumstances.

1. *Strengthening community participation and integration.* The main concerns of this kind of practice are to encourage the expression of views from all groups in the community and to achieve effective interaction among them, leading toward agreement on how to improve their common environment. Adjustment among groups and organizations and facilitation of cooperative relationships are important objectives. Murray Ross is a leading proponent of this view of practice.[11]

2. *Enhancing coping capacities.* This can be considered a variation of the first type. The concentration, however, is on improving means of communication and interaction in order to build up the ability of a community (or some segment of it) to cope with its environment and with change. Ronald Lippitt has developed a conceptual scheme based on this approach.[12]

3. *Improving social conditions and services.* The central goal here is to identify needs and deficiencies and to develop effective provisions and methods for solving or preventing social problems. This includes setting specific goals and mobilizing resources to achieve them. In their book Morris and Binstock concentrate on achieving changes in the policies,

[11] Murray G. Ross and Ben Lappin, *Community Organization: Theory, Principles and Practice,* New York: Harper and Row, 1967, 2nd edition.

[12] Ronald Lippitt, Jeanne Watson, and Bruce Westley, *The Dynamics of Planned Change,* New York: Harcourt Brace, 1958.

practices, or resource allocations of a formal organization, since in their view much of social planning (that is, efforts to resolve social problems) consists of attempts to do this.[13]

4. *Advancing the interests of disadvantaged groups.* In sharp contrast with the first type, the primary purpose here is to promote the interests of particular groups by increasing their share of material goods and services and/or by increasing their power, their participation in community decision-making, and their status. It is impossible to point to a single writer who reflects the full range of activity. We have chosen a paper by Charles Grosser to represent an important part of this type of practice. His paper, not intended to be as comprehensive a statement as those by Ross, Lippitt, and Morris, discusses neighborhood community development, by which he means "community organization with lower-class, minority group, urban slum residents."[14]

Our review will consider the purposes, strategies, and practitioner roles in each of the four types. But we shall also present the writers' views of certain social realities, because embedded in each approach are assumptions concerning the nature of the community and society and the processes of social change.[15] It is important to make a clear distinction between the *purposes* of practice and the *assumptions* on which it is based. The former rest ultimately on values, which do not require proof, nor are they susceptible to verification. Assumptions about social facts and forces, on the other hand, can and should be subjected to empirical study. For example, one can assert that self-induced change is better and more lasting than imposed change. That self-induced change is preferable in terms of democratic values cannot be argued. That it is more lasting is subject to demonstration and examination.

At a very general level it should be noted that these four works share a common set of values, although with different emphases. These can be stated briefly as respect for the dignity and worth of the individual, his right to a decent standard of living in terms of goods and services, and his right to struggle in concert with others for social improvements. At the same time there is an interest in interaction among groups with a

[13] Robert Morris and Robert Binstock, *Feasible Planning for Social Change*, New York: Columbia University Press, 1966.

[14] Charles F. Grosser, "Community Development Programs Serving the Urban Poor, *Social Work*, New York: National Association of Social Workers, 10, No. 3, July 1965, pp. 15–21.

[15] While Grosser's writing is rich in its analysis of strategies and tactics, his assumptions concerning the nature of the community and of social change must be largely inferred.

view to asserting collective control over the natural and social environment.

1. Strengthening Community Participation and Integration. In his writings, Ross is interested in achieving a "process objective," that is, in the wide participation of individuals and groups in identifying and acting on their community's problems, thereby enhancing community integration and reducing the impersonality, disorganization, and alienation of urban industrial society.

Ross recognizes the validity of working toward "a specific content objective" (the attainment of a particular reform or change) and a "general content objective" (effective planning, coordination, and development of a specific group of services), but he directs his attention to the "process objective." He also excludes from his purview "community relations," which he defines as the means of relating an agency to the community via public relations, the development of particular services, and the agency's participation in community affairs.

In order to move toward the process objective, Ross advocates the development of a "community association," as a vehicle for what he calls the "community organization process." The association should represent the major groups in the community and must involve their real leaders. The organizer maintains the association. He supports subgroups, avoids placing the association in competition with them, and builds the association's prestige. The worker provides emotional and symbolic experiences to participants and develops effective lines of communication within the association and out into the community. He neither overloads nor starves the communications channels of the association and avoids a pace that is too fast for the community.

It is the organizer's task to develop consensus. By proposing goals and methods of high acceptability, the worker sets up conditions that are conducive to reaching agreement. He also removes or circumvents blockages to cooperation by emphasizing common values, calming storms, mediating conflicts, tackling some blockages directly and serving as a model of good interpersonal relationships.

Ross identifies these roles for the worker in the basic task of building a community association.[16]

(a) As *guide*, the worker helps the community establish and reach its own goals. He is not a crusader. He does not take over responsibility for making decisions, but he is not passive. He can contribute his own

---

[16] Ross, *op. cit.*, pp. 200–228.

ideas as to what the problems and the solutions are. Moreover, he tries to recommend feasible targets for discussion and action.

(b) As *enabler*, the worker awakens and focuses discontent, facilitates its expression, and translates it into aspirations and "needs." The enabler also helps people to be realistic about problems and their resolution, the time required, and the obstacles to be anticipated. He sustains morale during the long process of organizing.

(c) As *expert*, the practitioner provides information and advice but does not make concrete recommendations. He is expert in community analysis and research; he knows the experience of other communities and he serves as a technical resource on these matters. He is skilled in evaluating "the cooperative process."

(d) The *social therapy* role consists of helping community leaders achieve self-understanding as a way of relieving tensions and blockages. This means dealing with deep and often unconscious material and should be practiced only by more experienced workers.

In all these roles, Ross looks on the practitioner as objective and non-judgmental. He must identify with the whole community and not with any part of it.

We shift now from Ross' choice of ends and means to his assumptions and to the practice implications he draws from these. He pictures the community as a composite of large subgroups, each of which develops its own cohesion. This may have the effect of increasing intergroup tension or of providing security for intergroup cooperation. It becomes critical, therefore, to determine the "fit" between each subgroup's values and the commonly held values of the community. Since leadership should reflect their subgroups, it is essential to know whether the leaders are really representative of their groups.

Ross assumes that people want change and that they are capable of changing and of developing problem-solving capacities through experience. He looks on technological development as the major source of social changes that have resulted in dislocations and high social costs. The motivation to plan is based on dissatisfactions with this situation and a desire to alter it. Self-initiated change of this type is more permanent than change imposed from outside.

Change will lead inevitably to conflicts, Ross assumes, but he wants to see conflict handled so that it will increase the community's tolerance for differences and its overall strength. He is persuaded that the development of skills in collaboration and "conferencing" will make conflict less irrational.

To the extent that problems and programs are significant to those involved, more successful integration will be achieved. A community's degree of integration (and its capacity for change) depend on such factors as the community's history and structure; the mobility of its population; its patterns of role definition and decision-making processes; on community values concerning cooperation and individualism; and on attitudes such as apathy and prejudice.

2. Enhancing Coping Capacities. Lippitt's objective is to strengthen the relationship of a "client system" to its environment, thereby building up its capabilities for adjusting to changes in the future. Lippitt's client system can be either an individual, a group, an organization, or a community. We shall concentrate on the application of his ideas to the community.

Lippitt poses three problematic situations and suggests strategies for each. One involves "faulty distribution of power." For this Lippitt calls for the creation of new centers of power outside the system or the making of internal changes to give a subsystem more power—essentially the strategy of Grosser's approach outlined below.

Second, Lippitt speaks of "the faulty mobilization of energy." The response to this is to develop insight through interpretation so as to re-channel energy and avoid internal conflict. The similarity to psychodynamic methods of treating emotional problems is apparent. He suggests further that the practitioner try to build satisfactions for the ailing part of a community by encouraging its particpation in decision-making.

Faulty "communication and perception of one's environment" is considered by Lippitt to be the third major source of difficulty in a community. This can be countered by an exchange of attitudes and feelings to achieve better mutual understanding of problems and solutions. This will make it possible for the system to take corrective action, much in the style of Ross.

This process depends on feedback. The practitioner or "change agent" provides information and corrects the client system's unrealistic perceptions. This leads to new behavior, which in turn changes attitudes and values. The change agent also tries to recognize connections among the subsystems in order to promote insights. He trains the client in problem-solving skills. He uses his authority when possible to change the situation and thus to trigger a chain of modifications in behavior, attitudes, and values.

Lippitt's change agent performs four main roles. The *catalyst*, similar to Ross' enabler, creates a climate for introspection and learning, improves communication, encourages belief in the possibility of change, and stimulates awareness of problems. The *expert* presents knowledge but does not impose his goals. The *implementer* builds new power centers, develops new programs, and on occasion uses legal authority to produce change. The *researcher* contributes to the development of skills and knowledge of the profession.

Beyond using a social system framework, Lippitt says little about the nature of the community. He sees a tendency toward stability in social systems in terms of both structure and process, including a tendency to retain existing patterns of solving problems. This stability is upset when established patterns of coping are rendered obsolete by external change.

Lippitt was proposing a scheme that would be applicable to various systems. He postulates that in small groups change is motivated primarily by outside forces. In organizations the threat to productivity spurs change. In the community, problems of internal disruption and conflict are the major stimuli. The change process can, however, be initiated either by the system itself, by a "change agent," or by a third party.

Strains among the parts of a system, in the face of its need to maintain its functions, lead to the development of problem-solving procedures and structures. This may proceed from pain, from an awareness of better alternatives, or from the acknowledgement of discrepancies between the system's values and its actions. Hostility toward change stems from distorted perceptions and ignorance of reality. Lippitt anticipates that resistance will arise from (1) a system's fear of its inability to make the necessary adaptations, (2) a reluctance to give up present satisfactions, and (3) ties to other systems.

CHANGING THE DISTRIBUTION OF RESOURCES

The writings of Ross and Lippitt stressed the building of stronger intergroup relationships in the community and the development of the capacity of the community as a system to deal with its problems. The two other approaches that are summarized below are concerned with changes in the use and allocation of resources and with ways of obtaining the decisions that are required to produce such changes.

3. Improving Social Conditions and Services. Morris and Binstock take as their task analyzing how the policies of a formal organization can be changed, since this is frequently the means of improving services and reducing social problems. Their framework is constructed from the point of view of a single actor "engaged in an attempt to achieve a goal." The actor is the planner, although "it is difficult to distinguish planners from their employing organizations. In some measure, their interests, motivations, and means are those of their employers."[17]

The planner uses his understanding of cause-effect relationships to select a "preference goal," which becomes the guide for his subsequent decisions and actions. In order to achieve change in the direction he desires and to economize his efforts, the planner assesses the relationship between (1) his influence for achieving his preference goal and (2) the resistance of the organization whose policies he wants to change. To make this calculation the planner needs to define the major interests of the "dominant faction" within the target organization.

With the target defined as this dominant faction, the planner examines the "pathways" through which influence can be brought to bear. These *pathways* are

> Obligation
> Friendship
> Rational persuasion
> Selling
> Coercion
> Inducement

The planner must select from among his own resources those that are most appropriate to the situation. These *sources of influence* consist of

> Money and credit
> Personal energy
> Professional expertise
> Popularity
> Social standing, political standing
> Control of information
> Legitimacy and legality

Based on his analysis of the problem at hand, the planner tries to match his influence resources to the pathways at his disposal. If a good "fit" between the two is lacking, the planner may do one of the following: alter his preference goal, substitute another goal or target organization, or increase the resources he is using.

Morris and Binstock assume that the community consists of individuals and groups with different and often conflicting interests and needs. They

---

[17] Morris and Binstock, *op. cit.*, p. 17.

make the assumption about organizations (and by extension, the community) that power tends to gravitate into fewer hands. In the large organization this constitutes the "dominant faction." Thus, formal organizations will operate and relate to each other largely in accordance with the major interests of their dominant factions.

These authors assume a tendency toward equilibrium that is not upset until and unless an unsatisfactory state of affairs arises. In that case, change will be possible. Thus, planning requires that there be dissatisfaction on the part of an organization and a commitment by the organization to work for change. The planner (and his organization) will intervene out of (1) concern for human need, (2) a desire to learn or experiment, (3) a response to an outside force, such as legal requirements, or (4) a desire for a change that will help to achieve another goal, such as acquiring resources for a purpose other than the change at hand.

Organizations will resist changes that threaten their cohesion, their ethos, or their autonomy. The degree of resistance is related to the major interests of the organization's dominant faction. It is easier to overcome resistance if the organization is dominated by only one faction. Factions within an organization, however, will respond differentially to various types of influence.

4. Advancing the Interests of Disadvantaged Groups. Grosser represents one approach to community organization work with disadvantaged groups. He states that the purpose of the activity is engaging "the poor in the decision-making process of the community, both to overcome apathy and estrangement and to realign the power resources of the community by creating channels through which the consumers of social welfare services can define their problems and goals and negotiate on their behalf."

Grosser views influence (as well as such resources as wealth, knowledge, social position, and access to officials) as unequally distributed in society. In order to promote the interests of the urban poor, two primary strategies are needed. One is to strive for a larger share of the goods and services dispensed by the agencies of city government and to press for elimination of injustices and denials of rights in the provision of these services. The other, which is the means to the first, is to arouse and organize people who "have been systematically socialized into apathy and inaction" and to teach them what are appropriate targets and tactics for their collective actions.

What roles are specified for the worker whose job is to organize these actions? There is, in Grosser's view, some value (although limited) in the role of *enabler*, since "self-imposed actions growing out of a community's assessment of its own needs have a value and permanence that do not inhere in actions imposed from the outside."

The *broker* role, however, becomes particularly important in working with and for the urban poor. Grosser says this role was first suggested for social work practice by Wilensky and Lebeaux in 1958 when they called for guides "through a new kind of civilized jungle." The broker would put people in touch with "community resources they need but can hardly name, let alone locate." Grosser expands this to collective brokerage, that is, the worker seeks administrative and policy changes that affect whole classes of persons rather than a single individual.

Frequently, the broker role is found to be "insufficiently directive," and it is imperative for the worker to function as an *advocate*, a role taken from the field of law. Here he must "provide leadership and resources directed toward eliciting information, arguing the correctness of a position, and challenging the stance of the institution." The worker becomes, as a result, a "partisan" in a social conflict. His "expertise is available exclusively to serve client interests. The impartiality of the enabler and the functionalism of the broker are absent here."

This commitment to one side in conflict situations implies an *activist* role for the worker in which he rejects a neutral or passive stance. Pointing to the myth of neutrality of professional workers who traditionally have urged people to visit dentists, contribute to the Red Cross, and support the PTA, Grosser asks "why should not tenants who are without heat also be urged to withhold rents, parents with grievances to boycott the schools, or citizens without franchise to take to the streets in legal public demonstration as a means to redress their grievances?"

On the organizational form that work with the urban poor should take, Grosser points out the tremendous variety of forms of voluntary organizations in middle-class communities and the "proliferation of styles, purposes and patterns of participation" in them. "Neighborhood work" he writes, "has been conducted with groups on the basis of common cultural patterns (hometown clubs), common social problems (welfare or housing organizations), physical proximity (building or block organizations), social movements (civil rights groups), specific task orientation (voter-registration campaigns) and the operation of a resource center (storefronts)." He concludes that attention needs to be given to developing effective strategies rather than to debating the merits of alternative structures for community development or neighborhood work with the urban poor.

Broadly speaking, all four schemes are oriented toward the achievement of social changes and toward both the improvement of social provision and the strengthening of relationships and problem-solving capacities. But each writer specifies his primary goal in different terms. Lippitt has the most general goal of helping a system relate more effectively to its environment. Morris accepts any objective set by the planner, although this is always related to some specific change in services or social conditions. Thus, the "specific content objective" that Ross excludes is the core of Morris and Binstock's scheme as it is of Grosser's, whose purpose is to enhance the position of a particular group. Ross' goal is better participation and cooperation in community problem-solving.

Given these differences it can be expected that the schemes would diverge in their strategies for achieving change. Ross calls for the development of a structure or a "community association" as the principal means for strengthening integration. Lippitt relies on the relationship between the change agent and the system to develop understanding and improve functioning. Morris and Binstock call for rational goal-setting modified by calculations of feasibility, that is, the availability of resources to overcome the resistance of the target organization. And Grosser looks to the stimulation and organization of poor people as the major strategy in their struggle to gain greater benefits from the society.

Nevertheless, these writers are in agreement that the source of social change is to be found in the dissatisfactions of groups who experience the "cramp in the system," as Long puts it.[18] Ross and, to some extent, Lippitt place a high value on self-initiated change and consider it more likely to last. Morris and Binstock and Grosser based their notions to a greater extent on the use of influence and other resources to press change on organizations that can be presumed to be resistant.

All anticipate some resistance to change, but the divergence in goals leads toward different targets. Ross would like to overcome divisive and destructive tendencies among groups in order to build common values and consensus on community goals. Lippitt is interested in overcoming the client system's internal resistance to change in general. Morris and Binstock's planner wants to overcome resistance in the organization-to-

---

18 Norton E. Long, "The Local Community as an Ecology of Games," *American Journal of Sociology,* LXIV, 1958, pp. 251-261. Reprinted in Mayer N. Zald, *Social Welfare Institutions,* New York: John Wiley and Sons, 1965, pp. 255–256.

be-changed, and Grosser's scheme involves group action to wrest benefits from the nonpoor and from the beureaucracies and decision-makers who control resources.

There is general agreement among the writers on the pluralistic nature of the communiity and the tendency of the constituent parts to protect and advance their own interests, although Morris and Grosser state this proposition more forcefully than Ross and Lippitt. Morris and Grosser tend to view change as occurring through a clash of interests represented by adversaries. Ross and Lippitt see possibilities of change within an integrated system.

The clearest differences emerge in terms of power and conflict. Ross seeks to resolve conflict by eschewing the use of power. Morris and Grosser predicate their schemes on the acceptance of power and conflict as facts of community life and the use of both to solve problems. Lippitt would like the client system to be able to use both cooperation and conflict appropriately to cope with its environment.

Two of the works covered in this review give attention to the adjustment of tactics in the light of experience during the change process. Lippitt speaks of choosing modes of behavior appropriate to each encounter in the relationship between change agent and client system. Morris and Binstock emphasize the importance of continual feedback and reassessment and correction of tactics throughout the process, including modification of the planner's goals if that appears necessary to insure that they will be achieved. Both say that choices of tactics can be made before, during, and after encounters with the target or client system.

PLANNED AND UNPLANNED CHANGE

While the four approaches differ substantially from one another, there is one respect in which they are similar. Essentially they are all based on a rational planning model that proceeds from a primary goal to an examination of alternative strategies and then, as noted above, to the choice of particular tactics or actions. Inherent in all these approaches is the assumption that planned change in human affairs is indeed possible. We have not examined that assumption up to this point and it is timely to do so.

Planned change is an aspect of the more general phenomenon of social change and can best be discussed in that context. Contemporary theories emphasize that there are many sources of social change. Etzioni, for example, lists technological, economic, political, religious, ideological, demographic, and stratificational factors as potential sources of change.[19] Most theorists assume that developments in the various areas of the social system take place at different rates and at times move in contradictory directions. They see social change as a result of the interaction and adaptation among these subsystems. For instance, the movement of rural people to cities may both reflect and stimulate alterations in their values, their economic status, and their political activity. The significant characteristic of such changes is that they are not planned by a central authority. Indeed, theorists agree in general that most social change does not take place through deliberate planning.

Changes that are not planned come about in many ways through man-made events as well as natural disturbances. The largest source of unplanned change is found in people's day-by-day pursuits which, for those involved, are conscious and planful but are based on factors within the individual's limited view and control. These individual actions have cumulative and "unanticipated consequences" that create imbalances and tensions in the functioning of social institutions—clearly the case in the rapid urbanization process that is going on around the world. Sevareid put this succinctly when he wrote that "the greatest intellectual discovery of this generation is that the real cause of problems is solutions."[20]

A number of writers have held that deliberate change is a reaction to the consequences of unplanned change. Warren writes on this point that "most purposive change at the community level is a response to problems arising from the unplanned aggregate of individual decisions by persons, families, and organizations of one type or another as they pursue their interests and objectives."[21]

Moore formulates a similar view in which imbalance in a social system triggers action to restore the former equilibrium. He sees the following as sources of imbalance: (1) imperfections in the adaptation of man to his environment, which lead periodically to pain and discomfort and serve as a continuing stimulus to technological improvement; (2) inconsistencies in rates of growth and development among different parts of the social structure and its component functions (for example, population growth rates, development of economic resources, and in-

[19] Amitai Etzioni and Eva Etzioni, Eds., *Social Change*, New York: Basic Books, 1964, p. 7.

[20] Eric Sevareid, *The Progressive*, July 1968, p. 16.

[21] Roland L. Warren, "Types of Purposive Social Change at the Community Level," No. 11, Papers in Social Welfare, Waltham: Brandeis University, 1965, pp. 5–6.

novations in knowledge and values); and (3) disparities between expected behaviors, as defined by prevailing value patterns, and actual
behavior. The last calls either for adjustments in the values because
they are found to be unrealistic or control over the nonconforming
behavior.[22]

In the face of the long-range, powerful forces noted by Etzioni and
Moore, can conscious efforts at change make any headway? Recognizing
that these forces severely constrain efforts to plan, we are nonetheless
persuaded that planning is both possible and necessary. We begin with
the premise that planning involves the selection of a goal or objective.
It is a rational process in which there is a calculation of the relationship
between ends and means. Planning also involves some projection over
time. Finally, it is a deliberate process. Putting these elements together
into a rough definition, *planning is a deliberate, rational process that
involves the choice of actions that are calculated to achieve specified
objectives at some future time.*

Within this approach there are variations in detail and emphasis.
Some theorists and practitioners stress only the implementing aspects,
assuming the goal as given. Others include in planning the process of
determining the goal as well as devising and/or implementing the
means to carry it out. Those who include goal determination place
planning in a larger framework—as a process designed to solve social
problems or to promote social development. This latter, with which we
concur, is still encompassed within a rational model.

There is, however, a view of planning that breaks away from the
rational model altogether and substitutes a process approach. Instead
of specifying a goal and attempting to realize it, planning in this view
establishes processes of interaction out of which both goals and methods
of achieving them will be generated. This is related to what Lindblom
calls the science of "muddling through." It built on the notion that there
is no single rational solution to a stated problem, but that issues of
evaluation arise at every point among people who are working toward
the solution of a problem.[23]

There are echoes here of the discussion in sociology of the "rational
system" versus the "natural system."[24] Within the planning field, the

[22] Wilbert E. Moore, *Social Change,* Englewood Cliffs: Prentice-Hall, Foundations
of Modern Sociology Series, 1963.
[23] Charles E. Lindblom, "The Science of 'Muddling Through,'" *Public Administration Review,* Spring 1959.
[24] Alvin Gouldner, "Organizational Analysis," in Leonard S. Kogan, Ed., *Social*

notions of "incremental planning" have been posed as alternatives to the rational model. Webber, reviewing the newer conceptions of planning, combines concepts based on ecology, program planning, and development to emphasize an open-system approach, based on adaptive, self-regulating mechanisms. He finds that planning today is viewed not as a straightforward march toward an end-state but as an ongoing enterprise that merges "intelligence and purpose into evolutionary processes."[25]

On close examination it appears that these revisions of the rational model are somewhat less definitive than they seem to be. Purposes and goals are still involved in the process. However, the means-ends relationship is described in more complex and subtle terms. It is not to be viewed as a simple linear relationship but as an interacting chain in which both ends and means are subject to continuous redefinition and correction in the light of experience. Ends, in this light, are not merely the broad global social goals that may motivate a project. They are also the more limited, more operational goals that are defined and redefined progressively within an evolutionary process.

Another element in the challenge to overly rationalistic conceptions of planning relates to the scope of control that is claimed for a central planning process. The weight of evidence in theory, research, and practice indicates the severe limitations in the ability of any central planning body to control complex social processes in clear and economical relationships to a predetermined goal. That is the meaning of planning against which Webber argues in saying that "comprehensive planning is not equivalent to either centralized control or coordination. Its output is *improved coherence* among components. . . . It calls for a process of looking outward from one's own focus of activity in search of relations to other activities and in an attempt to fit the one to others" [emphasis in orginal].[26]

Given these appropriate modifications, planning continues to represent a rational process about which there is a tradition of optimism in Western cultures. In the United States there has been a vast body of experience in planned social change, which was touched on in Chapter 2. Certainly some of the efforts to redress injustices failed—or have taken far longer than had been anticipated by those who saw a human

Science Theory and Social Work Research, New York: National Association of Social Workers, 1960.

[25] Melvin M. Webber, "Systems Planning for Social Policy," in Ralph M. Kramer and Harry Specht, Eds., *Readings in Community Organization Practice,* Englewood Cliffs: Prentice-Hall, Inc., 1969, p. 418.

[26] *Ibid.,* p. 424.

need and tried to respond to it. Today there are currents of pessimism in this country, not only over the means of achieving change but over the very possibility of righting wrongs by concerted thought and energy.

The task, as we take it up in the chapters that follow, is to seek out opportunities for effecting change within and despite the strong currents that are the result of diffuse decision-making. This means understanding obstacles that are placed in the way by such ponderous forces as deeply held values or the resistances of organizations to change. And it means finding strategies for overcoming those obstacles. William James put this in a few words, as we saw in Chapter 2, when he said, "The world resists some lines of attack on our part and opens herself to others, so that we must go with the grain of her willingness."

CHAPTER 4

A Framework for Practice

PURPOSES, PROCESSES, TASKS

Our survey of conceptual developments in the previous chapter revealed great differences in the objectives, strategies, and activities of community organization and social planning. Each of the works summarized there dealt with selected aspects of a field of practice and each sought to generate propositions applicable to its particular area. Some of the earlier attempts to define practice that we noted in Chapter 3 reached for general formulations that would apply to the whole field. The more recent tendency is to recognize the great diversity of the field. This, in our view, is necessary both for theoretical development and for empirical testing of practice.

But to recognize diversity raises the question as to whether there are linkages among different segments of the field. In an attempt to identify such connections, some writers have suggested *typologies of practice* that would comprehend the varieties of assumptions and approaches reflected in the work of Ross, Lippitt, Morris and Binstock, Grosser, and others. One particularly comprehensive example is the "three models of practice" described by Jack Rothman as "locality development and organization," "community planning," and "social action."[1]

Rothman's three models are differentiated on twelve dimensions, in-

---

[1] Jack Rothman, "Three Models of Community Organization Practice," *Social Work Practice 1968*, New York: Columbia University Press, 1968 (Copyright, National Conference on Social Welfare), pp. 16–47.

cluding goals, assumptions concerning problems, orientation toward power structure, conceptions of the client being served, conceptions of the role of the practitioner, and strategy, tactics, and techniques. The essential characteristics of the three types may be summarized as follows.

Locality Development and Organization. The goal is self-help and the integration of community groups. The target is the total community, regardless of class cleavages. It is assumed that there are common interests among the different groups and the strategy is directed toward achieving communication and consensus among them. The practitioner serves as an enabler, catalyst, coordinator, and educator. The community is, however, self-determining.

Community Planning. The focus of this model is on problem-solving in regard to substantive social problems. The practitioner serves as expert, fact-finder, and analyst, and as a program implementer and facilitator. His clientele is made up of consumers or recipients of services. Either consensus or conflict may be employed as a strategy. A basic assumption is that change can be brought about through rational decision-making.

Social Action. The goal is a change in power relationships and resources. The clientele are disadvantaged segments of the community and the practice is one of helping them to become organized, to crystallize action issues, and to engage in conflict-oriented action against the power structure.

These are "ideal types" and it is not to be assumed that the models are found in practice exactly in the form described. Each model, however, brings together a number of elements (for example, goals, strategies and roles) that express the basic nature of that kind of practice. The value of such an approach is that it clarifies the logical relationships among the elements and thus contributes to the development of principles of practice based on such relationships.

Rothman went on from the typology to derive propositions of practice, indicating which "model" of practice would be most suitable under a given condition. Thus, the "locality development" model is most appropriate to situations where populations are homogeneous and where consensus exists on major goals. Social action is more appropriate in a situation characterized by subgroups whose interests are antagonistic to one another.

Given the present state of knowledge and research, such propositions can be adduced only to a limited extent. Rothman recognizes that the typology in itself will not suffice to provide practice propositions. "The practitioner," he writes, "should also become sensitive to the mixed uses of these techniques within a single practice context as problems require such blending and organizational situations permit adaptations." In general, however, typological approaches such as Rothman's assume that there are necessary connections between such factors as organizational context, ideology, purposes, methods of practice, and the like. While this may be partially true for some segments of activity, many dimensions cut across one another in a complex matrix.

The work of these writers contributes to the building of a theory of practice, provided that their contributions are used heuristically rather than as definitive guides. Each implies a distinctive *methodology*. Each of the methodologies suggests relationships that may exist under certain conditions. But for the most part, these are hypothetical rather than demonstrated relationships, since only a limited amount of systematic research has been done in the field.

The use of typologies has tended to equate certain fields of activities— for example, community organization of low income groups or village communities in underdeveloped countries—*with specific techniques,* such as militant protest or nondirective education. To the extent that such connections become guides for action, they tend to reinforce two difficulties. One is the tendency to consider a particular field of activity as self-contained and to minimize its interdependence with other areas of practice. This is the case, for example, with self-help efforts that are limited to the neighborhood and are not linked to non-local resources and services. Or, conversely, efforts at coordination and planning of social services can fail to take account of the need for organized channels for participation on the part of people being served.

The other limitation of equating certain fields of practice to specific techniques is the tendency to limit the options available for action. Just as the auspices and purposes of social-change efforts vary over a wide range, so too do the methods that can be employed. There are un- doubtedly connections among auspices, purposes, strategies, and methods. And if these were properly established, they would make one method of intervention more appropriate under certain conditions than alterna- tive actions. Some beginning insights into such connections have emerged, but there is not yet enough knowledge to warrant firm conclusions as to the relationships among various dimensions of practice.

On the other hand, in a field where political and ideological issues are so intimately involved, values tend to determine actions, especially in the absence of reliable data. At the present time statements as to what methodologies are appropriate under certain conditions frequently represent philosophical value positions or at most untested hypotheses. These are undoubtedly legitimate, provided they are understood as such. To build them into typologies that then become guides for practice eliminates the possibility of experimenting with alternative methods in order to test the assumptions.

It should be clear that practice encompasses many dimensions. In order to generate propositions about effective strategies and methods, one must take account of such variables as sponsorship, ideology, differences in power position, organizational structure, and others. Each of these could be further elaborated into subcategories, resulting in a bewildering matrix of factors that would have to be incorporated into a comprehensive theory of practice.

This situation is similar to a general problem that besets the social sciences when they deal with phenomena that have many dimensions and many relationships among dimensions. It calls for sorting out factors that vary with one another and factors that vary independently of each other. Because of the difficulty of gathering data adequate to permit such complex multivariate analysis, it is apparent that the development of practice theory in community organization and social planning will be a long, slow process requiring both careful research and creative insights. Organizing the experience of practitioners for this purpose has barely begun, and it is clearly not possible at this time to present a coherent "theory" of community organization and social planning that provides a firm base for predicting the effectiveness of particular actions or methods.

Indeed, there is a reason not to seek an overall theory at this time. This is the dynamic nature of current practice and the difficulty as well as the undesirability of setting firm boundaries around its functions. There is a tendency in the models that have been proposed to identify professional practice with one or another approach. While definitions and boundaries are necessary in the clarification of a professional field, they can, if used excessively or prematurely, prevent that field from discovering its own potentialities. The diversity that now exists is an asset in enabling this field of practice to engage in experimentation and innovation.

Our examination of practice has persuaded us that there is no single methodology that fits all the dimensions of this field and that there is little consistency in the extent to which the various dimensions of practice are correlated with one another. Thus, a particular kind of structure is not necessarily associated with one purpose or ideology, nor does it require one set of strategies or the performance of only certain roles by the practitioner. For example, an organization sponsored by a client group may be directed toward self-help or toward organizational change; it may engage in educational or conflict tactics; it may have an ameliorative or a revolutionary ideology.

In most situations, more than one of the practice models reviewed in the previous chapter are at play. Frequently a practitioner may have to switch from one to another at different stages in the development of a program. Thus, a social planner who is concerned with the development of a service program may need to organize a social-action effort in order to gain support for the program. Whether or not the planner can himself undertake that action is a matter of his location, organizational commitments, and autonomy, but it is not necessarily excluded by the fact that he is working within the context of a planning model. If he is not able, because of these constraints, to undertake the action himself, he still needs to be aware of social action as a possible or necessary approach and alert to others who could carry out this task.

The differences that we shall emphasize in elaborating our framework should not obscure the unity of purpose that we assume to underly variations in practice. We take as our point of departure the assumption that social change is the general purpose informing all activities in this field and that community organization and social planning are concerned with formulating and implementing changes on the organizational level in order to cope more effectively with social problems. But concretely, what kinds of changes are to be achieved?

In his classic formulation of community organization, Lane regarded the central purpose to be the adjustment of needs and resources. This theme continues to run through all aspects of practice, but it needs to be refined and expanded. Relating needs and resources is of concern to the neighborhood organizer in a low-income area who is helping disadvantaged people obtain resources not now available to them; it is also basic to the social planner in a government agency who is responsible for deploying resources to meet a need that has been defined by public policy.

The older formulation was limited, however, by the relatively narrow functions of the social welfare system as then defined, which meant primarily the voluntary health and welfare agencies. The notion of balancing needs and resources was translated, too often, into the narrow function of ·distributing voluntarily contributed funds to existing service agencies. "Need" by such a definition was not what people in the community required but rather what agencies required for their specific activities. A much broader approach to the conceptualization of needs and resources is of course required. While the measurement of "need" poses complex issues, the tendency now is to seek both better indicators of social need and a fuller expression of preferences on the part of people directly affected. The current efforts to revise the ways of providing welfare, educational, and health services to the poor reflect this.

The Lane formulation of adjusting needs to resources may now be recast as a process of finding solutions to social problems by redistributing three factors—*resources, functions,* and *decision-making power.* Practice, then, is concerned broadly with these three elements and with the issues inherent in bringing about their redistribution. This may be stated briefly as follows:

1. *Resources* How are money, manpower, and other scarce resources to be distributed among service functions and organizations? How will shifts in the way these are distributed affect various socioeconomic groups?

2. *Service functions* Where and by whom are different services to be performed? To what geographical units, governmental or voluntary, of what size, is responsibility to be assigned for specific functions in health, education, income maintenance, social services, manpower development, community relations, and other social needs?

3. *Decision-making power* Who is to decide the questions cited above? Who is to exercise control over policies, programs, and resources, and how are these responsibilities to be distributed among different groups in society?

Any of these elements, or a combination of them, may be a target of change, but change in one will have repercussions in the other. Thus, an effort on the part of a neighborhood association to increase the power of local residents requires specification of the functional and structural form that such a change would take. One way would be to mobilize pressure on existing decision-making bodies to include representation from underrepresented groups. Another way is to press existing organizations to adopt specific policy recommendations of residents concerning functions and resources. Still another approach would be to alter the locus of decision-making so that control of certain functions and resources is transferred to different structures. The agitation for community control over public schools is an example of the last approach.

It is equally the case that achieving a change in one of the three elements may require, as a matter of strategy, a change in another. For instance, altering the distribution of program funds among agencies may necessitate first a shift in decision-making authority from one body to another or a change in the membership of an existing authority. The interlocking of these elements argues, in our view, for accepting as inextricable parts of practice the two traditional themes—strengthening social provisions and improving people's problem-solving capacities and relationships. The field of practice ties these two together in a common enterprise in which planful approaches to the solution of problems are fused with the mobilization of people to decide and act on their problems.

Assuming this definition of the purposes of practice, do we find similarities when we look at the range of tasks performed by practitioners in the field? Is there in fact some commonality among the kinds of practice represented by the writers we have discussed in this chapter and the previous one?

One common element involves the problem-solving process that practitioners employ. Writers from Lindeman on have developed schemes to describe this process.[2] It is usually presented in terms of a number of steps or stages, often with the implication that these are taken in sequence. Writers differ in their terminology and in the number of steps they identify, but their schemes are similar. We conceive of the process in this way:

1. Defining the problem.
2. Establishing structural and communication links for consideration of the problem.
3. Study of alternative solutions and adoption of a policy.
4. Development and implementation of a program plan.
5. Monitoring and feedback.

We elaborate on these phases of problem-solving in the next section, but first we want to make some general observations. It is not being suggested that these tasks are (or should be) performed in a prescribed sequence. A specific project may begin in the middle, so to speak, in the sense that some steps have been taken previously and the practitioner is introduced into the process with certain givens. This is the situation when the basic policies have been accepted and the requirement is to design and launch a program to carry out the policies. Nor does the process proceed neatly from one stage to another. The tasks are continuous, with peaks of certain activities at particular times. A spiral-like quality is characteristic of these tasks in that they are done over and

---

[2] Harper and Dunham, *op. cit.,* pp. 168–175.

over in the course of most projects, each time in a somewhat different way.

As the practitioner moves through the problem-solving process, he engages in tasks that require both *analysis* and *action*. We use the term "analytical" to refer to the intellectual work involved in problem-solving. These are the tasks the practitioner must perform in order to make choices as to what he will do, when, and how. He must continually analyze the situation in which he finds himself, the problem he is trying to overcome, and the objective he is trying to achieve. And he constantly engages in assessing the relevant conditions in the environment which affect the nature of the problem and the possibilities of achieving his objective.

The other type of task, to which we give equal weight, is *interactional*. This connotes the actions undertaken by the practitioner in relationships with other people—to communicate his proposals and ideas, to elicit their thinking and activity, and to provide the atmosphere, conditions, and resources which make it possible for others to pursue agreed upon objectives. These interactional tasks are guided and evaluated by the practitioner's analysis. Action in turn provides the material for analysis. The interrelationship is essential and continuous. The combination of these two types of activity is implied in most recent definitions of community organization and of social planning. Kramer and Specht define community organization as follows:

"Community organization refers to various methods of intervention whereby a professional change agent helps a community action system composed of individuals, groups, or organizations to engage in planned collective action in order to deal with social problems within a democratic system of values. It is concerned with programs aimed at social change, with primary reference to environmental conditions and social institutions. It involves two major and interrelated concerns: (a) the processes of working with an action system, which include planning and organizing, identifying problem areas, diagnosing causes, and formulating solutions; and (b) developing strategies and mobilizing the resources necessary to effect action."[3]

This definition includes, on the one hand, working with an action system and mobilizing the resources needed to produce change and, on the other hand, diagnostic and planning tasks.

[3] Ralph M. Kramer and Harry Specht, *op. cit.*, pp. 8–9.

Kahn defines social planning succinctly as "policy choice and programming in the light of facts, projections, and application of values."[4] The process is viewed as consisting of four essential elements: (a) definition of the planning task, (b) formulation of policy (the standing plan), (c) programming, and (d) evaluation, monitoring, and feedback. Kahn deliberately limits himself to the intellectual content of the planning functions, which are included in Kramer and Specht's concept of "working with an action system."

Both definitions, however—and this would be true of any that can be put forward at the present time—are lacking in precision. The difficulty with the Kahn definition lies in the questions raised by such terms as "choice" and "values," which are built into the definition. Immediately, one must ask whose choices and whose values, and how are they determined? Kahn does not assume these matters to be given, since he sees the expression of preferences as an indispensable part of the "definition of the planning task." His scheme assumes, however, that somehow an "action system" has come into being that can make these choices and filter the preferences. The planner is one who assists in that process— although it is not altogether clear how functions and responsibilities are divided between the professional planner and the planning group. But Kahn's scheme does not deal at all with the process of bringing a planning group into existence.

Kramer and Specht focus more sharply on the professional "change agent" and on his interaction with an "action system." They include in their definition not only planning but also "organizing," that is, both the intellectual process of defining problems and proposed solutions, and the activities that stem from those plans, involving mobilization of necessary resources to achieve a result. They go on, however, to develop a typology of community organization that is based on two models, *community development* and *social planning*, each of which represents a distinctive clustering of goals, activities, and techniques.

Community development is described as "efforts to mobilize the people who are affected by a community condition . . . into groups and organizations to enable them to take action on these social problems and issues which affect them."[5] Social planning, on the other hand, "refers to efforts directed toward integrating the different action systems of the community with other systems of the local community and/or with

---

[4] The most comprehensive development of social planning methodology is to be found in Alfred J. Kahn, *Theory and Practice of Social Planning*, New York: Russell Sage Foundation, 1969, p. 17.

[5] Kramer and Specht, *op. cit.*, pp. 10–11.

extracommunity action systems, and efforts aimed at bringing about reforms in the attitudes, policies, and practices of large private and public agencies, including legal, functional, and operating systems."

It is our contention that social problem-solving encompasses most if not all the elements included in the definitions proposed by Kahn and by Kramer and Specht. In our view planning is sterile without mobilizing people and organizations to put new policies and programs into effect. By the same token, organizing people to achieve social change requires planning to guide both the ends and means of their efforts. One can equate "organizing" with the *interactional* tasks to which we have referred and "planning" to the *analytical* work of the practitioner. These two kinds of activity are complementary to each other in the various phases of the problem-solving model that is elaborated below.

The table on page 62 is an attempt to illustrate the analytical and interactional tasks that fall within different phases of the problem-solving model that was outlined earlier. It must be borne in mind that the five steps in the problem-solving process are not carried out mechanically and that any attempt to categorize them must necessarily be highly abstract. The table is suggestive of the nature of practice tasks and is meant to apply to a very broad range of situations. The "problem," to cite a few examples, may be how to improve a service program that appears to be ineffective; how to develop a new provision for an emerging need; or how to alter a standing public policy that seems to be obsolete. The tasks are presented from the point of view of the practitioner.

A SOCIAL PROBLEM-SOLVING MODEL

We take up now in some detail the problem-solving process that was earlier described as consisting of these aspects or phases:

Defining the problem that is to be addressed or "solved."

Building a structure or communications system for addressing it.

Examining and selecting from among alternative solutions, policies, and lines of action.

Taking the action steps necessary to implement the chosen policy in programmatic form.

Revision of the above decisions and actions in the light of continuous monitoring, evaluation, and feedback.

Defining the Problem. The way in which a problem is formulated will strongly influence how it will be handled in the succeeding phases of problem-solving. To illustrate, the same set of facts about a population in

Table 1.   Analytical and Interactional Tasks by Phases of Problem-Solving

	Analytical Tasks	Interactional Tasks
1. Defining the problem	In preliminary terms studying and describing the problematic aspects of a situation. Conceptualizing the system of relevant actors. Assessing what opportunities and limits are set by the organization employing the practitioner and by other actors.	Eliciting and receiving information, grievances, and preferences from those experiencing the problem and other sources.
2. Building structure	Determining the nature of the practitioner's relationship to various actors. Deciding on types of structures to be developed. Choosing people for roles as experts, communicators, influencers, and the like.	Establishing formal and informal communication lines. Recruiting people into the selected structures and roles and obtaining their commitments to address the problem.
3. Formulating policy	Analyzing past efforts to deal with the problem. Developing alternative goals and strategies, assessing their possible consequences and feasibility. Selecting one or more for recommendation to decision-makers.	Communicating alternative goals and strategies to selected actors. Promoting their expression of preferences and testing acceptance of various alternatives. Assisting decision-makers to choose.
4. Implementing plans	Specifying what tasks need to be performed to achieve agreed-upon goals, by whom, when, and with what resources and procedures.	Presenting requirements to decision-makers, overcoming resistances, and obtaining commitments to the program. Marshalling resources and putting procedures into operation.
5. Monitoring	Designing system for collecting information on operations. Analyzing feedback data and specifying adjustments needed and/or new problems that require planning and action.	Obtaining information from relevant actors based on their experience. Communicating findings and recommendations and preparing actors for new round of decisions to be made.

"poor health" can be interpreted in quite diverse ways. One way is to put the emphasis on the lack of adequate income, which would account for bad housing and nutrition. Or the problem can be conceived of as the need for a new program that stresses health education. Or the problem can be formulated as non-use of medical services that are easily accessible to the population in question. In other words, the formulation of "the problem" to a large extent sets the direction for thinking about it and acting on it. For this reason, we devote considerably more attention in this chapter to problem-defining than to the other aspects of problem-solving, which are discussed more fully in subsequent chapters.

The first issue that arises at the point of problem identification is whether to accept a current formulation as provided by an existing service, organization, profession, or interest group or whether to define the problem in more "objective" terms, based on a body of data that will somehow describe the condition more adequately and therefore presumably provide a better guide for intervention. The planner is frequently enmeshed from the outset in a variety of prejudgments and constraints that stem from the auspices under which he is operating and various other factors. The theoretical model is nevertheless useful in defining some of the tasks that need to be performed, since the planning process necessarily rests on an appraisal of the situation that is to be affected. The exercise of appraising the problem with as much freedom from predefinition as possible provides an opportunity to consider a range of alternatives in addition to those that may already exist in the minds of relevant actors.

A related issue is the question of boundaries. On the one hand, the planner seeks to understand the problem in its broadest dimensions in order to consider all of the factors that may be relevant to his work in the later stages of policy development and program implementation. The kind of information that is brought into view and the way it is organized have an important effect on subsequent decisions. "A knowledge-organizing scheme," writes Kahn, "is in a sense also a planning framework."[6]

On this basis, Kahn calls for "a systematic review and appraisal of relevant research in an applied field."[7] General sources of data, such as census studies, trend studies, statistical series, and breakdowns of aggregate data that pinpoint the characteristics of particular subgroups and geographic areas, are all important checkpoints in the first approaches to a problem. This calls for knowledge of the sources of data that might be relevant and skill in the assembling of such material so that it can illuminate alternative responses to the questions.

A striking example of this skill in recent years was Molly Orshansky's analysis of poverty in the United States.[8] Orshansky's contribution was to

---

[6] Kahn, op. cit., p. 79.

[7] Ibid.

[8] Mollie Orshansky, "Counting the Poor: Another Look at the Poverty Profile," Social Security Bulletin, Vol. 28, No. 1, January 1965, p. 5.

develop a measure of poverty that was related to size of family and cost of food. She then applied this measure to census data and was able to show in a way that had not been demonstrated before the numbers and characteristics of families of different types (farm, nonfarm, male or female-headed, employed or unemployed, and the like) who were living below the poverty line. This innovative approach to the subject provided a framework for the discussion of poverty for years to come and was a starting point for new approaches to the planning of antipoverty programs.

The other side of the picture is that data cannot be used effectively unless they are gathered in relationship to some focus or question that has been adopted at least as a tentative basis for pursuing knowledge. To quote Kahn again,

"Planning without adequate investigation of relevant realities, relevant social facts, is utopian thinking or travelling blind. Planning that assembles volumes of data without imposing criteria of relevance and priority in the appraisal is useless ritual."[9]

If he is to exercise any independence and creativity in identifying problems, the practitioner is called upon to raise new kinds of questions around which data can be organized. What can stimulate this kind of innovative thinking? Where can the practitioner turn for fresh insights about a problematic situation that will help him in the early part of his analysis?

A general response to this question is to point to theoretical materials in the areas of *social behavior* and *institutional analysis*. The former deals with the behavior of people in relation to social systems and includes such subjects as role theory, group dynamics, small-group behavior, communication, and decision-making and is drawn from psychology, social psychology, anthropology, and microsociology. Social science knowledge applicable to institutional analysis comes from macrosociology, economics, and political science and includes content on community analysis, organizational theory, social stratification, power structures, and the like.

Such an answer is too general, however, and begs the question, since it fails to indicate what theory or theories the practitioner can apply to his analytical work. First, we must state our conviction that as of this writing there is no single grand theory of (or for) the practice of community organization and social planning. Theoretical systems, such as classical Marxism, that attempt to explain all of social reality seem to

[9] Kahn, *op. cit.*, p. 71.

have limited utility as tools for the tasks with which most practice is concerned, although the works of Marx, Freud, and others undoubtedly throw light on the genesis and persistence of many social problems.

The practitioner can, however, make use of theories that deal not with all of society but with a complex of problems such as poverty, delinquency, or family instability. In recent years this has been done with theoretical approaches to "the opportunity structure," to "powerlessness," or to "the culture of poverty." But the risk inherent in using a single explanatory model for a complex social reality is that it tends to restrict the perspectives to which the practitioner is exposed and to limit his ability to explore dimensions of the problem and approaches that are not contemplated in the model he has chosen.

For the most part practice problems are situational and not at the level, for example, of searching for a solution to poverty. This suggests the use of theories that fall in the middle range and deal with more limited problems. Given the present state of knowledge and its application to practice, it also suggests that the practitioner must "try out" for heuristic purposes a succession of theories that may help him to formulate the problem at hand. Let us take an illustration.

Assume that a service agency is challenged by an organization of its consumers on the grounds that the agency is no longer providing the service required by its mandate. The practitioner would first ask himself what he knows empirically about the situation that would help him to understand how this discrepancy developed and why it persists. Using the heuristic approach he would then try to marshal knowledge and theories from other sources in order to assist him in comprehending better the information he has and in order to suggest explanations he had not considered, thereby also indicating the kind of additional information he should gather.

This kind of stimulation from theorists and social researchers would lead him, for instance, to think of factors and processes both internal and external to his agency. Useful insights might come from Selznick, for example, and his work on cooptation or Etzioni's work on the disparity between ideal and real goals.[10] Blau and Scott might inform him of how

---

[10] The approach to the use of theory outlined here is based primarily on Armand Lauffer's unpublished paper, "The Social Science Component in Professional Education for Community Organization in Social Work," New York: Council on Social Work Education, 1967. Philip Selznick, "An Approach to a Theory of Bureaucracy," *American Sociological Review*, **VIII**, February 1943, pp. 47–54; "Foundations of the Theory of Organizations," *American Sociological Review*, **XIII**, February 1948, pp. 25–35; *TVA and the Grassroots*, Berkeley: University of California Press, 1949; and also Amitai Etzioni, *A Comparative Analysis of Complex Organizations*, New York:

the principal beneficiaries of an organization act to control it. Thompson and Levine would open up the possible importance of inter-organizational exchange processes in accounting for what has occurred in the agency.[11] Price might offer propositions on the influence of external factors on the organization's effectiveness, and Warren's analysis might lead him to search out the sources of horizontal and vertical inputs and their effect on the choice of consensus as opposed to conflict strategies.[12] Banfield and Wilson might direct him to new sources of personal influence and Katz and Lazarsfeld to those of political influence; Merton might lead him to focus on alienation, ambivalence, and the latent functions of changing goals, while Gouldner and Argyris, in different ways, might lead him to examine the behavior of the actors within the agency.[13]

Thus, various theories are used in succession, each yielding different information and insights. At this proceeds, the problem is continuously reformulated until it is defined in useful, operational terms, that is, until the practitioner can use the formulation to guide his strategies for intervention. This heuristic approach has its own limitations, of course. Each theory has only limited capacity to offer plausible explanations. Moreover, their very specificity limits their usefulness in producing practice principles that are generalizable to other situations.[14] Nevertheless, the

Free Press, 1961; and *Complex Organizations: A Sociological Reader,* New York: Holt, Rinehart and Winston, 1969, second edition.

[11] Peter Blau and W. Richard Scott, *Formal Organizations: A Comparative Approach,* San Francisco: Chandler Publishing Co., 1962; and Sol Levine and Paul E. White, "Exchange as a Conceptual Framework for the Study of Interorganizational Relationships," *Administrative Science Quarterly,* **5,** March 1961, pp. 583–601.

[12] James L. Price, *Organizational Effectiveness: An Inventory of Propositions* Homewood, Ill.: Richard D. Irwin, Inc., 1968 ; and Roland L. Warren, *The Community in America,* Chicago: Rand McNally & Co., 1963.

[13] Edward C. Banfield and James Q. Wilson, *City Politics,* Cambridge, Mass.: Harvard University Press, 1963; Elihu Katz and Paul F. Lazarsfeld, *Personal Influence,* Glencoe, Ill.: Free Press, 1955; Robert K. Merton, *Social Theory and Social Structure,* revised edition, New York: Free Press, 1957, and Merton *et al.,* Eds., *Reader in Bureaucracy,* New York: Free Press, 1952; Alvin W. Gouldner, *Patterns of Industrial Bureaucracy,* New York: Free Press, 1954, and *Studies in Leadership,* New York: Harper and Row, 1950; Chris Argyris, *Integrating the Individual and the Organization,* New York: John Wiley & Sons, 1964, and *Interpersonal Competence and Organizational Effectiveness,* Homewood, Ill.: Richard D. Irwin, Inc., 1962, and "The Individual and Organization: Some Problems of Mutual Adjustment," *Administrative Science Quarterly,* **II,** June 1957, pp. 1–24.

[14] Alvin W. Gouldner, "Theoretical Requirements of the Applied Social Sciences," *American Sociological Review,* **22,** February 1957, pp. 92–103. Also in W. G. Bennis, *et al.,* Eds., *The Planning of Change,* New York: Holt, Rinehart and Winston, 1961, pp. 83–95.

use of theory suggests to the practitioner possible explanations of the phenomena with which he is dealing and potential lines of action for affecting them.

To recapitulate, the formulation of a statement of the problem to be addressed requires the gathering of data in relation to theories or insights concerning the situation at hand. This involves a series of approximations that follow a rough logical order, although that is not necessarily the chronological order in which they are performed. As we pointed out above, information available through general sources, such as census reports and special studies, provides some guidelines to the parameters of a problem or condition. These data may also indicate variation among subgroups of the population that may be of particular interest, as well as variations over time. Previous research on the problem, including scholarly literature and the investigations performed by governmental and voluntary agencies, are other sources of information. The volume of such research, especially in the past decade, has multiplied substantially because many programs have required the collection of data on various social problems and needs as a condition for Federal grants to local communities. The critical analysis of such studies provides a useful resource.

Notwithstanding these sources of data, there is little information available in the form of general indicators that are directly relevant to planning, and much of the collection of data needs to be done during the planning process itself. Specific questions of description and measurement begin to arise almost immediately, and these can be pursued only through investigations tailored to the problem under consideration. These may entail survey research, studies of service statistics, and other forms of research.

But the inputs for problem formulation do not come only from these sources of "hard" data and quantitative measurement. As we have pointed out in earlier chapters, definitions of social problems are inherently matters of value judgments, and these differ from group to group.

It may be assumed that there is always more than one problem that presents itself. A choice is therefore almost always involved as to what priority will be given to a particular problem. Rational analytical techniques are generally not adequate to make this choice. At best, they can be used to indicate the dimensions of the problem and also the resources that are required within the existing state of knowledge to deal with the problem. However, the choice is largely in the area of preferences.

On the analytical side, the practitioner can make estimates as to the degree of interest and commitment that various organizations and groups may have in dealing with the problem and the capabilities and resources that can be brought to bear. However, much of this is not fully calculable, and interactional tasks must be relied upon to test out these matters through a presentation of the problem and an exploration of interest and capabilities in dealing with it. This requires channels of communication and structures for sustained interaction, and this requirement brings us to another phase of problem-solving.

Building Structure and Communications. Since planned change is a process that extends over time, the development of structure is not a single act but one that takes different forms, depending on the stage reached in the development of a project. The earliest stage may be viewed as a "preplanning" or "preamble" phase, where informal explorations are taking place to ascertain various perceptions of a problem, need, or purpose and no specific proposals have yet emerged. A practitioner who is acting at this "preplanning" stage finds himself engaged to a great extent in informal activity rather than operating through an organized mechanism. A skilled, analytical process of exploration should be directed toward an evaluation of the state of thinking in the field about the general problem, the areas of concensus and disagreement, and the degree to which potential participants in the venture are being propelled toward change.

Out of such an analysis, there begins to emerge a picture of the issues that are involved in a choice of structure. For example, if exploration indicates broad consensus on the purposes that different parties wish to pursue, but differences as to what measures will be most effective, the structure can be weighted toward maximizing expertness in problem-solving. If, on the other hand, there are wide differences concerning values, purposes, and goals, there is a prior task of finding a mechanism that can achieve an agreed-on direction with sufficient legitimation to exercise influence on the problem being attacked. The traditional model of bringing the contending parties together so that they may find agreement is not the only way of achieving that purpose. Indeed, it may often be the wrong way. Another is to gather together a more homogeneous grouping that is agreed on a goal and that undertakes to influence others to change their practices in order to achieve that selected goal.

Most of the literature on community organization and planning has dealt with structure from one of the following perspectives: consensus, cooptation, or centrally planned change. *Consensus* refers to the traditional "council" model, criticized in the literature on the ground that "participation of all" leads primarily to trade-offs and the protection of the status quo. *Cooptation* is associated with the type of structure in which representatives of a minority view or interest are included within an organizational framework dominated by others but render legitimacy to the latter's purposes. This was the way in which the inclusion of representatives of the poor on antipoverty boards was frequently characterized. "Tokenism" would be the popular term for a structure making for cooptation of less influential groups. The third approach to structure focuses on the problem of achieving change through the *mobilization of influence*. A central planner—individual, group, or organization—with a purpose to fulfill organizes a structure designed to maximize his opportunity to achieve that purpose. The issues involved in building such structures have been discussed in some detail in political science and planning literature.

It should be noted first, however, that the approaches to structure that have been mentioned do not exhaust the possibilities and that other factors of equal importance to the practitioner have not been dealt with adequately in the existing literature. For example, a practitioner is frequently faced, in the early stages of the development of a project, with an inadequate level of existing interest in the issue or need that he is mandated to address. His target is not (or not yet) the conquest of resistance to change, but the kind of apathy that stems from lack of knowledge or concern about the problem. The purpose of the initial organizational efforts in such a situation is basically educational—to expose potential participants in the project to the problem situation in a way that may arouse interest and concern. Study committees frequently serve this type of educational purpose rather than being directed primarily to the discovery of new information.

Another neglected topic is the use of an organizational structure as the vehicle for confrontation of differences, conflict, bargaining, and negotiation. The type of structure that has been characterized as making for sterile consensus or dubious cooptation may, under certain circumstances, provide opportunities for genuine and productive confrontations. Antipoverty boards, as noted, may have served as instruments for cooptation of the representatives of the poor. They also served, however, in many instances, as channels for the expression of well-organized interests on the part of these representatives, bringing pressure to bear within the organization for their demands.

It would take careful assessment to determine the precise circumstances under which change can be achieved more effectively through participation of opposing groups within such a structure, as against the mobilization of pressures independently. In at least some of the experience of recent years, however, it seems clear that the pressure of the Federal funding agency, requiring that the potential beneficiaries of the program be represented, generated new forces that had not been present previously in the planning situation. Representatives of very different types of constituencies were forced by the common need for resources to confront one another. The resolution of the issue was neither consensus nor cooptation but a redistribution, to some extent, of the resources and power available, and therefore a genuine change.

Command over resources was the key to that situation and is, in general, the factor of greatest importance in relation to structure. The issue may be stated succinctly in the form of a proposition—that the effectiveness of any given type of structure for planning and action is determined primarily by its access to and control over resources. Both "access" and "control" are equally important. The traditional budget committee of a community chest, for example, had formal authority over resources but relatively little real control because of the underlying agreements built into the structure and the ability of the major participants to achieve their goals independently if their interests were not satisfied in the central body.

To recapitulate, the practitioner weighs and chooses among various kinds of structure in order to foster the interaction and communication he considers most germane to the problem at hand. These interchanges from many sources provide much of the input for the formulation of the problem and alternative approaches to its resolution. Earlier we suggested that the practitioner enriches this phase of problem-solving with the products of his own empirical and theoretical research.

Policy Analysis and Choice. Policy formation takes its point of departure from general statements of goals and values and leads into more specific program measures. It is an operational statement of a goal or goals. Some of the essential properties of a policy are continuity over time (subject, of course, to change) institutionalization in the form of law or regulation or statement of principle, and, most importantly, provision of an explicit guide to future actions.

Because policy involves both ends and means, it cannot be viewed only as a technical function. Policy formation is a process of making choices, as indeed is all of planning. The choices at the level of policy are, however, in a large measure choices of "values" in the sense that they determine the purposes that are to be served and the benefits to be sought. They involve, at least implicitly, a judgment as to desirable social outcomes. *A methodology of policy analysis is therefore a technique for making choices clear and explicit and for using data in order to achieve that purpose.* The literature in the field of social policy is concerned primarily with the substantive issues of social welfare, and there is little on the methodology of social policy analysis.

Kahn views policies as "standing plans."[15] They are general guides to further decision-making. Wickenden uses the same notion in referring to social policy as

" . . . a settled course of governmental or group action and viewpoint, typically incorporated in an institutional mechanism such as law, regulation, program, or statement of principles which in turn governs future decisions in the same area."[16]

Rein argues for a critical approach that will challenge all assumptions and reveal the value premises inherent in what are ostensibly technical proposals; he also argues for a careful delineation of costs of choices made and choices foregone. He suggests that policy analysis needs to take account simultaneously of three different frameworks that have been used: ideology, feasibility, and rationality. Questions are to be explored in relation to all three criteria.[17]

Discussion of policy choices poses the question of the role of the planner in the process of choosing. Dyckman argues that the planner "must have a theory of long-run client interests" in order to help shape goals, since these will not be given to him as a "set of well-ordered preference functions."[18] The planner is an instrumentality for the creation of aspirations and demands, not only for identifying them. Davidoff agrees, stressing the role of planner as advocate.[19]

On the other hand, Reiner's conception stresses the planner's role as analyst of alternatives and their consequences, with the implication that the planner presents choices rather than making them.[20] Webber does

---

[15] Kahn, *op. cit.*, p. 130.

[16] From mimeographed notes prepared by Elizabeth Wickenden for use in a course in urban planning at Hunter College, New York, N.Y.

[17] Martin Rein, "Social Planning: Welfare Planning," in *International Encyclopedia of the Social Sciences*, New York: The Macmillan Company and Free Press, 1968, pp. 142–154.

[18] John W. Dyckman, "Societal Goals and Planned Societies," in H. Wentworth Eldredge, Ed., *Taming Megalopolis*, Vol. I, Garden City, N.Y.: Anchor Books, Doubleday & Co., 1967, p. 258.

[19] Paul Davidoff, "Advocacy and Pluralism in Planning," *Journal of the American Institute of Planners*, 31, No. 4, November 1965, pp. 331–39.

[20] Thomas A. Reiner, "The Planner as Value Technician: Two Classes of Utopian

not deal directly with this issue, but presents a developmental view of planning in which the emphasis is on processes of interaction, mutual adaptation, and continuous analysis.[21]

How does the practitioner choose a "mix" between advocating a specific course of action and outlining the available options? These might include such factors as the state of knowledge concerning causes and solutions of a particular social problem, the sponsorship and organizational context of the planner's operation, and the degree of agreement or disagreement concerning values among the groups with whom the planner is working. Too little is known as yet to permit systematic formulations of such a guide. Ideology and judgment together will have to determine these choices for the present, with the hope that accumulated experience and research can provide more assistance over a period of time.

Paraphrasing several approaches that have been referred to above, a number of major elements in the methodology of policy analysis are outlined below.

1. *Ends-means analysis.* Looking at ends and means as a chain of interaction, analysis aims both at distinguishing between them (at any given point) and showing their interrelationships. This calls both for revealing value assumptions that may be hidden behind instrumental proposals and for questioning whether ideological statements propounded as goals are actually being made in support of instrumental technologies. An example of the former would be a proposal for a work relief program; of the latter, a call for additional professional services of a given type.

It is recognized that ends and means are subject to varying definitions and that such variations may involve questions of value; it is also recognized that ends and means vary over time. It is the function of policy analysis to identify these variations and to establish the alternative relationships between ends and means that are possible within a given situation.

2. *System analysis.* The term is used here in a loose nontechnical sense, although attempts are being made to apply more formal systems analysis techniques to problems of social planning, and it is to be expected that further work will be done in that direction. By system

Constructs and Their Impacts on Planning," in H. Wentworth Eldredge, *op. cit.*

[21] Melvin M. Webber, "Systems Planning for Social Policy," in Kramer and Specht, *op. cit.*, p. 424.

analysis we mean specification of the structures and relationships that the planning project might affect—what target group or groups, what spread of problems and conditions, what elements of social structure, what organizational fields, and the like.

Alternatives are present here as they are in the selection of ends and means. Considerations of value, rationality, and feasibility are involved in the choice among specifications of system boundaries, as they are in the delineation of goals.

3. *Benefits analysis.* Different policy choices will, it is assumed, result in different benefits. Differences in the types and amounts of benefits and in the degree to which different individuals and groups do or do not benefit are to be traced in relation to different policy alternatives. Costs, insofar as they can be anticipated, are part of benefits analysis, particularly in the quite usual event that benefits to some groups involve expenses for others.

4. *Resources analysis.* This entails a first approximation of the possibilities and constraints that will affect alternative policy approaches. Resources include not only funds but manpower and knowledge, as well as sanction and authority.

5. *Policy strategy.* The result of all of the choices outlined above is the selection, among alternatives, of a broad policy strategy that incorporates decisions as to the level of intervention and the target or targets of the effort, taking into account (subject to testing and correction by experience) both the benefits to be anticipated and the resources available.

The remaining two phases of problem-solving—program development and evaluation—are treated here very briefly, since these processes are taken up in some detail in the chapters on service agencies and planning organizations.

Program Development. Planning that limits itself only to policy analysis is incomplete from the point of view of practice. It is here that one of the distinctions can be made between academic and practice orientations. The former appropriately may stop with analysis, identifying values, choices and consequences, and developing theoretical frameworks for their evaluation. The practitioner needs to incorporate all of that into an action situation, which means building a program to operationalize the choices made.

Programming involves the detailed spelling out of implementing actions to carry out broad policies related to a goal. It is essentially a logistical type of activity, guided by considerations of effectiveness and efficiency in seeking a result.

Like any logistical enterprise, programming involves the mobilization of resources and their delivery to where they are needed. The following are the major elements to be considered:

1. Content of the jobs—what are the specifics that need to be done— what kinds of activities, programs, services; in what sequence and what quantities; and through what physical arrangements.
2. Resources—what is required to do the various pieces of work— capital facilities, manpower of what qualifications, and funds; where those resources are now located, who controls them, how they can be mobilized.
3. Feasibility—availability or nonavailability of resources; changes needed in order to achieve the objectives in policies, distribution of resources, creation of new resources, and the like; existence of acceptance or resistance; strategies for achieving necessary changes (conflict, negotiation, bargaining, and so on).

Monitoring and Feedback. Evaluating information and feeding it back to guide action applies to the problem-solving process in two ways. First, this describes a continuous activity that permeates the problem-solving processes we have been describing, that is, problem formulation, the building of structure, policy choice, and program implementation. Second, evaluation applies to the action outcome or end product of the total process.

With respect to the first meaning, we have indicated that interaction with various actors in a problem-solving situation turns up at every step new information on the problem itself and on perceptions and preferences concerning the problem. This is used, for example, to "correct" or modify earlier decisions about structure or the most appropriate policy to be adopted. It also means that the definition of the problem changes as the process goes on, that people's views adapt themselves to one another as they interact, and that solutions tend to be a choice among alternatives each of which represents some gains and some losses. Morris and Binstock make a contribution to this in their discussion of feasibility, which calls for the adaptation and modification of goals in response to resistance encountered.

The more popularly understood meaning of evaluation, however, applies to the monitoring of operations that takes place as a result of a problem-solving or planning process. Data are obtained on outcome and effectiveness and are used to make decisions on continuing, discontinuing, or modifying the policy or program under scrutiny. Analytical and interactional issues merge here. The technology of scientific evaluation or research, drawn from the social sciences, needs to be adapted to operating situations and often resistances are encountered to the methodology of the evaluator.[22] When evaluation takes place after a policy or program has been in effect for some time, the judgments that are made concerning its effectiveness—of the unanticipated consequences that followed its implementation—provide material for a new round of problem-formulation and planning.

THE IMPORTANCE OF THE ORGANIZATIONAL CONTEXT

Although the problem-solving process in the preceding section has been described in rather abstract terms, it is our contention that it is useful, with appropriate modifications, for understanding and guiding the practice of community organization and social planning in its many diverse forms. But from the outset we have stressed the *variability in practice* along many dimensions; this was reinforced by the markedly different emphases we found in the literature. It is essential, therefore, to relate the problem-solving model to some scheme or typology that sheds light on these differences.

Of all the differences in practice to which we have alluded, what appears to account for most of the variations is the *organizational context* in which the activity is conducted. Zald's sociological analysis of community organization practice lends support to this view; it is based on this central proposition:

". . . Whether the practitioner facilitates, fund raises, foments, or fumes— whether he plans, serves as a resource expert, counsels or agitates he is guided by the structure, aims, and operating procedures of the organization that pays the bill.

"Therefore, any useful theory of community organization practice must include concepts and propositions about how C.O. organizations shape practice, how such organizations are themselves constrained, and about what kinds of problems and communities can be shaped and affected by what kinds of agencies."[23]

---

[22] For a discussion of these problems see Howard E. Freeman and Clarence C. Sherwood, *Social Research and Social Policy*, Englewood Cliffs, New Jersey: Prentice-Hall, Inc., 1970, pp. 70–83.

[23] Mayer N. Zald, "Organizations as Polities: Concepts for the Analysis of Community Organizational Agencies," Office of Juvenile Delinquency and Youth Development, Department of Health, Education and Welfare, October 1965, p. 4.

There is widespread recognition among practitioners that the specific organizational situation sets both the opportunities and constraints that govern the practitioner's operations. One example is the conclusion derived from government-financed community action experiments of the 1960's that militant social action directed toward changing the political power structure requires organizational independence and autonomy on the part of the action group.

Although it is not yet possible to realize the full measure of Zald's aspiration to derive a theory of practice from organizational analysis, our framework tends to move in that direction. Its purpose is to explore the relationship of such organizational variables as structure, function, ideology, and sociocultural position to strategy, tactics, and practitioner roles. In keeping with our earlier observations, we are not suggesting that these relationships will hold consistently, since there are many dimensions that vary independently of one another.

The framework we suggest is a heuristic device that both permits an ordering of much of the content of practice and offers a general guide to the practitioner in making judgments and choices based on situational analyses. The focus on organizational contexts helps to identify the factors that need to be taken into account in making these analyses.

We have found three kinds of organizations that are distinguished by the central function associated with each, by their structure or form, and by the typical problems and tasks they present to practitioners in community organization and social planning. The three contexts of practice that constitute our framework are (1) working with voluntary associations, (2) community work with service agencies, and (3) interorganizational planning.

Voluntary associations cover a wide variety of groups and organizations based on a membership whose common interest is in achieving some change or improvement in social arrangements, institutions, or relationships. A *service agency* is a formal bureaucratic organization that has as its central purpose the provision of a service to a designated target population. *Planning and allocating organizations* are networks of formal organizations whose function is the determination of how to organize and deploy resources to deal with social problems.

Each of the contexts contains within it distinct purposes, ideologies, and other factors that determine the approaches and activities that are undertaken. The commonality in practice, to the extent that it exists *within* each of the contexts, derives from the practitioner's central task. Thus, his basic job in working with voluntary associations is to build and develop the association and to help increase its effectiveness in obtaining its objectives, whatever they may be. The task in the service agency is conducting relationships between the service system and the community in which it is based, which includes the clientele that it serves. Finally, the practitioner in allocating and planning organizations is responsible for the articulation of needs and resources through an interorganizational system.

The following review sketches the salient features of practice in each of the contexts, which are discussed and illustrated in greater detail in subsequent chapters.

Voluntary Associations. Class differences as well as differences in ideology play a particularly important role in practice with voluntary associations. There are significant distinctions between lower-class and middle-class associations. The former are typically composed of disadvantaged people who come together on their own initiative or under the sponsorship of some outside group to improve their immediate welfare, the general conditions of their environment, and/or their power position in the society.

To the extent that there are distinctive characteristics in the life of lower-class people, these help to determine the nature of practice and the problems that the practitioner must confront. Studies of lower-class culture point, for example, to problems of apathy and lack of participation in formal organization, thus suggesting the need for practice to include informal as well as formal methods of organization, appropriate methods of communication, and attempts to achieve early and concrete results. The outstanding characteristic of lower-class groups—their limited influence and their restricted access to power—poses the fundamental questions of strategy and approach.

A related issue is the basis on which people can be organized. Available knowledge is inconclusive and evidence is contradictory, for example, as to the extent to which neighborhoods are stable enough to provide a basis for organization in contrast with organization based on a common interest or status, such as being a recipient of public assistance. In lower-class urban neighborhoods at the present time, the major issue of this type is the interaction of class and race and the choice between them as the explicit basis for organization.

As against lower-class voluntary associations that have principally the power of numbers as a resource, middle-class associations have considerable resources of finances, skills, and personal influence. Some are set up primarily or exclusively to serve the interests of their own membership; some are of a more general humanitarian or "public interest" character, concerned, for example, with population planning or voter education. Others are action organizations designed to obtain a service or benefit from the larger society, such as groups organized by parents of children with special health problems or handicaps.

Many voluntary associations are manned entirely by volunteers and never reach the point where they need employed staff. However, there are others that employ staff, and these belong within the framework of practice that we are discussing. The practitioner needs to concern himself continuously with his relationship to his sponsoring association. It is at this point that various conceptualizations of the practitioner's role are pertinent. The voluntary association is the policy-making group and determines its goals and methods of work. On the other hand, as the work becomes more specialized in content and as professional staff is introduced, that responsibility is shared between the association and the practitioner. To what extent and in what areas the expertness of the practitioner becomes determining is a recurring issue.

The organizational characteristics of both lower- and middle-class associations provide the framework for the practitioner's decisions on a number of questions: where to place the priority in organizational effort; what groups to approach in what order, what information to gather; and what policy and program alternatives to present for consideration. The ideology of the organization supplies the general goals and tends to determine the strategies and tactics to be followed. A major issue arises, however, when there are important differences between the ideological orientation of the practitioner and of the organization that employs him.

A special problem occurs in situations in which practitioners are employed by an organization, such as a settlement or a community action agency, to serve a voluntary association whose goals may then diverge from those of the employing body. The risks and costs for the practitioner in such situations of conflicting loyalties will be examined in the following chapter.

Voluntary associations include limited *ad hoc* actions by small self-help organizations as well as the sustained efforts of large organizations, many of them statewide and national in scope, with broad social change goals. In both, the practitioner requires a perspective about his work that links the immediate tasks that he and the participants perform to the long-range goal of building the organization. This is not to say that the immediate tasks are unimportant. They are important as measures to correct certain problem conditions, such as the elimination of unsafe or unsanitary conditions on a city street, but these tasks must also contribute to the development of the participants' capacity to engage in collective action on other issues in the future.

Service Agencies. The nature of a service agency and its changing relationships with its environment—that is, with consumers or clients, sources of support, and those who influence or set policy—set the community organization and social planning tasks for the practitioner. He should be viewed as a change agent responsible for improving the agency's performance of the service it is set up to render. The responsibility for relating the service organization to its community, although a general administrative responsibility, can be thought of as a planning and organizing task, carried out sometimes as a full-time job and sometimes as part of the work of executives and administrators.

Changes in conditions outside the agency produce pressures, demands, and opportunities that are transmitted to a number of points within the organization. These changes set the tasks of gathering and analyzing information about conditions and needs. This information is then used for making decisions about readjusting services, monitoring the implementation of new policies, and feeding the "intelligence" back for another round of analysis and adjustment. Thus, much of community organization and social planning work consists of program design and development based on assessment of needs and evaluation of adequacy of services. Other aspects of the work have to do with relationships to clientele and mobilization of resources and relationships with other relevant community groups.

Studies in organizational analysis and bureaucracy, an important focus in sociology since the time of Weber, provide concepts and empirical knowledge that can help to guide practice in this area. Specifically, experience in human service organizations is replete with examples of the differences between manifest and latent functions, the displacement of goals, and the inefficiencies of hierarchical control of operations that require individual judgment and flexibility. These points will be taken up in the following chapters.

Increasingly, practitioners are having to grapple with the issue of who is to control the policies of service agencies. An important task is the clarification of relationships between voluntary associations (especially those that take on the character of social movements) and service agencies. The dividing line is bound to be a fluid one in the period ahead, which makes it particularly important to understand the functional properties, opportunities, and constraints involved in each.

As we shall see in Chapter 7, for the practitioner's understanding of certain external relationships the notions of "interdependency" and "exchange" as developed by Levine and White and by Litwak and Hylton are important.[24] They provide guidance in identifying conditions that facilitate the acquisition of greater resources or lead to more effective use of existing ones.

Another set of constraining conditions concerns the difference between a "unitary" structure and a "federated" type made up of more or less equal parts. In his study of the National Polio Foundation, Sills pointed out that its strength was derived from the fact that, although it consisted of a large number of local units, its structure was highly centralized and controlled major functions, especially financing. Rein's study of Planned Parenthood Organizations revealed that those that were most successful in achieving their objectives were independent of the central coordinating structure. On the basis of this evidence, Morris and Rein developed a number of propositions concerning the relationships between structure, goals, and strategy, arguing that a unitary structure is more appropriate to goals and strategies of change, whereas a federated structure is compatible with goals of equilibrium and maintenance and a strategy of building consensus.[25]

Planning Organizations. This third context of practice includes planning in specific service and program areas, such as public welfare or manpower training; planning around problems such as juvenile delinquency, drug addiction or the needs of the aging; planning at the local or community level across both service and problem dimensions, as exemplified by welfare councils, antipoverty agencies, and the new human resources administrations; and, finally, large-scale social planning at the state and national levels. The basic functions included in these are coordination, allocation of resources, and innovation or change.

A dominant feature of all these settings is that organizing and planning take place through interorganizational relationships. Many important practice issues revolve around the type of dependence and the degree of interdependence that exist among the units involved. A critical question

[24] Sol Levine and Paul E. White, *op. cit.* Eugene Litwak and Lydia Hylton, "Interorganizational Analysis: A Hypothesis on Coordinating Agencies," *Administrative Science Quarterly*, **VI**, No. 4, March 1962; and Violet M. Sieder, "Community Organization in the Direct Service Agency," *Social Welfare Forum 1962,* New York: Columbia University Press, 1962.

[25] Martin Rein and Robert Morris, "Goals, Structures, and Strategies for Community Change," *Social Work Practice, 1962,* New York: Columbia University Press, 1962, pp. 127–145.

is the distribution of power or authority for decision-making and implementation. Although planners have some leeway in devising structures for interaction, to a great extent the focal points of power are fixed in an interorganizational situation and this constitutes an important constraint.

Another aspect of the issue of autonomy and dependence is whether the interorganizational body is advisory, informal, formal, or binding in its decisions. Sometimes the planning organization is simply a forum for exchange of views and does not purport to go beyond this. Sometimes it seeks the voluntary coordination of the policies of different groups and agencies. Sometimes the planning mechanism is itself designed to produce change, in which case the practitioners in it must consider the resistances to be overcome and the resources that can be tapped to achieve change.

The need for elaborate mechanisms of interorganizational coordination and planning arises from a recognition of the complex nature of human problems. A host of specialized services, programs, and organizations have developed to cope with particular aspects of problems. There are, for example, public housing programs for the poor, public assistance for the poor, and medical services for the poor. But at times there is little contact among the different services with a view to reinforcing each other in the interests of the recipients.

The difficulties of achieving effective coordination in the human services, despite repeated appeals on its behalf, are due in fact to a continuing tension between the benefits and pressures for specialization and the need and value of coordination. The two tendencies alternate in a cyclical pattern. Efforts at coordination are followed by new forms of specialization that in turn are labeled "fragmentation," and a further effort is made to bring about collaboration.

Another significant issue concerns the relationship between innovation and allocation. For example, in recent experience, demonstration programs in juvenile delinquency as well as antipoverty efforts have sought to encourage local innovation without having a coherent national policy. On the other hand, in the mental health field after the adoption of a framework of national policies, the principal task was to allocate resources across the nation. This is not to say that one approach is better than the other, but to suggest that they contribute to the attainment of different goals.

Efforts to conceptualize practice and to relate it to research have contributed in recent years to a growing body of knowledge that is particularly relevant to planning and allocating organizations, although

of importance also to practice in other contexts. Morris and his col-
laborators, as we saw in the previous chapter, have made inferences from
the findings of the Banfield-Wilson school of political science that
stress the pluralism of community power structure and especially of
community decision-making.[26]

Their main inference is that community organization and planning
efforts need to be highly focused and selective. They have challenged
earlier assumptions about broad participation and involvement and substituted schema for determining the relevance of selected means to
specific goals. Warren, elaborating on ideas advanced by Morris and
Rein, has filled out a typology to include not only change and consensus but several subtypes of each.[27] These are related to the nature
of the issue that is involved and the degree to which it is controversial.

The practitioner here as in the other contexts has a double responsibility. He must find his way into and through the politics and dynamics
of the process and he must relate to the content of the problem at hand.
Planning and allocating activities revolve around substantive policy and
program issues in specific fields of service. The building of practice
knowledge and skill therefore calls for improved technologies of measuring need, creating appropriate programs, distributing resources, and
evaluating outcomes not only in relation to political criteria but also in
regard to functional requirements.

Having examined briefly three organizational contexts in which
practice takes place, we should note the linkages among them. Planning
and allocating organizations assign resources and program responsibilities to service agencies. Some planning bodies seek voluntary contributions to finance their work; others are creatures of legislatures. In both
instances they must relate to voluntary groups that have interests in the
problems being addressed.

Service agencies study the needs that they are designed to meet,
evaluate performance in relation to need, and propose changes in function,
program content, and resources. The service agency may carry out these
tasks directly or through a planning organization. Increasingly the agency
must also relate to the pressures of voluntary groups.

A voluntary association can act as a generator of proposals directed

[26] Edward C. Banfield, *Political Influence, op. cit.* James Q. Wilson, "An Overview
of Theories of Planned Change," in Robert Morris, Ed., *Centrally Planned Change,*
New York: National Association of Social Workers, 1964, pp. 12–29; Herbert A. Simon,
Administrative Behavior, New York: Marinella, 1961.

[27] Roland L. Warren, *Types of Purposive Social Change at the Community Level,*
No. 11, Papers in Social Welfare, Waltham, Massachusetts: Brandeis University, 1965.

to service agencies or to planning and allocating organizations. Its functions include the formulation of goals, the organization of people to advance goals, the development of proposals, and the mobilization of resources to support programs. It is also within its province to seek modifications in programs, to resist programs that are inimical to its interests, and, finally, to seek the removal and replacement of services that are deemed undesirable.

The interrelationships among the three contexts of practice are circular and interactive. Modifications may originate anywhere in the system and the interactions are reciprocal among all the contexts. They may be visualized as follows:

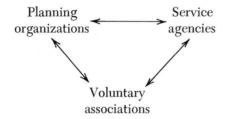

Planning   Service
organizations   agencies

Voluntary
associations

THE IMPACT OF VALUES

We have deferred until this point the discussion of the critical matter of ideologies and values that animate all three kinds of organizations as well as the practitioners who serve them. This important factor comes toward the end of the elaboration of our framework because it needs to be related to all the elements considered thus far.

An ideology incorporates proposals for change as well as a set of values as to what is desirable. Ideologies are based on different views of the nature of the problems that are being addressed, the causes of those problems, and how they can be overcome. Underlying these differences are even more fundamental views that people hold concerning the nature of the present social order and the degree to which existing institutions are capable of meeting human needs.

One approach is based on incremental change or adaptation and adjustment, another on institutional or structural change. The first would alter the operating policies of institutions in order to provide better benefits or to make better provisions for particular groups, such as a movement to reform prisons. The other approach is directed toward changing control over the institution, so that it will hopefully provide better benefits to the people who are dissatisfied and are seeking control.

Incrementalism is rooted in the acceptance of the existing social order and assumes that there are common interests shared by people regardless of their differences along economic, class, or ethnic lines or their special interests. This point of view rests on the values of cooperation and integration. The contrasting ideology calls for basic changes in the social order and sometimes for "changing the world." The difference between the two is, of course, difficult to measure. The issue of definition is in itself a reflection of ideology, since what seems to be a major change to one group may be merely incremental change to another. There are varying opinions as to whether major institutional change is in fact a realizable goal under the conditions of pluralism obtaining in the United States.

These ideological positions affect the stance of the practitioner. He brings his own commitments to his work. He must be aware of what these are and must be able to make them explicit in his dealings with people. But he is also a legitimate participant in the social interaction through which value choices are made by the people with whom he works. His distinctive role lies in helping to make the value choices clear and in tracing implications and programmatic consequences of alternative choices.

While value positions necessarily underly all practice, it does not follow that all of practice must share the same values. Values are translated into specific positions by the different social groups that sponsor organizing and planning efforts. Some make the definition in terms of a partisan interest or the public interest, or a single objective; others base themselves on the broad ideologies described above.

The translation of values into decisions and action is a dynamic process. It means identifying, progressively, specific objectives and concrete measures in a continuous ends-means chain. Choices must be made every step of the way, since the situation is usually such that not all values can be maximized simultaneously.

But value positions are not static. They emerge, develop, and are modified in the course of social interaction, including that between the practitioner and the people he serves. It can happen that people initiate a process on the assumption that they share an area of agreement and find, in the course of moving to more specific measures, that they are really in basic disagreement on their value assumptions as well as on their implementing proposals. The reverse can also occur. It is part of the practitioner's role to examine value issues continuously as the action proceeds.

In addition to the choices that the practitioner helps an action body to make, there are also decisions that he must make as an individual. Practitioners bring their own values to their work, and it is both inevitable and desirable that they should. Workers without conviction about the primacy of human needs would be poorly placed in this field. The important issue is what they do about their personal ideologies and commitments.

The choice of organization by a practitioner ought to be congenial to his own commitments. Too much disparity in goals and methods between the worker and his employers will result in dysfunctional conflict. On the other hand, the worker will usually find differences in purpose between himself and some of his employers. He does not forfeit his right and indeed his responsibility to make explicit his own opinions and to contribute to the debate that ought to precede decision-making. More, he is entitled to press his point of view and to try to convince others.

A problem arises, however, after basic decisions have been made and the practitioner whose views have not prevailed must face a choice between working within the policies adopted by his employing organization or, if the differences are deep enough and persist over time, removing himself and finding circumstances more in tune with his convictions. A particularly difficult decision is posed when a group adopts a policy or action that violates the practioner's sense of what is "in the public interest." Admittedly this is a concept that lacks objective, verifiable meaning. In the final analysis—and certainly in this context—what is in the public interest is a matter of judgment based on the practitioner's sense of values and guided perhaps by a code of professioinal ethics that has more general sanction. For instance, a decision by an agency to take an action that appears repressive in the eyes of the professional, or an action by a group that seems to him destructive of the rights of others, may induce the practitioner to disassociate himself from those who appear to be acting against the public interest.

The practitioner's choices are limited. By the very nature of his work, he must attach himself to an organization to be effective. He can choose on ideological grounds, for instance, to work outside the established agencies and to put his talents at the disposal of disadvantaged groups. In one sense he is then working outside "the System". But it is our contention that he must then accept the constraints of working within another system, and his freedom of action will be determined by the goals and strategies of the organization he has chosen to serve. There is an aspect of professionalism that comes into play here as well: the stricture not to exploit the role of practitioner for personal advantage or for purposes that subvert the will of the group or organization being served.

The practitioner can enter the picture at several points in the end-means chain. If he is early on the scene, he participates more fully in the original formation of the *antecedent* goals and structure. But whenever he enters, he brings more alternatives and options to bear on the situation. His basic role is that of critic—in the sense that he questions the decisions that are being made and examines them against other possibilities of which he is aware due to his expertness. His criticism can be applied to goals as well as to instrumental policies. It is one of the practitioner's critical functions to reveal the mixture of value assumptions and operational means that usually coexist within a particular statement of goals. This can lead to exposure of unintended value choices that have been made implicitly in the selection of a particular course of action, choices that may not be at all what the sponsors had in mind. This may open up differences in objectives that had not been recognized earlier. On the other hand, the practitioner's analysis may reveal that something that appears as a value may really be an operational policy and that there may be other policies that are equally compatible with the underlying value or goal but are more efficient in achieving it.

The choice of strategy and tactics is one of the key decisions facing all practitioners. Choices involve considerations of both what is desirable and what is calculated to achieve a proposed result. Values are again involved. Thus, for example, there has been a tendency in professional social work to accept certain tactics as conforming with values of client self-determination while rejecting other tactics as "manipulative" or as imposing the practitioner's point of view on the client.

One can visualize a continuum of strategies ranging from education and rational persuasion through the exercise of various forms of influence and authority to the use of coercion. The acceptance of methods of rational discourse, education, and persuasion as legitimate patterns of influence is associated with the values of democratic liberalism, and therefore primarily with middle-class positions. It has been pointed out many times, however, that these values are not always realized in practice, but that decisions are influenced very substantially by differences in the wealth, power, and social position of the parties to the process.

A significant issue of strategy is the choice between a "process" orientation as against a "task" orientation. An emphasis on process highlights the building of effective working relationships among the groups involved. This approach has been identified in the past with community organization and community development and it has been adopted both by radical social movements and by organizations such as welfare councils concerned with coordination. In contrast, planning has tended to focus on a specific task that has to be accomplished—the development of a program, the allocation of resources, the determination of particular needs.

The stress on process is based in large part on ideological considerations, but it also makes certain assumptions concerning its usefulness in achieving objectives. The major assumption is that involvement and self-determination are necessary for the development of a group's capacity to deal effectively with its problems. This rests in part on empirical evidence from small-group research about patterns of influence and the process of behavioral change. In part it is based on experience in situations that involve cultural changes, as in community development programs in developing countries. However, there has been little specification of how process and task orientations can be or must be combined under different conditions to achieve effective results. In practice there is considerable agreement that there is a complementarity between the two and that neither is adequate by itself to carry out community organization and social planning objectives.

All of the complex dimensions of practice that have been discussed up to this point come into focus in the actions of the practitioner. We come therefore to the *roles* of the practitioner, which are prescriptions as to how he should conduct himself in the pursuit of his tasks. We have extracted from the literature these typical roles.

Enabler. A practitioner who has no programs or prescriptions of his own to implement but is skilled in developing relationships with people and helping them to identify their needs and to develop the capacity to solve their problems. His expertise is in relationships and presumably in problem-solving, although the latter is not always very clear. He has no built-in commitments to particular strategies or conceptualizations of problems, but there is an assumption that the process of working together will make people more effective in dealing with their problems.

Planner. The major contribution of this role lies in the practitioner's command of the subject matter of the problem being addressed. He has expert analytical ability in defining the problem, examining its dimensions, and developing alternative solutions. He can spell out first- and second-order consequences of various alternatives. The tacit assumption is that it is possible to develop rational solutions to problems, given the proper tools and adequate knowledge. The planner himself is not necessarily the decision-maker but does take responsibility for evaluating the pros and cons of alternatives and for recommending a course of action to those who make the decisions.

Advocate. In this role the practitioner is committed to a cause that he pursues explicitly in conjunction with others who share his goals. He is expert in the techniques of achieving goals through organized action. He is not neutral. Although the concept of an advocate might be attached to any kind of cause, it has come to be associated primarily with work with disadvantaged low-income populations and with attempts to improve their conditions and increase their power in local communities or in wider political arenas. The role of advocate of consumer interests is growing in importance.

All of these roles rest on value assumptions as well as critical analyses of social situations. They all involve some kind of expertness. The difference, however, is in how expertness is defined. The major division of opinion is whether expertise lies in technical knowledge or in the skill of building and managing relationships. In our view, both types of expertise are needed and all three kinds of roles are required by practitioners in community organization and social planning.

Before examining the three organizational contexts we have identified, it is appropriate to summarize this chapter in the next six paragraphs in the form of a working definition of practice.

Community organization and social planning refer to activities in which organizational methods of intervention are used to meet social needs and counteract social problems. This requires that practitioners and the groups employing them find ways of redistributing resources, service functions, and decision-making power.

The activities include organizing people to act together as well as devising policies and programs to meet their objectives. These are linked together in a common enterprise in which planful approaches to the solutions of problems are fused with the mobilization of people's capacities to deal with problems.

The specific goals that guide practice are set by the values, ideologies, and responsibilities of the sponsoring organizations. The scope of effort varies from relatively small-scale adjustments in service programs to basic, long-range changes in social institutions.

The problem-solving process is characteristic of this field. This includes fact-finding as to the nature and dimensions of the problems being addressed; the building of structures for considering the issues; delineation and weighing of alternative policies and selection of one to be pursued; development of an appropriate program; and evaluation of results and modification of actions in the light of experience. As he moves through these phases, the practitioner engages in a combination of analytical and interactional tasks, that is, analysis of the situation as well as the use of communication and influence.

Research and conceptualization of practice are not yet at the point where specific methodologies can be advanced with certainty as to their outcomes. Too many interacting variables are involved to permit this at this time. Rather than describing and prescribing practice according to methods of achieving change, considerable variation in practice can be attributed to the organizational context in which the activity occurs.

Three basic contexts seem to shape practice—voluntary associations, service agencies, and interorganizational planning bodies. Each of these has characteristic functions and issues that present rather unique constraints and opportunities to the practitioner. However, no single methodology or role can be associated with each organizational type. The realities of the tasks call on the practitioner to perform some combination of the roles of enabler, planner, and advocate.

Throughout this chapter and the previous one we have said that empirical and conceptual work in this field has not reached the point at which one can talk about a substantial body of effective or "successful" strategies and techniques. Given this stage of development, the following chapters explore practice in three different contexts in the hope that an understanding of the obstacles and tasks facing practitioners under these differing circumstances will sensitize them to the decisions they will be called on to make and to the likely consequences of their judgments and actions.

CHAPTER 5

Voluntary Associations

GOALS AND CHARACTERISTICS

For more than two hundred years observers of this country have remarked on the proclivity of Americans for forming their own organizations to improve their communities and to advance the welfare of particular groups of people.[1] The tremendous variety in the purposes and activities of these voluntary associations bears out the observation that "the more differentiated the members of a community are, the more associations they tend to have—differentiated by occupation, place, or residence, race, religion, class, interests, way of life."[2]

In the last decade America's stark confrontation with racism, poverty, and war in Vietnam has quickened the tempo of organization of citizen efforts and given them new forms and directions. There has been an acceleration in the activity and militancy of organizations of the poor, racial and ethnic minorities, and students. And there have been successive waves of citizen participation related to governmental programs

[1] This is relative to other countries and does not mean that a high proportion of Americans participate in voluntary associations. Combining data from two studies, Wright and Hyman found that 47 percent of the families and 64 percent of the respondents belonged to no association and 31 percent of the families and a fifth of the respondents belonged to only one organization. See Charles R. Wright and Herbert H. Hyman, "Voluntary Association Memberships of American Adults," *American Sociological Review*, 23, No. 3, June 1958, pp. 284–294.

[2] Bernard Berelson and Gary A. Steiner, *Human Behavior: An Inventory of Scientific Findings,* New York: Harcourt, Brace and World, Inc., 1964, p. 265.

in urban renewal, delinquency prevention, mental health planning, the "war on poverty," Model Cities, and others.[3]

Against that background, this chapter will examine characteristics of voluntary associations for their implications for practice and then consider two distinctive fields of activity that involve working with voluntary groups—community development and social action. We consider first the general functions of voluntary associations in American society.

Ohlin, although writing specifically about local indigenous groups, describes in effect the functions of voluntary citizen organizations in general:

"In recent years, we have had renewed emphasis on the necessity of such involvement to preserve a pluralistic society. Such ideological restatements rest on the premise that the health and growth of a democratic system require constant creation of new channels for the articulation, aggregation, and communication of the unrepresented interests of submerged segments of the population at those points of decision which materially affect their welfare."[4]

Ohlin sees the following functions performed by such groups for society as a whole:

1. Successful indigenous movements redistribute and broaden the basis of social power and the exercise of authority. By limiting the arbitrary use of power or the development of exploitative practices, they reduce pressures toward deviance.
2. They heighten the personal investment of members in the established social order. In promoting personal satisfaction and a larger personal commitment and contribution, they enhance social stability, control, and morale.
3. They provide an arena for the training and recruitment of leaders for higher levels of organizational participation.
4. They promote a more flexible fit of the rule systems of major social institutions to the distinctive life styles of the local community. By facilitating such accommodations, indigenous organizations protect

---

[3] See Hans B. Spiegel, Ed., *Citizen Participation in Urban Development, Vol. I—Concepts and Issues,* Washington, D.C.: NTL Institute for Applied Behavioral Science, 1968, and George A. Brager and Francis P. Purcell, Eds., *Community Action Against Poverty, Readings from the Mobilization Experience,* New Haven: College and University Press, 1967.

[4] Lloyd E. Ohlin, "Indigenous Social Movements," in Mayer N. Zald, *op. cit.* p. 181.

the heterogeneity and cultural richness of the society and provide a broader base for cultural growth in many fields. By fostering the proliferation of subcultures or local styles of life, they furnish a buffer to the conformity demands of a mass society. By enlarging tolerance for certain forms of deviance, constructive channels are preserved for dissent.[5]

Typologies of Organizations. Ohlin's listing highlights the very broad and somewhat inconsistent functions of voluntary associations. One of the functions is to further the integration of individuals and groups with the larger society. Another is to promote change and redistribution of resources. Obviously, not all voluntary associations perform all of these functions. They differ markedly on many dimensions.

A number of organizational analysts have developed typologies of organizations that help to identify and to order these dimensions of variation. Blau and Scott, for example, use the criterion of *Cui Bono* (who benefits) to identify these classes of organization: Mutual benefit (for the benefit of its own membership); business concerns (which benefit the owners); service organizations (for clients), and commonweal organizations (presumably for the benefit of the publiic at large).[6]

The voluntary associations with which we are concerned in this chapter fall into the two categories of "mutual benefit" and "commonweal." A tenants' organization would be an example of a mutual benefit organization. Groups like the League of Women Voters or organizations seeking improvement of the "environment" are examples of the commonweal type.

Gordon and Babchuk suggest other dimensions that overlap the Blau and Scott typology. They highlight not "who benefits," but the nature of the benefit obtained. In operational terms the groups in which we are interested are *social influence organizations* "designed to maintain or to create some normative condition or change—outside the organization themselves. The NAACP, the League of Women Voters, and a Neighborhood Improvement Council represent this type."[7]

Gordon and Babchuk distinguish between these "instrumental" organizations and the "expressive" type where the activities are aimed

---

[5] *Ibid.,* p. 181.

[6] Peter M. Blau and W. Richard Scott, *op. cit.,* pp. 42–58.

[7] C. Wayne Gordon and Nicholas Babchuk, "A Typology of Associations," in William A. Glaser and David L. Sills, Eds., *The Government of Associations,* Totowa, New Jersey: The Bedminster Press, 1966, p. 25.

at the "immediate gratification of the participants." They observe that some associations have both functions and point to the American Legion as a case in point: "At the national level the Legion has registered lobbyists and a legislative program officially endorsed by its members, but at the local level it functions primarily as a club for convivial activities." At a later point, in the discussion of the methods and techniques used by practitioners, we shall return to the implications for practice of this duality in the functions of many organizations.

A familiar concept in organizational analysis that is relevant here is the distinction between "manifest" and "latent" functions, with the former referring to the instrumental purposes to which the organization is explicitly committed and the latter to the implicit rewards that the organization may confer on its members. Sometimes there is a contradiction between these functions and a tendency for the latent elements to displace the organization's instrumental goals. There is a tendency for organizations

"to turn away, at least partially, from their original goals . . . Typically it occurs through putting means in the place of ends, procedures in the place of goals . . . goal-displacement can also arise from getting a number of people involved who then want to follow their own ends . . . as in the case of the TVA (Selznick, 1953): this is sometimes viewed as the central dilemma of organizational life—in order to get some things done, you have to organize others to do them; as soon as you do, they want to get into the act of deciding what is to be done and how. Goal-displacement can arise from other roots as well: having to collaborate with people of different ideological persuasion . . . or from failing to respond to broad social changes."[8]

Among voluntary organizations this tendency often takes the form of turning from the members' original change-oriented goals to activities that are necessary to keep the organization itself intact. The staffs of these organizations become deeply involved in organizational maintenance tasks, and it is one of their persistent problems to avoid becoming engulfed by these demands. The pressure arises from the fact that it is not enough to recruit members; it is vital to see that the organization stimulates their participation, sustains their interest, and maintains the foward momentum of the group as a whole. Strategic questions, such as making coalitions with other organizations, may be crucial from time to time, but a great deal of the professional's day-by-day work consists of

[8] Berelson and Steiner, *op. cit.*, pp. 366–367.

training leaders, handling interpersonal relationships' and potential conflicts, and creating an *esprit de corps*. The issue confronting the practitioner, of course, is not which is the "right" activity to pursue—goal-directed tasks or organizational maintenance—but under what circumstances he must divert energy into building or rebuilding the organization whose existence is vital as a base for action.

Voluntary organizations function at every level of society. The residents of a city block may band together or they may belong to a larger neighborhood association. At the community level, that is, the city or the rural county, there are a great number of organizations concerned with housing, health, education, and the welfare of racial, ethnic, and religious groups. Increasingly, as problems are defined in terms that reach beyond the locality, voluntary associations organize on a metropolitan and a state basis and are in turn affiliated with national bodies.

The links between one level and another affect an organization's degree of *autonomy*. In his analysis of national organizations, Sills developed a typology of "corporate-type" organizations with a high degree of central authority and "federation-type" bodies where control is diffused among more or less independent units.[9] This same useful distinction can be made at other levels—in the instance of a city-wide association of neighborhood groups or a state organization composed of local chapters of a mental health association.

The matter of independence is also much influenced by the *sponsorship* of a voluntary association. Where the members constitute the only source of support and sanction, there will obviously be a maximum of autonomy. When a group is maintained by another organization, for example, through the provision of professional staff, its independence will be limited. Thus a local group sponsored by a Community Action Agency, a settlement house, or a municipal agency more likely than not will reflect the institutional interests and responsibilities of its sponsor.

The main reason why voluntary associations so often must be supported by sponsors is their need, especially among low-income membership groups, for resources that cannot be supplied by their constituents. They frequently require physical facilities for meetings or finances to cover operating expenses, but primarily they need the time and expertise of paid staff. Traditionally voluntary associations were organized and conducted in large part through the spontaneous activity of their members without professional assistance, but increasingly paid functionaries

[9] David L. Sills, *The Volunteers: Means and Ends in a National Organization*, Glencoe, Illinois: The Free Press, 1957, pp. 3–10.

are introduced either to organize new associations or to assist volunteers in the conduct of established organizations.

This is related to the fact that as informal groups grow in size and become more stable, there is a tendency to develop a division of labor and a structure to match it. In this connection, Chapin writes:

"Voluntary organizations having once started on their life career, grow and gain momentum toward formalization of structure. As growth in size of membership proceeds, structure subdivides into subgroups of smaller size and with different functions . . . . An increasing emphasis upon conformity and status develops, and the voluntary organization begins to have traditions. In short, the process of growth and formalization has run its course and the original 'voluntary' organization has become a full-fledged institution."[10]

Thus associations vary according to the degree of formal structure, ranging from small face-to-face groups with considerable informality to highly organized bodies with a hierarchy of committees and great dependence on professional staff.

Social class is a major variable that accounts for a number of significant differences among voluntary associations. To begin with, it is clear that participation in voluntary associations is unequally distributed among socioeconomic groups in this country.[11] It is greater among "urban residents, among those in the prime of life, among the married-with-children, among those moving up in the class system, among those with residential stability, and especially among people of more education and high socioeconomic status."[12]

Unlike lower-class people who suffer from a deficit of political power, middle-class people have resources that contribute to their greater influence in economic and political terms. They have considerable personal influence with legislators and administrators by virtue of the fact that these office-holders are often neighbors and friends with whom they generally can find many points of ideological agreement and common interests.

Frequently, the goals for which middle-class groups organize are presented as being "in the public interest." This formulation avoids the

---

[10] F. Stuart Chapin, "Social Institutions and Voluntary Associations," in Joseph B. Gittler, Ed., *Review of Sociology: Analysis of a Decade*, New York: Wiley, 1957, p. 263–64 (reprinted in Berelson and Steiner, *op. cit.*, p. 366).

[11] William Erbe, "Social Involvement and Political Activity," *American Sociological Review*, 29, No. 2, April 1964, pp. 198–215.

[12] *Ibid.*, p. 379.

stigma that can attach to the efforts of lower-class groups whose very intention of securing more goods, services, or power is interpreted as "special pleading" for one group at the expense of others. The fact is, of course, that middle-class groups who seek to advance or protect their vested interests are engaged in precisely the same kind of effort, but the challenge to the established balance of political power appears less threatening when such a group seeks to achieve or avert a social change.

To the extent that money is needed to support their organizational efforts, middle-class people are in a better position to collect funds for employing professional staff, for obtaining office space, and for printing educational and promotional literature. Moreover, the technical and professional skills of the participants themselves are of great value to their collective enterprise. These are the skills and experience of lawyers and engineers, of academics, architects, and publicists. Their knowledge of substantive problems is matched by the skill they have usually acquired in organizational work itself.

In general, the worker is expected to assist these groups in the use of such strategies as informal influence, legal action, lobbying, and community education that appeals to the public interest. He can assume some sophistication about organizational activity on the part of participants. Generally, they know how to collect information, communicate their ideas, and reach decisions through a committee structure.

Because lower-class people have deficits in precisely those areas in which the middle class has advantages—money, influence, and technical expertise—they must exploit their own resources. They have numbers that can be mobilized for a show of determination and strength and they have traditions of group loyalty that can be called into service. On the whole, however, the life experiences of lower-class people discourage them from seeking solutions to their problems through organizations.[13] Their problems and needs are intense and immediate and leave little time, energy, or optimism for organizational activity. Add to this their fear of retaliation, the high population turnover in low income areas, and the resistance of established agencies to change their programs and it is

---

[13] For a discussion of the characteristics of people in low-income communities, see Frances Piven, "Participation of Residents in Neighborhood Community Action Programs," *Social Work*, 11, No. 1, January 1966; papers by Herbert Gans, Jerome Cohen, S. M. Miller in Frank Reissman, Jerome Cohen, and Arthur Pearl, Eds., *Mental Health of the Poor*, Glencoe, Illinois: The Free Press, 1964, pp. 119–158; and Lee Rainwater, "Neighborhood Action and Lower-Class Life-Styles," in John B. Turner, Ed., *Neighborhood Organization for Community Action*, New York: National Association of Social Workers, 1968, pp. 25–39.

apparent that organizing the poor is markedly different from promoting the interests of middle-class people.

Neighborhood Organization. Despite the difficulties, organization of low-income groups has been widespread in America. Urban neighborhoods—the dwelling places of generations of working-class people, immigrants, and the poor—have long been concentration points for voluntary associations and for organizing efforts. Distinct patterns of neighborhood organization and action had emerged at the turn of the century. People were building their own organizations to protect their interests as workers in the expanding industries, to offer help to their incoming countrymen from Europe's farms and ghettoes, and to preserve and draw security from their cultural and religious backgrounds.

At the same time agencies such as the settlement houses offered services to help ease the immigrants' entry into urban life and to "Americanize" them. Political leaders proffered practical help in return for support at the polls. Health departments tried to educate and inoculate. Social reformers sought legislation to deal with serious social and environmental problems, and the upper class sponsored private agencies to assist the poor, uplift the fallen, and reform the deviant.

Later local citizens' organizations were developed, some by settlement houses or by welfare councils, to help the residents deal with the needs of their immediate locality. These were usually composed of individuals and of representatives of local organizations, churches, and social agencies. Often they were organized around a critical issue and then became more permanent bodies with a broad range of interests in housing, city services, intergroup relations, and health and welfare services.

During and since World War II, our cities have experienced an influx of large numbers of blacks and whites from rural and mountain areas of the South, and Spanish-speaking people from Puerto Rico and those who came originally from Mexico. The dominant white, native-born population has been made increasingly aware of its economic, social, and political discrimination against these groups. The rediscovery of their poverty and the recognition of inadequacies in employment and housing opportunities and in education and social services have led, in recent years, to an intensified pace of activity in urban neighborhoods. This is also true of the rural poverty of black people in the South, of people with Spanish surnames in the Southwest, of white people in Appalachia, and of native Americans on and off reservations.

There is thus a long tradition of efforts to deal with the problem of poverty and related social ills through activities that have a *locality* base. Implicit is the notion of some geographically bounded community as the appropriate framework for efforts to achieve social change. That assumption becomes explicit in programs or movements such as community development and social action that will be described later in this chapter. Much of the practice of community organization developed historically, as we have seen, out of neighborhood-based activities.

The reasons for adopting a neighborhood approach are not difficult to identify. Social problems obviously are not distributed evenly throughout urban communities. It takes no special search to identify certain neighborhoods as containing a high incidence of poverty, deviance, and all types of social problems. As indicated in our historical references, such neighborhoods have always attracted reform efforts, both indigenous and externally directed. Beyond such common-sense observations, support for a locality-based approach can also be found in some of the studies of low-income populations. The "culture of poverty" studies stress the fact that the geographical range of peoples' activities is much more limited for those with low income than it is for middle-class groups. While middle-class voluntary associations are based on specific, well-defined interests, lower-class populations, it is argued, need more holistic approaches if they are to be reached successfully. It is their common life in the neighborhood rather than specific segmented interests that provide the basis for organization.

Reasonable though such arguments appear, they are far from self-evident and are indeed increasingly subject to challenge on several grounds. Experience has indicated that generalized neighborhood organization appears to have little viability, but that the locality-based activities that have demonstrated some capacity for action tend to be those centered on more specific common interests. These tend to be related to class and/or ethnic identity.[14]

Another major issue highlighted in all of the appraisals of neighborhood-action programs is the limitation of the locality in being able to provide the remedies and resources for the social problems of its population. Warren, among others, has pointed to the "vertical relationships" in American society as having a much greater impact on setting the con-

[14] Of particular relevance are studies of the efforts that have taken place as part of the anti-poverty programs in the 1960's (George A. Brager and Francis P. Purcell, *op. cit.,* Ralph M. Kramer, *Participation of the Poor: Comparative Community Case Studies in the War on Poverty,* Englewood Cliffs: Prentice-Hall, 1969; Peter Marris and Martin Rein, *Dilemmas of Social Reform,* New York: Atherton Press, 1967; John B. Turner, *op. cit.;* Roland L. Warren, "Model Cities First Round: Politics, Planning,

ditions of life that affect low-income people than the "horizontal relationships" within the limited geographical locality in which they live.[15]

Suzanne Keller, describing neighborhoods as "local areas that have physical boundaries, social networks, concentrated use of area facilities, and special emotional and symbolic connotations for their inhabitants," points out that these four dimensions do not overlap predictively or significantly, hence the difficulty of defining or "building" neighborhoods.[16] She notes that in "changing urban areas, especially, the boundaries of neighbors with whom active relations are maintained do not coincide with historical, official, or physical boundaries of neighborhoods, nor with those of local facilities, nor with attachment to the local setting."

The experiences and observations of people who have done block-by-block organizing support Keller's view. Block organization is a time-consuming process that is perhaps more effective and lasting with homeowners, who feel a stronger stake in their property and their street, than do tenants, especially in areas of high mobility and transiency. For the latter, there is some evidence that block organization is too unfocused, too limited in what it can hope to achieve, and too difficult to sustain.

Block organization implies the hope that everyone on the block will participate. This calls on the organizers and the leadership to devote disproportionate amounts of time to enlisting and sustaining the involvement of the less interested, the less able, and the less responsive residents. This kind of organizing also puts considerable emphasis on attaining consensus, which may have to be maintained at the expense of efficient or quick action by the organization and the achievement of specific objectives. Some organizers who have attempted this have concluded that there are more dynamic possibilities in organizing around issues. In fact, block groups may become mutual-interest groups or may become active only in reaction to a critical situation. Issue-oriented groups appeal more selectively to particular categories of people, but may very well remain geographically based.

A useful comment on this is made by Von Hoffman, who takes as his premise that the purpose of organization is power. He writes:

and Participation," *Journal of the American Institute of Planners,* XXXV, July, 1969, pp. 245–52; Harold H. Weissman, Ed., *Community Development in the Mobilization for Youth Experience,* New York: Association Press, 1969.)

[15] Roland Warren, *The Community in America, op. cit.,* Ch. 3.

[16] Suzanne Keller, *The Urban Neighborhood, A Sociological Perspective,* New York: Random House, 1968, pp. 156-157.

"An organization needs three things: (1) a network of people spread out and in a position to reach and mobilize the inert majority; (2) continuity, and (3) money. The majority of small groups in the ghetto districts I am familiar with turn out to be potentially strongest in one of these three qualities . . . the right balance of network, continuity and money is engendered by an organizational program containing a balance or mix of goals or would-be pay-offs (which organizationally is all that a goal is) for the various groupings you need to recruit. For homeowners the program may be defense against venal building inspectors, for welfare mothers it may be defense against snooping welfare inspectors, for the unemployed it may be pressure on some well-known local firm that discriminates, for the church group or local civil rights sentiment it may be some sort of an assault on the local educational system. Hence it has been said that organizing of this nature is, at least in part, building up a community-wide set of interlocking log-rolling agreements; 'You scratch my back and I'll scratch yours, but if we don't combine, nobody's back'll get scratched.' "[17]

Despite obstacles and limitations, attempts persist to organize low-income populations on a neighborhood basis. This is due in part to the desire of both indigenous and external sponsors to overcome the chronic barriers to participation by lower-class people. The sponsors hope that involvement in a neighborhood-based association, which often begins with a concern for recreation for children, local traffic conditions, or garbage collection, will provide beginning experiences and encouragement for participating in more sustained efforts to deal with broader objectives.

Several of the issues that have been identified thus far as characteristically involved in working with voluntary associations can be explored more fully by examining two fields of activity—*community development* and *social action*. In both of these areas, we find a mixture of locality-based and special interest-oriented activities. Both types of activity were widely represented in the community action programs of the 1960's, which combined concern with the availability of opportunities with efforts to develop new collective attitudes and behaviors on the part of the populations in low-income areas.

Community development and social action can be considered as two fields of activity, each with a body of practice and a literature reflecting

[17] Nicholas Von Hoffman, "The Good Organizer," Ch. 4 in Joan Ecklein and Armand Lauffer, *Community Organizers and Social Planners*, New York: John Wiley & Sons, 1972.

its own assumptions, purposes, and strategies. It must be recognized, however, that the terms lack precision and general agreement as to their meaning and that the distinction between the two is blurred both in discussion and in reality.

The thrust of community development is to generate changes in attitudes, relationships, and behavior among people at the local or community level. Its major strategy is to develop self-help activities and to foster wide participation in them in the hope that people will be convinced through their own experiences that collective effort is necessary, desirable, and effective as a way of making improvements in their lives. The attainment of immediate and concrete objectives is seen primarily as a step toward the long-range goals of building a sense of community and understanding among people and groups. Community development stresses collaboration, not opposition or conflict. It is rooted in a local geographic base and has been a prominent activity in urban neighborhoods and rural areas in the United States and in Asian, African, and Latin American villages, much of the latter under the stimulus of the United Nations.

While community development programs have placed the emphasis on social change through self-help, the thrust of social action programs has been to seek changes in structural arrangements that govern the distribution of rights, privileges, and resources. Social action is directed at institutional targets in order to accomplish such changes as the passage of legislation, modifications in programs or practices of an organization, and increases in benefits accruing to a particular group.

As a concept, social action is not necessarily limited to a locality or to a particular class group. The term has in fact been used to describe the activities of middle-class and professional groups operating at local, state, and national levels to further specific objectives, such as changes in legislation, increased social security benefits, reforms in governmental practices, or licensing procedures for professional practice, to mention just a few of the many purposes that social-action activities may serve. In the past decade, however, the term has become associated more specifically with the organization of disadvantaged people in low-income areas, in a context that seeks institutional change and that typically employs strategies of confrontation, conflict, and negotiation. An important spokesman of this approach has been Saul Alinsky, whose point of view and activities have received wide publicity.

We shall now look in more detail at some of the components in each of these fields.

COMMUNITY DEVELOPMENT

The spirit and essence of community development are caught in these vivid words of Danilo Dolce, writing of his experiences in Sicily. He found that many people in both agricultural and industrial societies have no idea that development can proceed at a different pace or in a different direction from what they see around them.

"A man does not make an effort unless he knows that he, too, can influence development in a given direction.

"Thus, I learned that one must work with people to create new facts, at all levels, so that they can see, through their own experience, that things can be changed, and how this can be done, and to provide an opportunity for real communication between persons of many different backgrounds and walks of life. . . .

"The masses were beset by hunger and other evils; exploiters old and new were sucking their blood, worse than the lice. But these people, who in fact, were idle or nearly idle, for much of the year, would have been glad to work and bring progress to themselves and to others if only they had known what they could usefully do.

"Water in winter runs down the hillside and is wasted in the sea, and in summer, fields that might produce food for all lie parched and yellow; but how can you plan to build a dam if you have never heard of a dam? Manure is burned in heaps on the outskirts of many villages; how can you put it to good use if you do not know how to rot it and turn it into a valuable resource? Topsoil slides down from unplanted slopes, improperly cared-for crops and livestock produce low yields, while a large part of the population, often superstitiously regarding these evils as punishment from on high, stand around with their hands in their pockets. There is a living to be made for all; but the people do not know it.

"To build a dam was important because the water would bring to the parched land, along with bread, the green shoots of experience, the proof that it is possible to change the face of the earth; but it was important also because the building of the dam meant workers' union; a democratic management of the irrigation system, grape growers and other agricultural cooperatives. In other words, it meant the organizing of chaos; it meant the beginnings of true democratic planning."[18]

Dolce captures in this statement the basic elements of community

[18] Danilo Dolce, "What Have I Learned," *Saturday Review,* July 29, 1967, pp. 13–14. A moving account of the organization of a "community union" appears in

development: (1) the stimulation of awareness of problems and of possibilities, (2) the channeling of energy into self-help projects, and (3) the use of this experience to crystallize a new consciousness and to consolidate it through organization. All of this, it must be noted, revolves around the people of one locality. It is consonant with Rothman's "locality development" type of practice, which "presupposes that community change may be pursued optimally through broad participation of a wide spectrum of people at the local community level in goal determination and action."[19] Burke speaks of this in part as "education-therapy strategy," which is concerned with citizenship training in problem-solving and with developing self-reliance, and in part as a "behavior-change strategy" aimed at influencing individual behavior through participation in an organization.[20]

In attempting to capture the essentials of community development for brief summarization, one is faced with a very extensive literature that is, however, far from definitive on any dimension. There is no general history of community development, nor is there anything approaching a systematic evaluation of what has been achieved by projects that go under this title, however defined. The literature reflects many different conceptual approaches as well as fragmentary empirical material, mostly in the form of case illustrations.

Some writers approach community development as a social movement and/or social philosophy. Others describe it as a field of work related specifically to the organization of people living in rural communities in economically underdeveloped countries in order to help improve their conditions of life. Still others generalize from that experience and view community development as a methodology that can be applied to other fields, such as organizational work in low-income neighborhoods of American cities. In this last view, community development is not a field but a methodology. The descriptions of the methods, however, tend to be couched in great measure in terms of philosophy and to deal with purposes rather than techniques, or both together, so that it is often difficult to determine whether a particular way of working is considered a means toward an end or an end in itself.

Community development as a field has figured prominently in the work

Ecklein and Lauffer, *op. cit.*, Ch. 1, "La Causa and La Huelga," in which Cesar Chavez describes his work among Mexican-American agricultural workers.

[19] Jack Rothman, "Three Models of Community Practice, *op. cit.*, pp. 19–21.

[20] Edmund M. Burke, "Citizen Participation Strategies," *Journal of the American Institute of Planners*, September 1968, pp. 287–294.

of the United Nations. The working definition that the UN adopted in 1956 refers to community development as "the processes by which the efforts of the people themselves are united with those of governmental authorities, to improve the economic, social and cultural conditions of communities, to integrate these communities into the life of the nations, and to enable them to contribute fully to national progress." There was recognition that the governmental authorities had the responsibility to provide technical and other services to the local efforts, but the language called for "as much reliance as possible" on the initiative of the people themselves and urged provision of services "in ways which encourage initiative, self-help and mutual help and make these more effective."[21]

The self-help theme was characteristic of the early years of the programs. A review by the Indian National Planning Commission of the first three years of community development in that country commented that the main value of the program was to be found not so much in actual improvements achieved but "in the change in outlook effected among both the officials and the people." The working assumption was that those changes were necessary in order to overcome apathy and skepticism, attitudes that were considered at that time a major impediment to the achievement of economic progress.

A 1959 U.N. report spoke of three methods of changing social attitudes, each of which was typical of the program in a particular geographic area.[22] One method was "community education" involving the use of films and other mass media to change the climate of opinion in a country through mass education. A second approach emphasized "group dynamics" to be used in leadership training and informal or "social" education programs. In a third method the program itself was used as the educational medium, particularly where there was a significant economic component.

There have been inconsistent tendencies within the field of community development from its earliest days. Many statements can be found that define community development almost entirely in terms of changing attitudes and conducting educational activities at the small-group level, but there are other formulations from the same period that call for a broader framework. For example, an authoritative compilation in 1955 lists ten "basic elements," many of them founded on the principles of

---

[21] United Nations, *International Survey of Programs of Social Development,* New York, 1959, p. 156.

[22] *Ibid.,* pp. 156–157.

participation, education, and attitudinal change.[23] But equal weight is given to the importance of linking local projects with the wider resources and goals of the country and to the necessity of government assistance to community development programs. The point is made that community development aims to integrate the mutual-aid capacities of the local people with the service activities of social welfare departments and the economic and social planning activities of the central government.

The actual practice of community development seems in large measure to have been limited to the local level and to have proceeded in a relatively isolated fashion. This is due not only to the ideology of local self-help but also to the inadequacy of resources. Indeed, the record of community development as a field of work and program of social change in developing countries has been somewhat disappointing. The early UN surveys, published in 1959, indicated that some changes had taken place but that they were much less extensive than the enthusiastic promoters of the movement had hoped.

These UN surveys cast some doubt on one of the basic assumptions of community development—that there would be a correlation between an increase in community self-help activity and the achievement of better standards of productivity. The earlier evaluation of Indian programs indicated that new methods of work within the rural village were adopted by the individuals who were able to improve their own condition, but that this was not associated with an increase in joint action for the common benefit. On the other hand, in some countries where there was a considerable development of common action and a growth in community facilities, this was not accompanied by an increase of productivity.

In subsequent years it became clearer that the achievements that could be anticipated from local efforts alone were quite limited. In the light of these frustrations it is important to take note of the thinking of a group of experts meeting in 1969. They proposed a broad framework of social development in which agricultural policies would be designed to achieve not only a growth in productivity but also a more equitable distribution of the gains. This called for both land reform and a policy of agricultural employment. The experts warned that community development should not be seen in isolation; "otherwise," they stated,

---

[23] United Nations Bureau of Social Affairs, *Social Progress Through Community Development*, New York, 1955, pp. 8–13.

"there was a danger that it may become a way of evading the real problems and needs of the rural population."[24]

Another area of major difficulty was found in the relationship of the community projects to the political forces at work in the different countries. A prominent element in the original ideology of many of the community development projects was the commitment to a nonpolitical approach. This was based on the contention that political domination was one of the factors standing in the way of development itself. Political competition and factionalism were seen as obstacles, along with the rigidities of the kinship and caste systems, to the adoption of methods that would yield greater benefits to the population. The community development ideology avoided concepts of political conflict and struggle, relying instead on a process that would unite various groups in a common effort. Reliance was placed on voluntary associations as the sponsors for the community development projects, and there was an absence of working relationships with politically elected bodies in many of the countries.

Some negative effects flowed from this lack of integration between community projects and the political system. In some instances, by organizing populations that had previously been unorganized and by articulating demands, community development became in effect a political force, although this had not been anticipated in the planning. The projects became a challenge to existing authorities but were not in a position to pursue the challenge effectively. Community development became a political issue and came to be either opposed or dominated by political forces. In some countries community development work was associated with the decentralization of government functions and did in fact have a close relationship with local government. One of the early evaluations of the projects in India suggested that some of the best results were achieved where there was a strong tie between the projects and an active local village council that was the elective body.[25]

These lessons pose something of a dilemma to the ideology of community development. Tendencies toward national planning run counter to the tenets of local self-determination that are basic to the community development approach. The 1967 UN Report places considerable stress

[24] Commission for Social Development, United Nations Economic and Social Council, *Social Policy and Planning in National Development:* Report of the Meeting of Experts on Social Policy and Planning held at Stockholm from 1–10 September 1969, U.N. Memorandum 67-29312, p. 12.

[25] United Nations, *International Survey of Programs of Social Development,* 1955, p. 158.

on the need for national policies that will further economic and social development, and it points out that the "felt needs" of local populations may be incompatible with these national requirements. The Report nevertheless argues that ". . . what must be avoided at all costs, if the very spirit of community development is to be maintained . . . is the imposition of plans from above and the use of community development simply as a means of implementing action decided upon by the higher authority."[26] The resolution of this dilemma proposed in the Report seems to be more an expression of hope than a convincing prescription for action:

"What is necessary is an approach that leads in the first place to establishing *rapport* between the community and the practitioner so that mutual confidence is assured, and then gradually leading the community to think in terms of objectives for action that are sound and likely to make a contribution to the development process. In this way, there can be a measure of planning from below and of popular participation in development."[27]

As a result of all these factors, community development programs now occupy a somewhat different status in the United Nations than they did a decade ago. Whereas there had been a suggestion that community development might be in itself an instrument for major social change, today such programs are subsumed under larger programs of national and regional social development. Importance is still attached to community development programs as instruments for mobilizing resources, but that task is now seen as an integral aspect of programs that are broader in geography and in scope than the village-level efforts that have been most characteristic of community development work.

Although community development emerged as an ideology and a program out of experience in rural areas, it has been extended to urban communities in both the industrialized and developing countires. Clinard has provided one of the most comprehensive descriptions of this work in disadvantaged urban areas.[28] His book is a spirited argument on behalf of community development as an approach to the problems of urban slums, one that is superior to other solutions such as urban renewal and slum clearance or what he terms "social service" and "economic opportunity" approaches. The latter are ineffective, he argues, because they

[26] United Nations, *Report on the World Social Situation*, 1967, p. 99.

[27] *Ibid.*

[28] Marshall B. Clinard, *Slums and Community Development*, New York: The Free Press, 1966.

fail to arouse the motivation and participation of slum residents, do not reach those most in need, and do not correct the deviant behavior that exists within the slums.

". . . this (community development) approach relies directly on the slum dwellers themselves. If their apathy and dependence can be overcome and replaced by pride and a sense of initiative, the slum dwellers can make good use of 'millions of hands' and their own resources, meager alone but large when pooled, in trying to solve their manifold problems."[29]

Clinard's approach is very smilar to that which had been formulated in the rural programs. It is based to a major extent on the use of group educational processes. Change is expected to develop out of the group's perception of the need for change. The goals are not to be imported from the outside but defined by the group itself. Outside assistance is largely to facilitate the creation of a new type of social organization in which the group process can take place. Change is to be sought not only in external resources and institutions but also in the identity and self-image of the participants. On the other hand, there is some recognition of political elements, a demand for decentralization of some governmental functions, and a willingness to undertake conflict to achieve a shift in political power and transfer of resources.[30]

Clinard's analysis is based in part on experience in the Delhi project in India, where it was found that participation tended to be greater in projects that were smaller in size and in projects that were older, indicating that it takes some time for participation to be developed. On the other hand, the number of self-help activities undertaken tended to decline as the projects got older. More people participated in the organization and in the decision-making, but the volume of activity declined. Of greatest significance, however, was the character of the self-help activities. Most of them were in the recreational field and relatively few had an economic impact, which is consistent with the findings of the United Nations. To the extent that they were effective, they influenced the amenities of slum life rather than the underlying economic conditions.

COMMUNITY ACTION

Community development concepts played a prominent role in the American community action programs of the 1960's, where they became closely interwoven with social action objectives.[31]

[29] *Ibid.*, pp. 116–117.
[30] *Ibid.*, p. 313.
[31] There is a rapidly growing literature on community action programs. A few

Mobilization for Youth in New York City, one of the earliest and most comprehensive of these programs, may be taken as a case example for discussion of this intermingling of the two approaches. Mobilization for Youth (MFY) was located in an area characterized by low income, high delinquency, poor housing, and a large concentration of black and Puerto Rican people. Organized by a number of voluntary agencies, it was supported first by the Ford Foundation, then as a demonstration project financed by the President's Committee on Juvenile Delinquency, and later as a beneficiary of the Office of Economic Opportunity's antipoverty program. What follows is a brief review of the MFY experience.

In the field of housing, efforts were made to obtain code enforcement, but these proved to be laborious and discouraging. It turned out that housing was not a top priority for most of the people in the area, and there was a sense that improvement in housing, if not accompanied by a general raising of economic standards, would prove futile. The program set minimal and realistic objectives such as tenant education, some relocation service, and agitation for code enforcement in the most serious cases, together with demands for selective rehabilitation of housing.

Consumer education programs registered limited successes. Some cooperatives were formed. These efforts were evaluated as helpful on an individual level but not of sufficient magnitude to make basic changes in the system with which low-income consumers have to contend.

Legal services were made available to residents to protect their rights as tenants, consumers, and clients of social agencies. Lawyers not only acted on behalf of individuals but also began to use the courts to challenge and change the policies and practices of organizations that intimately affected the lives of people in the target area of MFY.

Mobilization was able, through its voter registration activities, to increase the numbers of those who registered and voted, but the numbers remained relatively low and were not adequate to make an impact on actual results. It was concluded that much more sustained efforts of political organization and education would be required.

examples are: *Annals of the American Academy of Political and Social Science,* September 1969; *Against Poverty; Readings from the Mobilization Experience,* New Haven: College and University Press, 1967; Irwin Deutscher and Elizabeth Thompson, Eds., *Among the People: Encounters With the Poor,* New York: Basic Books, 1968; Special Issue on "Citizen Participation" of the *Journal of the American Institute of Planners,* XXXV, No. 4, July 1969; Ralph M. Kramer, *op. cit.;* Sar A. Levitan, *The Great Society's Poor Law: A New Approach to Poverty,* Baltimore: Johns Hopkins Press, 1968; and Peter Marris and Martin Rein, *op. cit.*

Some of the most tangible results were obtained in connection with public-welfare rights and benefits. One of the earliest activities was a campaign to secure clothing grants for welfare clients, and this was quite successful. It provided an impetus to continuing organization of welfare clients that gradually became citywide in scope. Substantial gains were obtained in the form of welfare grants, and the organization became a vehicle through which clients were able to demand more respectful and equitable treatment for themselves from the welfare system.

Mobilization's history is marked by a number of distinct phases. Weissman summarizes them as follows.[32]

Phase 1—many scattered efforts to establish relationships and to work with a variety of voluntary groups in the neighborhood.

Phase 2—the coalescing of these scattered efforts into more systematic mass organization of pressure groups that would work on specific issues. This phase was characterized by militant pressure activity such as rent strikes and school boycotts.

Phase 3—a further stage, described as a "coalition," was achieved through federations of like-minded groups that were concerned with similar issues. The main example of this form of organization was the Welfare Rights Movement.

Phase 4—described as the "technical" phase, involved a mixture of social protest activity, characteristic of the previous two phases, with the development of social services and the establishment of more stable and formal social organizations with professional and nonprofessional staffs.

Mobilization, like many of the demonstration projects of the same period, had a multiplicity of objectives that were not always consistent with one another. Community development and social action approaches were mingled, and there was considerable emphasis on the coordination of services to make them more accessible and effective in relation to the needs of the population. All "models" of community organization were present in Mobilization's activities, with recurring issues as to which aspect of the program should receive priority and how the different elements would relate to one another.

All of this took place, however, within a framework of basic tenets that are characteristic of community development. Chief among these was the emphasis on involvement of the local people in determining their objectives and in carrying out the programs. In line with this

---

[32] Harold H. Weissman, *op. cit.*

emphasis, it had been one of the original MFY objectives to create an independent organization that would have the capacity to sustain social action programs on its own without outside help. It is the judgment of those reviewing the experience that this goal was never attained.

Under the pressure of immediate demands, effort was expended simply to achieve short-run objectives without regard to whether these were building an independent organization for the long run. On the other hand, services were introduced in response to the needs of the people being organized; the services made a contribution toward the development of the organization but without necessarily contributing to the goals of social action. It was found that the attempts to build an organization on a block basis were not adequate in themselves but that it became necessary to provide and create services. Block organizations thus tended to develop into community centers. One reason for this was that only a relatively small number of the people reached could be stimulated to take part consistently in organizational work, but larger numbers could become identified with the project through the use of concrete services.

Mobilization's historians reach the same conclusion that has been reported from the experience of underdeveloped countries. "Perhaps the most profound lesson of the Mobilization experience is that slum communities cannot solve their problems alone. They need outside help and resources."[33] The major accomplishment, they conclude, lay not in any of the specific services created or benefits obtained, but rather in identifying the social problems of the slums and making those problems a social issue in the eyes of the public at large.

There is, however, another conclusion that some have drawn from this same analysis. It calls for a sharper orientation of activity toward the organization of social movements based primarily on the low-income population and directed toward the formulation of a new power group capable of exerting influence on the political system. This was discussed in Chapter 4 in terms of Grosser's writing. The term *social action* is often used to identify this approach and to distinguish it from community development which, although it may include elements of social action, is generally not committed to the creation of a new political force as a central objective. The work of Saul Alinsky illustrates some aspects of the social action approach.[34]

[33] *Ibid.*, p. 186.

[34] A recent analysis of Alinsky's approach to community organization, which also contains references to available material by and about Alinsky, is Robert Pruger and Harry Specht, "Assessing Theoretical Models of Community Organization Practice:

Alinsky is fond of pointing out that Machiavelli wrote *The Prince* to tell the "haves how to keep it," while his purpose is "to show the have-nots how to take it away from them." He has given the greatest importance to building an effective organization to engage in the kinds of action that will convey a sense of power to its members and will reflect that power to its adversaries. Through the disciplined use of power, an Alinsky-type organization seeks to become increasingly effective in asserting its interest against those in authority who have hitherto disregarded the group or its members because they were perceived as powerless.

Another approach to social action is presented by Haggstrom in a paper that analyzes the organization of poor people. He also stresses the building of an organization.

"Action by the organization of the poor should be evaluated on the basis of its outcome in *organizational mileage* for the poor. For example, a demonstration at City Hall would not be evaluated on the basis of whether concessions were wrung from the city government. It would be judged on the basis of whether the organization had more power after the demonstration, and therefore had moved some distance toward a better world. The organization would have logged mileage only if it did not decline after having won the concession.

"Organizational mileage is a subtle and complex criterion of action. It can be used only by those who clearly understand where the organization, if successful, would go. Organizational mileage is mileage in the direction of a distant and fundamental goal; movement by an organization often does not add up to organizational mileage. It would, therefore, be important for the membership of an organization of the poor to acquire as rapidly as possible a sophisticated understanding of the journey which they are attempting. To some extent they must learn social geography and fashion a map based on that discipline in order properly to guide their organization in the direction of their goal."[35]

Alinsky as a Case in Point," *The Social Service Review*, 43, No. 2, June 1969, pp. 123–135. For an account of Alinsky's work in the black community of Rochester, see Ecklein and Lauffer, *op. cit.*, Ch. 3, "Alinsky Starts a FIGHT." See also bibliography in *Poverty and Human Resources Ab tract₃*, Vol. 1, No. 6, 1966, p. 167. See also Saul D. Alinsky, "Of Means and Ends," Chapter 12, and "Citizen Participation and Community Organization in Planning and Urban Renewal," Chapter 14, in Fred M. Cox, John L. Erlich, Jack Rothman, and John E. Tropman, Eds., *Strategies of Community Organization, A Book of Readings*, Itaska, Ill.: F.E. Peacock Publishers, 1970, pp. 315–323.

[35] Warren C. Haggstrom, "Can the Poor Transform the World?" in Irwin Deutscher and Elizabeth J. Thompson, Eds., *Among the People: Encounters With the Poor*, pp. 79–80.

Organizations of poor people differ significantly in terms of both their ends and their means. They are more or less focused on the kind of "distant and fundamental" goals that Haggstrom advocates; they are more or less given to the accumulation and use of power, as he and Alinsky recommend. Based on a study of local organizations in the community action programs of the 1960's, Austin identifies types of civic action associations, which vary according to two interdependent factors: autonomy and the use of contest methods to achieve their ends. He defines a "contest" situation as a struggle for power in which one side emerges as the victor. Austin's five types are:[36]

1. The self-help, mutual-aid, community development association. This is autonomous, focused on problems within its area, and does not engage in contest tactics.
2. The junior partner association. Here an outside organization develops the group to increase the effectiveness of service delivery or to participate in planning. It is focused on a particular area and uses non-contest methods.
3. The petitioner association. This is a local, autonomous organization concerned with getting action from organizations outside the area that are responsible for providing services. The approach may be aggressive, but contest tactics are not used.
4. The militant association is autonomous. It demands actions of outside organizations by use of contest tactics.
5. The service-providing association. Locally controlled, this type provides or controls direct services to an area. It is sometimes called a community corporation.

This is a useful typology. However, it describes means only as a dichotomy between contest and non-contest strategies. Two recent studies concur in the observation that among these organizations there is no simple, direct relationship between goals and strategies. Turner's study found that consensus and conflict strategies are both used to pursue both controversial and non-controversial goals. Hillman reported that "neighborhood organizations that are the most successful use many strategies and move flexibly from one to the other."[37] We return in the following

[36] David M. Austin, "Influence of Community Setting on Neighborhood Action," in John B. Turner, Ed., *op. cit.*, p. 34.

[37] Arthur Hillman, *Making Democracy Work, A Study of Neighborhood Organization*, New York: National Federation of Settlements and Neighborhood Centers, 1969, p. 92.

chapter to the choice of organizational goals and strategies and relate these to people's identification with locality, race, and social class. We want to close this chapter with some observations about the success of community action programs.

This chapter has dealt at length with the organization of lower-class urban residents in voluntary associations and has given less attention to middle-class groups or to organizing in rural areas. But because of the extent of activities in the ghettoes and barrios in recent years, it is important to summarize what has emerged from that experience, particularly by way of limiting factors that ought to be kept in mind.

First, it appears that low-income people respond more to efforts that are addressed to bread-and-butter issues of immediate importance to their daily lives than they do to complex policy issues. This affects the choice of both targets and strategies and must be taken into account in recruiting members and in the demands that are made on their participation.

Second, voluntary associations of low-income people are typically organized at the neighborhood level. They experience some difficulties in forming horizontal or vertical alliances or coalitions, in part because of the controversial nature of their demands, in part because of limited skill in organizational matters.

Third, lacking financial and other resources, these self-help associations must for the most part look to other organizations for support and staff. These sponsoring organizations, governmental or voluntary, are usually part of the established institutional network of the community, with ties and interests that place restrictions on the freedom of movement they can permit the groups they sponsor. The pull toward autonomy and away from this dependence and control constitutes a major problem for the staff who must, in a sense, serve two masters.

The study conducted by Turner and his associates of what they call "self-help associations" noted that while paid workers and members of these organizations had difficulty in defining success, it was obvious that many of them felt that they were accomplishing something. Seen from a broader perspective than that of just one citizen self-help group, there are criteria for success that are not dependent on the success or failure of a specific action. Actions of problem-oriented self-help groups may have an *accumulative* effect. One group protesting urban renewal in its neighborhood, for example, will be unsuccessful and the area demolished, but if enough groups protest urban renewal throughout the country, then it is possible that wholesale bulldozing will not be seen as a viable means for improving housing. Or, the demands by an organization for a black school principal may not be met at that particular school, but the following year there may be several new black school principals. The original action may produce results that are widely separated from the initial protest. Thus, the total impact of a citizen self-help group is difficult and may be impossible to assess from the perspective of one particular group at a particular point in time.

Several contributors to the Turner report made their own assessments of the accomplishments of local organizations in the community action programs.[38] Rothman suggested that local groups can achieve improvements in some services, develop people's political skills, benefit them psychologically, and build constituencies for broad national efforts. Another view was that these local groups are most effective in forcefully communicating to the rest of society the unmet needs of their members, but that they can do little beyond this. Slavin argued that the primary purpose of such organizations should be to make institutions more responsive, not simply to produce new services. Rainwater stressed political organization and moving into the major parties as the route to better economic conditions.

In his epilogue to the report Turner argues the necessity of using these "lower-level mechanisms" as counterweights to the strong tendency to "push decision-making toward the more rarefied levels of geopolitical interaction." This very challenge, however (as we have seen in the experience of community development under United Nations sponsorship and in Mobilization for Youth) is a difficult one for local organizations to meet.

If they are to grapple with the most serious problems of their constituencies, these associations must have an impact on the centers of decision-making that control employment opportunities, public-assistance levels, housing, education, and health care. These centers are located beyond the boundaries of the ghetto, the neighborhood, and even the city. The main switches that control the flow of these goods and services are found more and more in Washington and to a lesser extent in state capitals. Moreover, affecting changes at the source of these decisions involves just those long-range, complex policy issues that are most difficult for these associations to handle.

Recognizing these limitations does not imply that grass-roots community organization is ineffectual or wasteful of the energies that go into it. These issues are posed, rather, to suggest that careful analysis of lines of responsibility and control and of cause-and-effect factors are

[38] Turner, *op. cit.*, pp. 39–51.

needed in attacking social problems in order to trace them to their sources and to find the levels of influence and channels of action that are most germane. Some problems require the mobilization of action on a state or national scale; some are local in character. The problem of air and water pollution cannot be solved by action directed against a few industrial firms within one city; it requires the attention of whole states and regions and the powers of the Federal government. By contrast, if many parents in a school district find the performance of their school board or administrator to be unsatisfactory, this is an appropriate target for their efforts to bring about change.

In terms of community development, the United Nations is now striving to relate these programs to national planning. But, as we noted earlier, this creates a dilemma, because it strains the ideological commitment of community development to local self-determination. There are several ways of dealing with this dilemma. One is to redefine the functions of community development in such a way as to make them compatible with the ideology. Biddle, one of the leading theoreticians of community development, in reviewing the failure of community development programs to achieve some of their more ambitious goals, suggests that "community developers should come to look upon themselves, not as nation-builders or as economic problem-solvers, but as educators."[39] He goes on to reaffirm the basic tenets of the community development methodology. It is education not in the sense of formal instruction, but as a process of involving people in experiences from which they will learn ways of enhancing their capacity for self-directed activity. The "community developer" is a guider of the group process. He interprets people's experiences to them and thus helps them to derive lessons for their own guidance.

Given the finding of historians that people in need require "outside help" in addition to their own resources, another approach is to make the target of educational efforts not those in need but the public at large. Making the electorate and political leaders more aware of social issues and potential solutions has to a limited extent been one of the accomplishments of the activities of the last decade.[40]

This leads to still another way of solving the dilemma—that is to seize it by the horns and to seek broad social-change goals by organizing new political forces to oppose the policies of existing governments. This is the path of assertive social action. Here, we have seen, the outcome is

---

[39] William W. Biddle, "Deflating the Community Developer," *Community Development Journal*, **3**, No. 4, October 1968, pp. 191–194.

[40] *Ibid.*, p. 186.

also a mixed one. New and effective interest groups have been formed, such as the Welfare Rights Organization, that have won some concessions, developed organizational skills among the new leaders, and exposed some problems to public consciousness.

The weight of the evidence indicates, however, that neither community development nor social action undertaken at the local level by disadvantaged people have thus far produced powerful social movements, political realignments, or significant changes in the distribution of rights and resources. They have, on the other hand, stimulated more awareness of the needs of disadvantaged people, developed more effective spokesmen for them, and brought about some limited modifications in the structures and practices of those bureaucracies that are most vulnerable to local pressure.

CHAPTER 6

Working with Voluntary Associations

DEVELOPING INFORMATION AND RELATIONSHIPS

Whatever one takes as a point of departure—the people of an area or an issue, a community development approach or a social-action stance—there are significant similarities in working with voluntary associations for social-change goals. This is consistent with our thesis that the organizational context largely determines the issues and tasks facing the practitioner and that these in turn shape the methods that are appropriate.

Using the problem-solving framework outlined in Chapter 4, we begin with the practitioner's initial task in working with voluntary associations: defining the situation he is entering. This involves gathering and analyzing information about the area, the problems, and the people relevant to his purposes and simultaneously establishing relationships with those who will be involved in the action. These activities correspond to the analytical and interactional tasks noted in the framework. The organizer's first explorations help him to obtain a beginning view of the problems he will be confronting and to define his role vis-a-vis the people with whom he will be working. The process of defining the situation thus involves an interplay between analysis and action—between the gathering of information and the development of relationships.

In some of the traditional prescriptions for community organization practice, considerable stress has been placed on conducting surveys as a way of defining the problems on which action should be undertaken. In the development of action projects with voluntary organizations, however, the effective use of information is dependent on a definition of the purposes for which the information is being sought. It is necessary to have at least a beginning viewpoint as to the definition of the problem being attacked in order to determine what kind of information to seek and how best to obtain it.

Generalized approaches to community surveys, for example, stress the gathering of data concerning the characteristics of a population, as well as inventories of community institutions, organizations, and resources.[1] Such suggestions do have some value as starting points for a worker to become acquainted with the characteristics of an area, since his frame of reference for undertaking the development of an organizing effort has been defined as having a local geographical base.

Decennial census information that provides demographic and housing data according to census tracts with an average population of 4000 provides a way of obtaining a quick impression of basic demographic characteristics of the population, such as age, family composition, nativity, length of residence, occupation, ethnic groupings, and the like. It is also helpful to identify trends, such as population turnover or changes in characteristics of the population, by comparing successive census enumerations and using special census reports or analyses on specific subjects. Similarly, it is useful to have some general picture of the network of services and associations located in the area, since they offer a potential for implementing the action purposes of the effort that is being developed.

However, the utility of such generalized information-gathering is quickly exhausted. Almost at the outset, there is a need to begin to answer the question of purpose more specifically. Typical of a more focused approach to the use of surveys is a recent manual on organizing, in which the questions raised are related clearly to the social action objectives of the work being undertaken. Surveys are to be directed, not to obtaining a general picture of the population, but to locating certain dynamic elements in the situation, such as where decision-making power is located and what the relationships are among various power groups.[2]

To make a comprehensive inventory of the structure and functions of the institutional network in a neighborhood is a formidable undertaking. There is, however, no need for a general survey of all organized activities unless there is a specific program objective for doing this. It is more likely

[1] A classic and comprehensive guide for conducting a community survey can be found in Roland L. Warren, *Studying Your Community*, New York: Russell Sage Foundation, 1955, pp. 306–347.

[2] Martin Oppenheimer and George Lakey, *A Manual for Direct Action*, Chicago: Quadrangle Books, 1964, p. 15.

to be important to have a resource file of certain types of service agencies or membership organizations. Mapping organizations can be facilitated by keeping in mind a number of analytical dimensions.

1. Organizations that perform neighborhood-relevant functions as distinct from those that are located in the neighborhood but do not perform such functions.
2. Categorization of organizations according to the degree to which decisions governing their functions are made inside the neighborhood or outside of it.
3. Organizational structure—that is, social agency, membership organization, delegate body, and mixed types.
4. Public or voluntary organizations.

Oppenheimer and Lakey discuss how to assess the power structure of a whole community not a neighborhood. They ask "which people, families, and business concerns, which politicians, ministers, and educators have the authority to make decisions which influence the behavior of other individuals."[3] In the search for powerful leaders and groups, the authors note:

"The elite will vary, of course, with the kind of community—in an area of large plantation-type agriculture, there will be one kind of elite. In a more commercial and industrial area, there will be another. Important parts of the decision-making elite may not live in the city. Above all, it is important to remember that elites do not always agree among themselves. They have interests which differ and sometimes conflict."

Initial Steps—Differential Approaches. Given some beginning picture of the area or population to which the practitioner is addressing himself, the initial steps that he takes in entering the situation and the way he presents himself and interprets his purposes are important determinants of the ensuing development of the action project. To illustrate, we shall draw on three quite different approaches that are described in the companion volume of case materials.

In one situation a team from a university, taking a community development approach, worked with embittered, suspicious white mountain people. They began by building personal relationships, using a nondirective approach and emphasizing that they had no specific objectives and programs in mind. In the second case an organizer opened an office in a low-income public-housing development and, under a contract with the

---

[3] Oppenheimer and Lakey, *op. cit.*, pp. 15–29.

Housing Authority, set about organizing the residents "to bring services to the projects and to bring people out of the projects and to services." The organizer immediately set in motion a door-to-door survey that served to generate two-way communication between the organizing staff and the tenants. In the third case a community organization specialist for a city planning commission was assigned to organize a predominantly black neighborhood so that its people could make recommendations and "deal with the city" in connection with urban-renewal planning. The worker's first move was to make contact with groups with political importance in order to solicit their help in arranging a series of meetings for discussion of the city's urban-renewal proposal. It is worth looking more closely at each of these situations.

In the first case a team of organizers went into an area in Appalachia in which both human and physical resources had been despoiled by the coal industry.[4] The staff that came to Straw Hollow from the State University's Institute for Regional Development had studied the economic and social history of the area. They knew, for instance, that 87 out of 93 families depended on some form of relief, that those on the county welfare roles "knew their meager checks were dependent upon their good behavior," and that the people had withdrawn into silent bitterness. The organizers visited the community, trying to establish contacts and get acquainted.

"Although they introduced themselves as staff and students from the university, they offered no specific program. 'Whut you all goin' ta do out hyer?' was the usual question. 'What can we help people do?' was the usual reply.

"I suppose their wandering around, their refusal to make decisions about what to do for the people's welfare, their non-directiveness must have been very disquieting for the residents. A preacher who had warned that they might be dangerous outside agitators could not find anything to accuse them of agitating about. Some residents must have decided the visitors were freeloaders (they did accept invitations to meals at people's homes on two occasions), or goof-offs or gold-bricks. The one thing they were not seen as were representatives of the outside community's exploitive and degrading institutions."

Later a husband and wife on the organizing team decided to rehabilitate a one-room school in Straw Hollow and live there. As they

---

[4] Ecklein and Lauffer, *op. cit.*, "Hollow Hope: Community Development in Appalachia" in Chapter 5.

worked some of the teenagers and younger children came by to watch and several offered to help. When they finished they decided to give a Thanksgiving feast as a way of thanking their new neighbors for their help. Describing their experience, the organizers comment:

"Of course not everyone came. Fact is, we hardly knew anyone in the hollow. We had decided not to go out aggressively to meet people, but to let it happen naturally as we met them on the road, at the Post Office, as they came by to check on who we were and what we were doing, etc.

"The next day about fifty people or more, many of whom we had never seen, came by to look or to introduce themselves. We had them in for coffee. It was like an open house. And then we realized something that hadn't really occurred to us before. Our home was a familiar building to them. Many of the parents and the grandparents and some of the older children had gone to school there. It had been a community building. It still was the largest single room in the hollow, and it seemed natural for it to become a community building again. Had we kept it strictly to ourselves we would have been like squatters taking over something of theirs.

"Our success in patching up our living quarters suggested to us that we might be able to get a 'clean-up' or 'face-lift' campaign going before the winter set in and it got really cold. We failed in getting any support at all . . . . To make a long story short, by Spring we had a folk craft co-op going, sent some things to an exhibit at the University, and arranged for the sale of some items . . . . Not once had we suggested to anyone that we wanted to help him seek a job, but after a while young men and older boys began coming in regularly asking for help. . . ."

By contrast, the organizer in the public housing project explains that he uses a survey as a standard procedure for opening up new neighborhoods to organizing efforts because it offers a "quick, easy way to get information and to build a support network."[5] He continues:

"It didn't take more than a couple of days, what with residents looking around as we moved office furniture in, and as some of our staff hung around the parking lots and entrance ways in the early mornings and late afternoons, to find out what the real problems were. The old folks needed protection—too many muggings and petty robberies right in the buildings themselves. Mothers needed day care help. Teenagers needed recreation facilities, tutorial help, jobs. The men needed jobs and job

[5] Ecklein and Lauffer, *op. cit.*, "The Survey as an Organizing Technique" in Chapter 5.

training. Everyone needed help with transportation. The management of the project was often arbitrary in establishing rules. Residents weren't involved, and earlier attempts at developing a tenants' council resulted in a takeover by a very vocal lady and a small group of henchmen. The place was demoralized. People just wanted out. If there was no hope of escape, there was no hope of improvement either.

"Now, we didn't need a survey to find all this out. We were told quick enough. We knew pretty much on the basis of informal discussions what the results of a survey might bring out.

"The canvassers who went from door to door did not just ask questions and leave. They stayed and talked . . . about anything people had on their minds, and about why we were there, in the project. A twenty-minute interview could easily stretch into an hour. It was never time wasted. We identified potential leaders, located the disinterested, got insights into the politics of the housing authority. Most important, we began establishing communication links. Not just between ourselves and the people . . . but among them too. Bringing residents along and having them do some of the canvassing was very helpful. They were able to dispel some of the mistrust people showed strangers.

"A survey can give you accurate information. It can furnish you with knowledge about conditions that don't get reflected in any formal document. It is a way of getting known and of establishing relationships. It helps you begin to focus on an organizing issue. And it educates your staff and whomever else you want to use in canvassing."

However paradoxical it may be to give someone the task of organizing a voluntary association, this was precisely what the city planning commission worker was asked to do in the third case illustration.[6] He was to develop a local organization that could speak for the neighborhood residents and negotiate on their behalf with the city's urban renewal planners. As he moved into a ghetto area he found it "a maze of power conflict . . . black-white feelings, working-class versus professional, political blacks versus anti-city hall blacks, etc." He decided that he had to thread his way "step by step so that at each point or layer I would be able to involve key individuals and groups and gain sanction of the people on that particular level." He began with two black groups at the YMCA, a businessmens' organization and a professional group.

"I met with both of these groups and they arranged for a series of meet-

---

[6] Ecklein and Lauffer, *op. cit.*, "Preparing a Neighborhood for Urban Renewal" in Chapter 6.

ings where the city proposal could be discussed. This brought the proposed study immediately into the open and for a month there were a series of meetings. Several things were gained by this. I became visible. People knew that I was willing to come and explain and interpret what was going on.

"Notice, I was Jewish, I was white, I was middle class; I had all of these strikes against me. But notice what I was doing; I was preparing the way for the next level, to get to the proposed renewal area and talk to the people there directly.

"I met with a minister's group, some black professionals, some home-owners. These were all a series of meetings and by this time (5 or 6 weeks) people were getting to know me. There was no formal group but people in the target area were beginning to receive signals about the city's intention to study this area. I did not know who they were, but they began to react to the rumors and at one of the meetings we were invaded by a group of 30 or 40 of the home-owners who had heard about the proposal. They wanted to know what was going on and why we were not dealing with them.

"I welcomed them into the meeting and told them I was a guest and was prepared to talk to anyone without regard to their group affiliations. From this point on the shift began from the YMCA and other power groups to the local people."

These three cases reveal some of the factors that the professionals took into account as they moved in and began to define the situation in which they were working. The unobstrusive, rather slow approach of the team in Appalachia was consistent with their goal of developing a local organization capable ultimately of working on many fronts for the welfare of the people of Straw Hollow. By contrast, the city planning specialist moved directly and swiftly toward his objective of setting up a structure to deal with urban renewal planning. In one situation the organizers were sensitive to the importance of personal and kin relationships and in the other the organizer made use of existing organizations and their lines of communication out into the community.

In all three cases there was an initial period of building trust and credibility, drawing from people their views of their own situation and presenting to them the scope and the limits of the organizer's role. The critical significance of the personal element is made clear in this comment by another organizer:

"When you're dealing with people down town or in some big organization, it's important to tell them who you are—your title, what you expect to accomplish, etc. You play it like an organization 'rep.' But when you're in the neighborhood, people don't want to know your title. They want to know *you*. Can they trust you? Are you afraid of getting your hands dirty? Are you going to play square or just promise the world?"[7]

Ordinarily an organizer enters a situation with the legitimation of the organization that places him there. This inevitably constricts his freedom of action, but the lack of legitimating auspices can also pose serious problems for the organizer, who must then win acceptance entirely on his own. Moreover, the absence of legitimation in the case of volunteer organizers can also mean the lack of a clear-cut mandate or function. This has proved to be confusing to both the organizer and those he seeks to organize, as was the case with a group of students who found that some of the difficulty they encountered in organizing a neighborhood project was

"rooted in the fact that most citizens of the neighborhood, despite our ideological pronouncements, wondered why we had come there in the first place. This distrust increased as our promises, which emerged more out of our ideology than out of what was materially possible, persistently outran our accomplishments. Of course, many people in the neighborhood broke a promise or two during the course of several months, but for us such failures were different."[8]

The building of relationships means dealing with the hesitations, fears, and hostilities that stem from situational factors and cultural and psychological resistances to the organizer and to the organizing process. For example, workers reported at a conference on organization that it was very difficult to organize white mountain people, in part because they do not ordinarily attend formally organized meetings. They stay close to their families and their life is centered around their children. Add to this bitter interfamily hostilities and the worker faces the risk of alienating one faction if he is able to make friends with another.

People's willingness to talk about their situation depends on such factors as the previous relationship of the practitioner to the people with whom he is in contact and the history of the problem under discussion and of efforts to cope with it. Ease of communication also depends on the meaning of the subject in terms of the shared values and cultural patterns of the people involved. A discussion of parochial schools will

---

[7] Ecklein and Lauffer, *op. cit.*, Chapter 5, "Getting to Know You—Talking At or 'Rapping With.'"

[8] Ecklein and Lauffer, *op. cit.*, Chapter 4, "A Tutorial Project in Harlem."

have different meanings to various religious groups. The consideration of water fluoridation for a community has brought out very sharp differences among otherwise united groups.

Out of his preliminary contacts with residents and organizations, the organizer forms a preliminary and tentative picture of the patterns, trends, and problems of an area. He has, moreover, in the very process of exploration, made beginning contacts and collected impressions of the interests, capacities, and relationships among various groups and individuals within the community. The picture that emerges is inevitably a mosaic of perceptions and opinions that not only differ from person to person, but, more often than not, contradict each other. Because the mosaic is composed of partially accurate and incomplete perceptions, the practitioner must seek out many sources of information in order to build up a rounded representation of the situation.

The college students working in Harlem discovered, in this connection, that there were substantial conflicts of interest within the area:[9]

"It quickly became apparent that sex, age, and particular places of residence made their own particular and conflicting concerns . . . Mothers of younger children, for instance, expressed a need for a child-care center: among the older boys and men the problem was to get jobs, the younger students felt trapped by the local school system; some tenants wanted to do something about their dilapidated homes; some persons wanted more space for recreational purpose; some tutees wanted their own hangout; some parents wanted more ways to get together with each other; others only wanted peace and privacy.

"A general conflict was evident between the older and younger generations of the block. The young people wanted more freedom of movement. . . . The parents generally wanted to enforce 'respectability'."

At some point the organizer adds up his impressions and information and assesses the picture he has formed as a basis for deciding on his next steps. This point in the process is well illustrated in an account of the organization of tenants in a public-housing project by a group of students and faculty of a social work school.[10]

The organizers had spent some time "hanging around benches talking to mothers" about what they thought was wrong with the housing project as well as talking with the project manager, who suggested names to

[9] *Ibid.*

[10] Ecklein and Lauffer, *op. cit.,* Chapter 7, "Organizing Tenants in Low Income Public Housing," by Lawrence Grossman.

them for a tenants' group. After interviewing some of these people and deciding that an organization built by them would not be action-oriented, the organizing staff devoted two days to taking stock of the situation.

They found that the social conditions in the project deprived people of self-respect and inhibited the achievement of "community or general well-being among the tenants." The organizers analyzed this into several components: the manager's monopoly of power and of information as to what the "rules" were; the tenants' lack of access to decision-making authority; the stigma attached to the project by the larger community; and the manager's encouraging of tenants to inform on each other as a control measure. They found further that tenants developed certain styles of response and adaptation to these conditions, the basic types being (1) acceptance of the situation and retreat into passivity; (2) anger at the management; (3) manipulating the management for individual gain; and (4) identifying with the management and striving to separate themselves from the mass of tenants.

Out of this analysis the organizers defined their broad aims and carefully selected the initial leadership. They set as their general goal the development of a powerful tenants' organization, the systematic restructuring of the destructive features in the environment, and the development of political skills "to facilitate the emergence of dignity and the kind of communal interaction that would support self-esteem." The staff had done explicitly what organizers do more often implicitly, that is, convert the results of their reconnaissance into a framework of goals, a process to which we now turn our attention.

SELECTING PROBLEMS, GOALS, AND STRATEGIES

Once having acquired some understanding of a local situation, the practitioner confronts the task of setting priorities among different problems and different modes of intervention.

The choice of a problem, Ohlin points out, "significantly determines the activities the movement will engage in, the form of organization, the population segments involved, the sponsoring agents or groups, and the means employed to achieve goals."[11] He goes on to say that "we need better criteria for selecting those development problems most amenable to indigenous organizations with different levels of experience, scope, and competence" and suggests these as tentative criteria:

[11] Ohlin, *op. cit.*, pp. 181–182. A particular action episode may begin, of course, with one or more of these factors already established, including the prior choice of a problem.

1. What is the degree of indigenous awareness of the target problem?
2. What is the level of intensity of indigenous concern about the problem?
3. What is the relative importance of the problem to residents in relation to other problems that they may have?
4. To what extent are remedial actions and appropriate organizational means either visible or accessible to interested indigenous persons or groups?
5. What do the indigenous members of the community perceive as the probability of immediate or long-range solution?

The process of choosing problems to work on throws into sharp relief the division of labor between the organizer and those with whom he works. Whether he follows an enabling role or a strong leadership role, *the practitioner must make decisions to guide his own activities.* This notion is expressed in an organizing manual:[12]

"You must have a *plan*. Some organizers start by going around and talking with people they plan to organize. They try to discover a common problem the people feel, and then call a meeting to figure out what to do about the problem. Most *successful* organizers, however, analyze their community, factory, school or profession carefully before they start. They know the basic political problem of the group. And they develop a *plan* to solve that problem. Then they take the plan to the people they plan to work with, change it to meet individual needs, and go to work."

McSurely's statement assumes that the practitioner "knows" what the basic problem is and that he makes his plans accordingly. But there are different ways of conceptualizing "the problem," and quite different goals and actions flow from these conceptualizations. A recent paper suggests two approaches that differ although they are not necessarily inconsistent. One emphasizes improvement in the situation of *the individual* and the other improving the position of a *whole group or category* of people.[13]

Using the terms "individual mobility goals" and "group mobility goals," Blum and his colleagues point out that goals related to group mobility challenge the general ideology of individualism in America and are therefore much harder to achieve. These goals, he points out, will be accomplished primarily through changes in social policy at the state and

[12] Alan McSurely, *Getting and Keeping People Together,* Louisville, Kentucky: Southern Conference Education Fund, 1967, p. 3.

[13] Arthur Blum, Magdalena Miranda, and Maurice Meyer, "Goals and Means for Social Change," Turner, *op. cit.,* pp. 106–120.

Federal levels, while individual mobility goals can be achieved to a greater extent at the local level.

The experience of the late 1960's has provided ample evidence that attempts to improve the status of deprived racial or class groups are perceived as serious threats by blue-collar workers and middle-class suburbanites. The objective of helping "motivated" individuals to make it up and out of the ghetto is more likely to permit the building of alliances with middle-class groups, especially when there is agreement on the use of non-controversial strategies and tactics.

A crucial choice among goals and activities for a voluntary association, roughly parallel to Blum's group and individual mobility goals, is inherent in the dilemma of *services* or *political action*.[14] A commitment to services would provide opportunities for disadvantaged people individually to participate more fully in the benefits of the society. A political orientation would shift power to disadvantaged groups so that they can exercise more control over resources and create their own opportunities.[15]

Political activity, however, sometimes requires the provision of services to attract people into an oragnization. Certainly among low-income people there is an enormous demand for assistance on an individual basis, which cannot be disregarded lightly. There is the incident, perhaps apocryphal, of the neighborhood organizer who knocked on a door to tell a resident about an important meeting and was told, "My son is out of work and I'm sick but I can't afford an operation." The neighborhood worker faced a difficult choice. If he were to permit himself to respond to each person's call for help, he would be utterly engulfed in a sea of troubles and diverted from his primary purpose of building the organization. On the other hand, if he ignored completely the personal needs of neighborhood people, his usefulness and credibility would be severely limited and he could expect little response to his organizing efforts.

In operational terms the service approach usually means assisting people to make contact with existing programs. This is the concern of many people and organizations: the friendly neighbor, the clergyman, the policeman, the caseworker, the physician, and others. Many of the local associations that were part of the anti-poverty programs in the early 1960's stressed this kind of "reaching out" to influence people to use legal, employment, health, and other programs.

[14] Perlman and Jones, *Neighborhood Service Centers*, Washington, D.C.: U.S. Department of Health, Education, and Welfare, Office of Juvenile Delinquency and Youth Development, 1967, pp. 70–74.

[15] Arnold Gurin and Joan Levin Ecklein, "Community Organization for What?— Political Power or Service Delivery," *Social Work Practice, 1968*, New York: Columbia University Press, 1968, pp. 10–15.

Linking people to services may go well beyond giving them information or even of arranging an appointment and escorting them there. It often entails convincing an agency by persuasion or pressure to alter its way of delivering its service. This kind of intervention to protect people's rights seemed to be required in Straw Hollow, where job-hunting by the men usually ended in failure, frustration, and lethargy.

"One young man, a recent father, told us that he wouldn't go on ADC: 'I haven't sunk that low yet!' He had been to the Employment Office in Charlestown on many occasions and filed applications. He was told once that he was due to enter a welding training program soon, but the next time he went, he was told that there was no application in the files for him. This happened twice and he was furious and desperate.

"We went to work on his case and, after some fifteen phone calls, managed to locate and expedite his application. The problem had been one of communication. He had no phone and his neighbors had not been home when the crucial call came through. This would have happened again except that we made our phone available as a backup and made sure he got the word. He is now in the training program and we are considered wizards at dealing with those matters. As a result, we have a constant demand upon us as aides in tracking down lost applications, advising on employment matters, making appointments for kids at the Department of Employment Security."[16]

Connecting people to programs has been described as the work of a "broker" who guides people through a new kind of institutional "jungle." This role is "facilitative, usually neutral politically."[17] A more forceful stance is taken by the "advocate" who represents his client or client group in much the same kind of relationship that a lawyer has with his client. The advocate is frankly a partisan, whose purpose is to advance the interests of his clients.

One alternative to brokerage and advocacy on an individual case basis is to organize a new service. This can originate in the desire of a small, informal group to undertake a self-help program. For example, a group of mothers can organize a play group for their children and operate it as volunteers, possibly with the technical assistance of a worker from a settlement house, a neighborhood center, or the municipal recreation department. Self-help activities very often begin with a concern about

---

[16] Ecklein and Lauffer, *op. cit.*, Chapter 5, "Hollow Hope: Community Development in Appalachia."

[17] Arthur Hillman, *op. cit.*, p. 51.

children—arranging parties, vacation outings, or bus trips. They may develop into mutual baby-sitting arrangements, car pools, credit unions, consumer education, beautification and clean-up campaigns, or consumer cooperatives. These may be or may become part of the regular program of some service agency, especially when the program calls for resources (funds, full-time staff, or specialized skills) that are beyond those of the original self-help group. Another possibility under these circumstances is for the worker to help a local group to prepare a program plan and proposal for support by some governmental agency, foundation, or voluntary organization.

Still another alternative to linking people to existing services or organizing new ones is to group their grievances and to take collective action, sometimes through the courts, against the very institutions responsible for providing services, such as the school, welfare department, police, or housing authority. Mobilization for Youth formed a number of groups around common needs primarily as a means of stimulating and organizing social action. "The justification of the use of social brokerage in a program oriented toward social action is the expectation that the informal groups which emerge out of individual needs will develop an interest in community problems."[18] However Mobilization for Youth and others found, as we have seen, that this expectation was fulfilled only to a limited extent.

The difficulties of combining political organizing and services under the same program or structure arise from both internal and external considerations. Internally, the attempt to combine both functions involves bringing together two rather different approaches and styles of operation that may be in conflict. In political action, the focus is on environmental conditions and the common problems arising from them. Proposed solutions call for changes in those conditions. Services, however, are directed toward meeting individual needs. Those oriented to services may feel that social action ignores or overrides or even in some cases accentuates the problems of individuals. Social actionists will see services as dealing on a one-to-one basis with problems that can only be dealt with by more general measures; they will often decry a policy of "picking up the pieces" or of adjusting the individual to an unsatisfactory environment rather than modifying the environment so as better to meet the needs of individuals.

Externally, the difficulties of harmonizing the goals of political action and of service to individuals revolve around relationships to agencies

---

[18] Ecklein and Lauffer, *op. cit.*, Chapter 4, "Social Brokerage and Social Action."

and the community generally. A service program that is identified as political in purpose will attract some people while excluding others who might be equally in need of the services offered. More seriously, controversy generated by political action may antagonize agencies so that important resources cease to be readily available and an organization's ability to help the individual is impaired. In view of these considerations, proponents of services and social action may each feel that their operations are adversely affected by the presence of the other and that separation would enable them to pursue their own objectives more effectively.

There are nonetheless advantages to combining the two functions. Social action and service programs have common long-term objectives in terms of enabling people to cope with their life situations more effectively. Insofar as the two approaches differ in emphasis, style, knowledge, and skills involved, each is a necessary corrective to the other. Without such correctives, social action programs might ignore the needs of the individual in the interests of the wider cause, while service programs might ignore the importance of social conditions and attempt to deal with community problems as though they were individual pathologies.

At the operational level, service agencies are a major source of information to neighborhood organizers concerning the problems of people in the area, the way social conditions impinge on individuals and families, and the possible effects of different measures on the population. Agencies may also act as expert resources in developing the objectives and program proposals of neighborhood organizations.

It is the task of the practitioner to seek an optimum solution to goal-setting that yields the benefits to be derived from different approaches while mitigating the negative results of contradictory elements inherent in such combinations. The example of this issue we have chosen—social action as against a service orientation—illustrates a pervasive element in the goal-selection processes of voluntary associations. While elements of both these goals may frequently be present in many situations, there seem to be real difficulties in trying to give them equal priority within a single organizational effort.

The practitioner is therefore faced with the need to choose, or to help guide the choice, in one direction or the other. That choice is obviously a matter of values. However, it is equally an issue of rational calculation based on an analysis of the societal position of the voluntary association, its access to resources, and its capacity to deliver on one or another of the goals it chooses. A group that is in a position to organize a service program will need to engage in certain types of social action that are relevant to that function, but will probably have difficulty if it extends its purposes to more generalized types of political action. Similarly, social action programs or social movements that have as their central objective a change in political relationships may find it necessary and desirable to undertake service functions, but will need to limit their scope to those elements that help to strengthen the basic organizational purpose.

Developing Strategies and Programs. The strategies and activities of voluntary groups stem from their ideologies and their purposes, particularly from the decisions made as to the mix between a service orientation and a political stance. Since we have ruled out of our purview those activities calculated only to promote friendship and personal satisfactions within a group, the programs in which we are interested inevitably throw a voluntary association into relationships with other organizations. The satisfaction of goals, especially those calculated to achieve some change, depends on these relationships.

Warren has worked out a typology of strategies for achieving "purposive change."[19] His three types are related to the extent of agreement among actors in terms of their values and interests.

Collaborative strategies are based on the assumption of consensus or a common base of values and interests. Agreement on specific proposals can be obtained by overcoming poor communication, misinformation, or inaction.

Campaign strategies apply where the actors do not agree that an issue exists or on how an issue should be resolved, but there is nevertheless a likely prospect of reaching agreement on a proposal. Here the strategy is one of educating, persuading, or pressuring reluctant or recalcitrant actors to realize that their interests will be better served by agreement to the proposal.

Contest strategies, where there is dissension on the issues at hand, call for pursuit of one actor's goal in opposition to other actors. Some contests take place within accepted social norms; some violate these norms.

There has been little empirical study of what strategies are most effective under what circumstances. Burke, speaking of "community power strategies," points out that members of the "power structure" must first be put in the position of willingness to negotiate, and this occurs only after they have been pushed to do so.[20] He goes on to make these observations:

"The conflict strategy works best for organizations committed to a cause

[19] Roland L. Warren, "Types of Purposive Social Change at the Community Level," *op. cit.*

[20] Burke, *op. cit.*, p. 292.

rather than to specific issues or services. In securing the involvement of individuals identified with the basic cause, the organization serves as the unifying vehicle for achievment of individual aims. There is, then, little necessity to include the participants in the goal-defining process. Agreement is assumed. But on specific means to achieve the goal, disagreement may arise. Because the participants are emotionally involved in the ends, detached, pragmatic analysis of alternatives is difficult. Concerns are immediate and give rise to impatience, which, coupled with emotional involvement, can often lead to internal squabbling and dissension. . . . The effectiveness of the strategy appears limited in duration. Maintaining citizen interest appears to be the chief difficulty. The organization has only its goal, its idealized purpose, to sustain interest and create satisfaction. . . . The emotional commitment required is too personally enervating. Often the leader of the organization is forced to depend upon exhortations or the manufacturing of crises to recharge interest. Membership dwindles, or frequently the organization changes, tending to rely less upon conflict tactics and more upon cooperation."

Blum and his associates call attention to the fact that contest is designed to lead to negotiations and that contest *per se* seldom resolves problems.[21] They report that it is at the point of negotiation, after successful contest activities, that self-help organizations have had their greatest difficulty. Organizations that have been able to maintain their initiative through a relatively long period of confrontation, then find it difficult to resist the diversionary tactics or superior resources of the power structure, to successfully withstand the pressures of continuing negotiation, or to prepare acceptable compromise solutions. They may also lose the commitment of their members, who can become disappointed and disillusioned when they find that their contest activities have not by themselves brought about a resolution of the problem, but have only brought them to the stage of negotiation, albeit with a new and stronger position from which to negotiate.

There are no simple and universal guidelines by which to decide on the appropriateness of negotiating, but some clues are suggested in a pragmatic manual on the subject. "The most important reason to sit down with your opponent," the manual states, "is to make sure they are your opponents, that is, that they are the people who can meet your demands, and that they are not the wrong targets."[22] The manual goes on to state

---

[21] Blum *et al., op. cit.,* pp. 112–118.

[22] Alan McSurely, *How to Negotiate,* Louisville, Kentucky: The Organizer's Library Series of the Southern Conference Educational Fund, 3, 1967.

that the group and its organizer must estimate carefully in advance the power of their opponents, their own power, and their preparedness for backing their stated positions with action. They must plan the negotiating "scenario" in advance and must insure that the group's demands and the opponents' response are reduced to clear, simple writing.

Negotiation requires that leaders be delegated the authority to speak for the group, that structures exist that will support their actions, and that they have available to them the knowledge and expertise necessary to negotiate successfully. Blum notes that a major lack has been the inability of local associations to gain access to expert knowledge. Without this they are overwhelmed when asked to suggest a solution. He argues that self-help organizations must have available to them experts in such areas as law, welfare, housing, and manpower training if they are to be able to negotiate on equal terms with powerful and well-informed opponents.

Based on his findings, Blum raised a series of critical questions: Can an organization that successfully utilizes contest be successful in negotiations? Do self-help organizations that rely on consensus attract members with different characteristics than contest-oriented organizations? If so, will organizations organized for contest always use contest and those organized for negotiation always use negotiation? Does the community label an organization as one that uses contest or concurrence and does this impose a restriction on the means it can utilize?

These considerations notwithstanding, lower-class associations have increasingly been using forceful methods—sit-ins, demonstrations, picketing, and activities designed to disrupt the operation of the target system. Some of these tactics involve the use of "symbolic participation" and the management of impressions through the strategic use of small numbers. This has become a particularly cogent tactic when it is used to exploit television coverage.

The targets of contest strategies may respond in several ways. They can make real concessions in order to protect themselves. They can attempt to "buy off" the leaders of a protest group by special privileges. They can make token concessions and try to buy time. But disruptive methods may also generate increased resistance, backlash, and the use of sanctions. A sponsor may feel compelled to withdraw support or staff from a voluntary association. A target organization may invoke legal processes or use political power to thwart or destroy an organization.

Organizations need to be able to shift strategies in order to cope with resistances. The Girard Street Association case illustrates this.[23] The

---

[23] Ecklein and Lauffer, *op. cit.*, Chapter 7, "The Rent Strike on Girard Street."

Association's leaders had decided that while other aspects of their program would improve the block somewhat, "a real improvement in the lives of the residents could not be made without extricating them from the housing stranglehold in which the landlord's greed and racial discrimination held them." A young attorney volunteered his time and with his help this program plan was formulated:

"The Association would conduct a detailed housing survey of the bad apartment buildings on the street, make a catalogue of violations and then he, as an attorney for the Association, would complain about these violations to the Bureau. Thus between the hopeless tenant and the irate landlord a third, unevictable party would be interposed. . . .

"It took six months for a trained lawyer, backed by the detailed surveys listed above, to force a landlord to make partial repairs in one apartment building. Even then, the repairs were not satisfactory . . . . The fact that the tenants bear the burden of proof and that a most persistent effort is necessary to require the landlord to make even minimal repairs is well understood by slum landlords . . . . It was plain that they resented having to deal with an organization which could overcome the handicaps placed in the way of individual tenants—lack of know-how, lack of time and vulnerability to retaliatory eviction."

The Girard Street case illustrates an important point about the relationship between ends and means. Legal action to enforce the housing codes against slumlords proved, in the end, to be extremely slow and ineffective in achieving results. Then, the serving of an eviction notice to a woman and five children living in appalling conditions "gave the Association a chance to test another approach to the issue of housing in the slums." A rent strike was organized to force the landlord to make repairs. Again the legal battle was long and frustrating and it ended in defeat when the Association could not afford the costs of appealing to a higher court. Bitter and discouraged, the Association members turned to still a third strategy:

"What was needed was a direct, simple approach that would produce results within a reasonable time. In searching for it the Director learned of the existence of another block organization which had developed a new approach to the problems of slum housing. This block club was organized by two young men who decided that the only way to improve the houses is to buy them. This they began to do. They repaired the houses themselves and then rented them to tenants who were willing to collaborate with the block club to keep them in decent shape. Thus

Better Homes, Incorporated, was organized in July, 1962, as a nonprofit housing corporation under the Nonprofit Corporation Act of the District of Columbia."[24]

The shifting of program strategies as a result of feedback from experience as well as the use of a battery of simultaneous actions represent matters for analysis and choice by the practitioner and the association.[25] One such strategy is the making of *alliances.* Drawing on guides suggested by Morris and Binstock, a worker can help the association he is serving answer these questions: How and in what way is the prospective partner relevant to the objectives of the association? How strong is its position on the problem at issue? How influential is the organization and what other resources can it bring to bear?

Both opportunities and risks are associated with alliances. One way of compensating for deficits in power and expertise is to form coalitions. Blum concluded that the prospects are poor for lower-class, disadvantaged associations to make alliances with working-class groups, but that opportunities are more promising with middle-class organizations. When alliances with middle-class groups are set up as temporary relationships to deal with specific issues, they can be effctive, provided that there is agreement not only on goals but on means as well.

Of interest in connection with the choice of strategies are the findings of Turner and his associates. They asked how lower-class associations actually made these decisions and found that rational processes of setting objectives and then developing programs to meet them were rare. They concluded that members and staff tend to deal with specific problems on a crisis basis or in response to the desires of articulate members. There was a lack of ideology that looked beyond the crises at hand. In effect, the associations set modest and limited goals that focused "on how to make existing community-service programs work better rather than on designing new alternatives to solving problems."[26]

It would be a mistake to view the development of an organization and the setting of its goals in static terms as if both function and form were fixed. Most informal voluntary associations, certainly at the neighborhood level, tend to disintegrate after a short period of time, usually once the crisis is past. Many that do achieve some stability become formal

[24] *Ibid.*

[25] For a description of the differential use of tactics such as leafleting, a delegation to the mayor, a public rally, legal action, and other means, see "SCEF Responds to a Crisis" in Ecklein and Lauffer, *op. cit.* Chapter 3, where a white group expresses its support for blacks in a crisis situation.

[26] Turner, *op. cit.,* p. 14.

organizations and frequently undergo modifications in their original objectives.

BUILDING THE ORGANIZATION

Probably the most consistent and demanding task in working with voluntary associations is the building and maintenance of an organizational base from which to operate. This corresponds to that phase of the problem-solving framework that we referred to as "developing the structure." It is apparent that this is carried on throughout the life of an association. Recruiting members, handling internal problems, and locating and training leaders call for some understanding of patterns of participation and communication.

In their study of citizen self-help associations, Turner and his associates noted differences between the groups that were more oriented to middle-class patterns and those that had distinctly lower-class membership.[27] The former were the older, larger organizations and were more highly structured internally; they served as secondary groups for their members. The lower-class associations were smaller, with less internal structure and differentiation, and they tended to serve as primary groups in which individual needs—especially those of the leaders—often seemed to overshadow organizational goals. In general, associations that are small, not highly specialized internally, and homogeneous in their membership are more attractive. This is also true when the members have considerable power relative to the officers.[28]

The less-structured organizations that Turner studied tended to engage more directly and more often in power conflicts. It was also found that the lower the socioeconomic status, the more likely decision-making would be done informally, but the more necessary it seemed for the members to have help with managing the organization and determining a course of action.

Most of the groups covered in the Turner study had less than 100 members and were not well known among their potential constituency. It is unrealistic to expect that all eligible or potential members will take part fully and consistently in the work of an organization. This is not an achievable objective in any socioeconomic group, but is doubly difficult to obtain among people who are burdened by the grinding, daily demands of work, money worries, caring for children, and running a household. This unrealistic expectation also ignores differences that exist among

---

[27] Turner, *op. cit.*, pp. 13–25.
[28] Berelson and Steiner, *op. cit.*, p. 380.

individuals in terms of their interests and energies, their commitments to other groups, and their leadership ambitions and capacities.

Organizations that are larger than a few people who meet informally usually consist of a core or leadership group and a larger fringe of people who may be activated on special occasions such as a public meeting or a demonstration. Some individuals who are in the core of one group are on the periphery of other groups. Others have the energy and the desire to play leadership roles in a number of organizations either through formal office-holding or informal but effective participation behind the scenes. One can think of participation as a series of concentric rings, with the leaders at the core and circles of followers becoming less and less identified with the group. Outside the circles are the non-joiners, who may nevertheless be drawn into specific actions from time to time by people with whom they have close personal ties.

There is a strong tendency, despite these realistic limitations, to put great stress on recruitment and participation. Blum found that the neighborhood organizations they studied measured success by the number of members they had. He noted:

". . . much of the organization's energy then went into getting members and keeping them, but nothing happened in the organization because its energy was dispersed in just trying to get members rather than developing directions, goals, and strategies that might attract members. This numbers game was a dominant theme and yet some of the most successful organizations were those that never had a large ongoing membership but were organizations that could turn out large numbers of people when they had to."[29]

It was not generally recognized that active participation in an organization is usually limited and that it fluctuates depending on issues. Even organizations that could activate large numbers for specific actions were viewed as unsuccessful when they could attract few people during periods of planning. Although a major allocation of energy went into recruiting and maintaining membership, many associations were ineffective because "of minimal abilities to mobilize and to achieve disciplined responses from their greatest resource, namely, their constituents."

Attempts are often made to recruit people to a group through the broadside distribution of written material or the use of radio, television, and the press. Experience, especially in low-income urban neighborhoods, has shown that these methods have limited usefulness in an educational

[29] Turner, *op. cit.*, p. 126.

or informational campaign. They have often been found wanting if they are relied on to motivate people to take some desired action. This may be because the message is misunderstood or "not heard" due to discouragement or apprehension about "trying something new."

More effective, although it demands much more time, patience, and shoe leather, is direct person-to-person contact. Word-of-mouth communication, particularly when it is carried out by accepted and trusted local communicators, appears to be more successful in attracting people. This has been found to be the case in organizing activities such as campaigns to register voters or to "get out the vote" on election day. Indeed, neighborhood workers have learned, as did political party workers long ago, that personal contact to inform people or persuade them to do something may require them actually to assist or accompany the person to the place in question—a local employment office, a clinic, or a neighborhood meeting.

As people associate themselves with an organization, the organizer finds himself concerned with group processes such as decision-making, internal conflict, and the emergence of leadership. The organizer must help the members deal with these processes not as a therapist but from the point of view of assisting the group to achieve change in its environment.

It is generally accepted that most organizations of any size will function through a leadership subgroup. Leaders emerge over time out of the crucible of a group's experience, but the organizer can and inevitably does play a part in this. Alinsky, Chavez, and other experienced organizers caution against accepting too quickly and permanently the "first generation" of leaders who appear on the scene apparently ready, willing, and able to lead. Von Hoffman puts it this way:

"But you will notice too that the reasons for your picking the first leaders (and you know it's you who pick them) say nothing about how they will wear over a period time. That respectable clergyman can turn out to be a timid jerk; the lady who was so good at sounding off in front of the judge may be good for nothing else, and that big freedom fighter can look like a vain egomaniac living off the reputation of a deed done many years ago. The lesson I draw from this is that at the beginning keep the organization very loose, spread the responsibilities and the conspicuous places around. This permits you and the new membership which you are supposed to be recruiting, to judge the talent, and it keeps things sufficiently porous so that new talent isn't blocked off."[30]

---

[30] Nicholas von Hoffman, *Finding and Making Leaders*, New York: Students for Democratic Society, p. 4 (mimeographed).

McSurely offers some criteria for identifying good leaders:[31]

1. He is in front of the group—but not too far in front.
2. He is sensitive to the needs and problems of members.
3. He watches silent members to see what their silence is saying.
4. He talks openly about signs of a power struggle, and reassures the group about his own strength.
5. He lays hidden issues and personal interest on the table.
6. He doesn't get sucked into other people's despair.
7. He knows how to listen, to reflect to the group, to run a meeting, to make confrontations, and to comment on group problems.

One of the organizer's tasks is to train leadership in the skills of negotiation. In this incident, a neighborhood worker explains some of the hazards and recalls the devices he used in preparing a delegation for a negotiating session.

"The Housing Administrator had agreed to come to a meeting of our housing council. What usually happens at such a meeting is that everyone gets bogged down in details and nothing gets accomplished. I decided it was necessary to structure the meeting. I met with a group of local council members before the meeting and we listed all the grievances and they decided to bring each grievance and get an answer from him on the spot. In meeting with ten people before the meeting, each one was given an assignment and told to sit at different places in the room. Ten people can do a lot. It wouldn't occur to them alone to stand up and make a statement. Sometimes they forgot what they are supposed to say. Others just sit and nod during the whole meeting and don't say anything. This way with the ten people who are coached sitting around the room, a lot got accomplished at that meeting."[32]

Another task is to help the members of an association develop decision-making machinery and procedures. It is impossible to specify what degree of formality is appropriate for a group without knowing its history, purpose, stage of development, and the previous organizational experience of its members. There is a risk, however, of over-formalizing a group's structure and procedures. For example, some groups become prematurely concerned with the adoption of a constitution and by-laws rather than with the development of common goals and working relationships among their members.

[31] Alan McSurely, *Common Group Problems,* Louisville, Kentucky: The Organizer's Library Series of the Southern Conference Educational Fund, 1967, pp. 1–2.

[32] Comments made by a practitioner in an anti-poverty program and excerpted from an interview conducted in 1966 by a member of the staff of the Community Organization Curriculum Development Project.

Thus far the internal structure and operation of a voluntary association have occupied our attention. We turn now to the relationships between such an organization and the larger community of which it is a part. It is in the nature of these groups that membership in them is selective, since it is based on a voluntary act of participation. When such associations become broader movements and speak for large constituencies, the problem of whom they represent and how they—and the professional staff—are held accountable to their constituents becomes more serious. Quasi-political measures may come into play. Attempts were made under the anti-poverty programs to use a voting procedure to select representatives of urban neighborhoods to serve on the board of Community Action Agencies. These efforts had only limited success because of the generally low level of participation in the voting.

Austin observed that in heterogeneous neighborhoods some self-help associations seek representation from various groups. This requires the association to operate on the basis of consensus.[33] Other associations limit themselves to a small core of like-minded individuals. Austin comments that "one of the significant contributions of professional assistance to an association may be an analysis and assessment" of the local situation and the reality factors within which organizing can be done.

Other forms of representation involve the election of representatives of small associations to larger councils with which they are affiliated for common purposes. Here there are also problems of accountability, communication, and democratic control. Jurisdictional disputes arise, with rival claims among associations as to their legitimacy as spokesmen for particular groups. The management of such issues through techniques of education, negotiation, and contest is an integral part of practice.

When block clubs or neighborhood groups are related to each other through district or citywide structures, this opens up possibilities for having greater impact on a community and its institutions. But this also brings other problems, one of which is the "leadership drain." The active and able people in neighborhood associations tend to become absorbed in these higher-level activities, thus depriving the local groups of a scarce resource. Exposed to wider influences and stimulation, the leaders become separated from their constituencies, who sometimes feel that the leaders have been captured by "the Establishment."

The development of a hierarchy of organization, while it may strengthen the local groups in some ways, also tends to limit their freedom of action by subjecting planning and decisions to groups at higher

[33] David M. Austin, "Influence of Community Setting on Neighborhood Action." in Turner *op. cit.*, pp. 76–96.

levels. This touches on what is undoubtedly the most critical issue in organizing voluntary associations, especially among lower-class people —the autonomy of the organization. Typically, self-help groups are organized by a sponsor, such as a Community Action Agency, a national organization, a church, or a settlement. Or if they begin from an indigenous nucleus, they later seek outside support and staff help.

This was a long-standing issue well before the community action programs of the "war on poverty" brought it to the fore in cities and counties across the country. Years earlier, local groups formed and serviced by settlement houses, community centers, and welfare councils had been hobbled by their ties to their sponsors. In the case of neighborhood associations served by welfare planning agencies, it was reported that "social action issues are a continuing source of potential embarrassment to the central financing bodies to which planning councils are related."[34]

In its original proposal, Mobilization for Youth anticipated the strains and dilemmas in this relationship:

"There is, of course, a contradiction inherent in the proposal to establish lower class community organizations under Mobilization's sponsorship. Mobilization is responsible to a wide variety of groups. Issues with which lower-class organizations deal may threaten some of these groups, in which case pressure may be exerted to control the fledglings. Unless they are formed spontaneously under the impetus of an inflammatory issue, lower class groups cannot be organized without the financing and support of such established (i.e. middle class) organizations as Mobilization."[35]

Later Mobilization looked back on its experience and reported:

"The advantages of social protest for social action may constitute disadvantages for sponsoring agencies. The activities involved in social protest are difficult to supervise. When the participants challenge repressive statutes, it is not always possible to predict or control the outcome of their action. The issues underlying social protest are always controversial. Any agency that becomes involved in social protest is perceived by the public as being on one side or the other since the issues are not formulated in a way that permits the agency to play a mediating role on middle ground.

[34] Robert MacRae, "Community Welfare Councils," *Social Work Yearbook 1957,* New York: National Association of Social Workers, 1957, pp. 189–190.
[35] Mobilization for Youth, *Proposal for the Prevention and Control of Delinquency by Expanding Opportunities,* New York: August 1962, 2nd edition, pp. 136–137.

"Organizational autonomy is thus most problematic in the area of social protest. A sponsoring agency is often held responsible for the activities of indigenous organizations which, if independent, are not accountable to the agency. Experience has taught the Community Development Program to specify the nature and limits of Mobilization for Youth's commitment to social protest in agreements with new organizations. This helps to protect the agency from public involvement in activities it considers unwise. Since, however, social protest has proven to be an effective strategy for increasing the participation of the poor, Mobilization for Youth has confirmed its commitment to such activities. In order to help groups attain their goals, Mobilization for Youth must be prepared to support them in their struggles. The traditional claim to neutrality sounds like an expression of fear to individuals who risk much to protest."[36]

Grosser examines a number of models for sponsorship of neighborhood organizations.[37] The antipoverty model used government funds to provide staff to indigenous groups and provided some freedom of action for them. These pilot, demonstration organizations offered some flexibility, but "their separation from continuing institutions also modifies their ability to produce lasting change." The church sponsors neighborhood organization as a way of expressing "its historic concern for justice and for man" with considerable ability to "sustain the hostility of the welfare system." These models, in Grosser's words, "do not resolve the interest difference between the sponsors and the organization. They merely suggest various structures within which these differences can be contained without disrupting both parties."

THE PRACTITIONER'S ROLES

When people organize their own group, the inexorable process of institutionalization means that the organization's functions become more specialized and its structure more differentiated. Certain tasks come to be seen as too onerous or too skilled to be performed by the original members and are delegated to paid employees who often come from the membership itself. Historically, this development has spawned a new professional group that becomes increasingly concerned with methods and technology as distinct from (and sometimes in opposition to) the value commitments and goals of the original founders.

[36] Mobilization for Youth, "Action on the Lower East Side," Progress Report and Proposal, July 1962–June 1964, pp. 77–78.
[37] Charles F. Grosser, "Staff Role in Neighborhood Organization" in Turner, *op. cit.*, pp. 137–139.

In order to carry out the responsibilities we have described, practitioners play a variety of roles: communicator, interpreter, expediter, broker, advocate, enabler, expert resource, agitator, and supervisor. The worker performs multiple roles, often simultaneously.[38] A paramount issue related to these roles is the practitioner's relationship to the members of the association.

By definition these associations emerge out of a desire to produce change, but the tendency to become institutionalized raises problems because specialized roles, functions, and structures usually reduce the group's flexibility and militancy. Shall the organization buy efficiency at the expense of pursuing its change objectives? If the staff assumes greater responsibility and authority as the organization grows in size and complexity, control by the members is jeopardized. The practitioner must seek a balance here, as Haggstrom points out in a passage that is applicable to many situations, not only to organizing the poor:

"Normally, the organizer makes his expertise available to the members of the organization and helps them acquire the skills and knowledge necessary to maintain the organization. . . . The organizer must sometimes assert vigorous leadership and, in addition, he may have to fill roles which the members have not yet learned to fill. Very early, however, the members themselves should be expected to be responsible for the maintenance and functioning of their organization. . . . On both sides there would be critical evaluation. . . . The organizer would therefore be a partner in a mutual effort with the membership, a partner to be dealt with openly and honestly, neither manipulating the members as objects nor being an object manipulated by them."[39]

Working out this relationship and the division of labor between organizer and members hinges in part on the degree of directiveness on the part of the worker. Much has been made of the argument, advanced especially by protagonists of community development methods, that the worker must work "with" and not "for" people. Traditional community

---

[38] Discussions of this subject can be found in Charles F. Grosser, "Staff Role in Neighborhood Organization" in Turner, *op. cit.*, pp. 133–145; Hillman, *op. cit.*, Chapter II on "Role of Staff," pp. 49–62; George A. Brager and Francis P. Purcell, *op. cit.*, Chapter IV on "The Low-Income Nonprofessional" and Chapter V, "New Roles for the Social Worker."

[39] Warren C. Haggstrom, *op. cit.*, in Irwin Deutscher and Elizabeth J. Tompson, Eds., *op. cit.*, pp. 97–98.

organization principles stressed "indirect" or "enabling" methods and tended to label more directive approaches as "manipulation." The issues were thus posed in moral rather than instrumental terms. Increasingly it is recognized that the model of the practitioner as strictly a non-directive catalyst is unrealistic. The rationale for the worker's presence is that he has something to contribute. Often he will have brought a group into existence and will have been its sustaining force in its early stages. Whether the group is new or old, the worker will be constantly influencing the members' perceptions, understandings, and decisions.

The organizer of a social action group interviewed in the field stressed, with undoubted sincerity, that the group must make its own decisions. Yet it was clear that he and the agency that had employed him had previously decided the category of people to be recruited into the group, the nature of its activity, the problem it was to be concerned with, and the methods it was to adopt. For organizers to pretend they have no objectives can be self-defeating, since the implicit objectives that are generally present are likely sooner or later to come to light. McSurely makes short shrift of what he calls the "intruder hang-up." "Of course organizers are intruders," he says. "Our objective is change, and if we do not intrude on the existing systems . . . then we are not doing our job. So part of the solution to the intruder and short-timer hang-up (besides deciding about our own values and goals) is to: (1) accept our role of intruder, (2) figure out what our job is."[40]

This description of an early phase in the organization of a militant black group shows how Alinsky's staff man made clear his role.

"Chambers defined his role as constantly trying to push people into doing things they wouldn't otherwise do. He moved through the community and kept widening his contacts. He set goals and he set tests, such as telling the leadership that if they could not produce sixty pickets for the demonstration, it should be called off. He suggested program ideas such as negotiating with landlords who were holding back on maintenance and also complaining about their tenants, and suggested arranging to reduce the rent for a 'house mother' who would then keep order in the house. He saw this as a prelude to starting tenants' clubs later on. It seems clear that Chambers screened and selected the issues for action. He resisted efforts to involve the organization in service programs, as for example, when it was suggested at one meeting that FIGHT participate in the literacy program by providing teachers; he felt that this was not a central concern of the organization."[41]

[40] McSurely, "Hang-Ups," Louisville, Kentucky: The Organizer's Library Series of the Southern Conference Educational Fund, 2, 1967, p. 6.
[41] Ecklein and Lauffer, *op. cit.*, Chapter 3.

These observations should not be interpreted as arguing for directive rather than non-directive methods under all conditions of organizing work with voluntary associations. The point is rather to pose the choice between such approaches in relativistic and pragmatic terms rather than as matters of basic principle and value commitment. In most situations, we have argued, the sponsors of the organizational effort do in fact have an objective, and the practitioner should acknowledge it and deal with it in a straightforward manner.

It does not follow from this argument that the practitioner does "for" people, takes over, and "manipulates" the group with whom he is working. A typical objective of work with voluntary associations of all types is to help them strengthen their decision-making processes and operational effectiveness. That objective can be recognized explicitly by both the worker and the voluntary group. It then becomes the basis, mutually understood, for the conscious use of the worker as an educator and enabler who will help the group explicitly to improve its collective functioning. As this happens, the worker's views on goals, strategies, and techniques, which he will continue to have and to express, will be subject to increasingly competent review and criticism on the part of the association's members.

The widespread employment of paraprofessionals in the poverty programs of the 1960's was based on the desire to (1) expand services to the poor, (2) substitute local people for middle-class professionals who had been traditionally reluctant to work with low-income clients, (3) provide jobs for poor people, (4) have the new "nonprofessionals" serve as role models in deprived communities, and (5) perform a "bridging" function by having indigenous people interpret the community to the professional and vice versa.[42]

Experience with the employment of local people in neighborhood work, stretching back long before the anti-poverty programs, would seem to support some of these aims and expectations. Previously unused abilities have been disclosed and put to worthwhile use; new opportunities have been opened for some; and the presence of indigenous workers has had an impact on the policies and practices of organizations in which they have worked. But some troublesome issues remain. The very qualities for which indigenous workers are valued—spontaneity, personal style, directness, informality, and partisanship—may be dysfunctional in circumstances in which more formal methods are required. Nor are low-income people a homogeneous group. Background, language, ethnic origin,

---

[42] Frank Reissman, "The Revolution in Social Work," Mobilization for Youth, Inc., November 1963, unpublished.

and style, while they may make contact easier with some groups, will by the same token make it more difficult with others. Mobilization for Youth came to the conclusion that "one major failure has been the inability of the nonprofessional to facilitate communication between the low-income resident and conventional persons and institutions.[43]

A further complication arises when local leaders become paid workers of an agency serving their area. Some find it difficult to shift from a "leadership" role to a "helping" role. The possibility of performing in too directive a manner under these conditions is apparent in the remark of an indigenous worker that "a chairman and secretary were elected to assist me in planning for the group."

Some advocates of the use of indigenous workers have emphasized the dangers of "professionalism" and have felt that paraprofessionals should not be encouraged to remold themselves in the professional image. On a retest questionnaire distributed to Mobilization for Youth workers after two years, the indigenous workers were no better than the professionals in predicting the responses of local residents. On the original test they had been much more accurate. Despite this, it seems reasonable to prepare workers to deal more effectively with the demands of their jobs. There is a natural drive on the part of indigenous workers toward training, motivated not only by personal career aspirations but also by the assumption that this will increase their effectiveness. A selection process takes place in which agencies seek the most promising indigenous workers or association members for training and professionalization.

There are several levels of responsibility in work with voluntary associations. More experienced workers and, for the most part, those who have had professional training, may be engaged not in grass-roots work but in the development of overall strategies and in the supervision of "ground level" workers. The following comments of a supervisor discussing the summer training of college students as grass-roots organizers point to some of the factors that enter into such supervision:

"It is imperative that the supervisor be somebody who knows a lot about community organization, because the college students are acting on intuition and they need someone to channel their energies. They need immediate support, because they experience everything as a crisis. They especially need support over problems of non-attendance at meetings. This kind of supervision is crucial for the first couple of months. I knew people in the community and this helped a great deal. The main task of

[43] George Brager, "The Low-Income Nonprofessional: An Overview of His Role in Program," presented at the *National Conference on Social Welfare*, Los Angeles, May 1964, mimeographed.

supervision was that of getting the students over the frustrating part of organizing the neighborhood councils. The frustrating part is that many people promise to attend meetings and then only two people show up. The other aspect of supervision was the teaching of techniques and strategies to be carried out before meetings, such as working with the chairman and anticipating difficulties in a meeting before they happened."[44]

We noted previously dilemmas and ambiguities that affect even the most experienced workers when they are caught in the middle between the people whom they are serving and the sponsoring organization. They can also be caught between their professional and ideological commitments and their loyalty to their constituencies. This was clearly at issue in the action described in "Black Students Take Over."[45]

"Being black in white America can be difficult enough. But being a black employee in a white institution because one is black, is particularly difficult. The job becomes almost impossible when one has to represent the institution's administration to its black constituency while helping the blacks organize themselves effectively to deal with the same administration. That's the position many black university employees find themselves in as representatives of dean of students' office, and coordinators of Black Studies programs, etc. When the inevitable conflicts arise, it is easier if one can identify entirely with one side against the other. That is rarely possible; too many questions always come up.

"As an employee of an institution, to what extent can one ethically organize from within or gather support from without in order to change the organization's basic policies? At what point are one's actions ethical and at what point is one's occupational behavior unethical? Who defines ethics? One's constituency or one's employer?

"By the time I came on the scene, many of the blacks saw themselves in an adversary position. What they were asking for or suggesting at first, they were not ready to demand. I tried to convey these feelings to the Deans and administrators. Although many were well aware of them, they tended to dismiss what I thought were legitimate grievances as the unrealistic demands of 'a group of extremists,' 'black nationalists,' 'radicals,' or 'unbalanced kids.' I was frankly disturbed by these labels. If you define someone in narrow terms, you are limited in your behavioral responses. When I worked with street gangs years earlier, for example, I found that behavior towards an outsider was standardized in accor-

[44] Comments made by a practitioner in an anti-poverty program and excerpted from an interview conducted in 1966 by a member of the staff of the Community Organization Curriculum Development Project.
[45] Ecklein and Lauffer, op. cit., Black Students Take Over, Chapter 4, p. 1.

dance with whether he was defined as a 'punk,' a 'stoolie,' a 'square,' etc. If a guy was a 'punk,' you could 'stomp' on him. In fact you were not only justified but almost duty-bound to do so. The labeling process was no less pronounced on the student side."

Another story of role-strain is told by the administrator of a community action agency:

"I hadn't been at the agency for more than a week before a group of para-professionals, representing all 8 neighborhood centers, came to my office with a list of grievances and a set of demands. Their concerns really pointed up the problems in our program . . . they were complaining about how their work kept them out of touch with what was 'really happening' in the community.

"I specifically instructed the para-professional community workers to make contact with as many community groups as possible. If we were going to create some real changes in the community, it wasn't going to be through the neighborhood councils and center boards alone. I wasn't sure of what the end results might be, but I knew that increasingly the militants and even former block club and council members were looking at the neighborhood councils as irrelevant. The Panthers, Muslims, welfare rights groups, other Black nationalist organizations, church groups, gangs and fraternal organizations each had their own programs. I felt it was as much our job to encourage them and to give them staff help as it was our job to develop our own constituencies. . . .

"The mayor, you can imagine, is not too happy. The city administrator is hardly pleased, what with the 'flak' he has been getting from the mayor, the cops, the public works supervisor, etc.

"Interesting thing about neighborhood groups. You organize them as your constituency hoping that they will give you the backing and support you need to conduct your program or push for reforms. But if you are successful, if you give them their head and help them become really independent, they take on a life of their own. And they begin to put the pressure on you just like on everyone else . . . even more so, because you are the most visible and easily accessible."[46]

In these situations the staff people are indeed caught in the middle, with resulting conflicts in identification. It is likely that for some time to come practitioners will have to learn to live with this anomalous position, playing a mediating role between their employers and the people they

---

[46] Ecklein and Lauffer, *op. cit.*, Chapter 4, "Unleash Your People, and You Stand to Lose Your Job," p. 2.

serve. This is not, of course, unique in the annals of professional services. But the strains become more visible in conflicts between the organized disadvantaged and the established institutions because the issues are sharper and more explosive.[47]

Although this chapter and the previous one have concentrated on the organization of voluntary associations primarily among the urban poor, these activities reflect the basic functions of voluntary groups of all kinds in contemporary democracies, as defined in the quotation from Ohlin at the beginning of Chapter 5. All these organizations exert influence on institutions to come to grips with the social problems they have identified. The targets of many of their efforts are service agencies and these form the subject of the next chapter.

[47] Turner, *op. cit.*, pp. 39–51.

CHAPTER 7

Service Agencies

Our focus shifts now from voluntary associations engaged in self-help and social action to the other major line of development in dealing with social needs and problems.[1] We refer to agencies that deliver a variety of social services. The proliferation of these service organizations is one of the hallmarks of industrialized, urban societies.

Common to all service agencies in the fields of health, education, social welfare, and manpower is the concept that certain benefits ought to be provided to people to meet needs that have come to be recognized as collective responsibilities. These organizations are in every sense agents or agencies of society, whether they are public and tax-supported or are financed through voluntary and philanthropic contributions. Both kinds of agencies represent group decisions that certain human needs cannot be left to the market to satisfy.

Judgments concerning what constitutes a problem or need that requires social action and responsibility are in part culturally determined. They differ, for example, between the conditions of economic scarcity in developing countries and the conditions of greater affluence in industrialized areas. In the former, food, housing, and other basic provisions constitute needs for masses of the population. In the latter, social problems arise from the maldistribution of more plentiful goods and services.

The purposes and functions of specific service agencies can be examined by asking what needs or problems they are established to meet. Another way of putting this question is to inquire what kinds of people

[1] This chapter incorporates material drafted for this textbook by Violet M. Sieder, Professor of Community Organization at the Florence Heller Graduate School for Advanced Studies in Social Welfare, Brandeis University, Waltham, Massachusetts.

are eligible for their services—all people, all those of certain ages, or only those who cannot afford to pay for services on the open market? This is a fundamental question in the planning and development of services and, as we have seen from the beginning of this book, decisions are based ultimately on commitments to certain values or value systems, such as the responsibility of the family to care for its own members or the right of the very young or the very old to society's protection and support.

Moreover, the responsibilities or functions of service agencies are not static. Indeed, change in service systems is a characteristic to which much of the practice of community organization and social planning is addressed. In this chapter and the one that follows we shall use the field of social welfare to illustrate the types and characteristics of service agencies in general and to indicate the issues and tasks they pose for practitioners.

Historically, the definition of what constitutes the field of social welfare has evolved from a relatively limited and narrow concept, sometimes called "residual," to a broader or "institutional" notion of the function of social welfare in society. The residual approach looks on social welfare as concerned with specific disabilities and difficulties, such as old age, blindness, poverty, or desertion. The provision of services to meet these contingencies faced by marginal groups, Wilensky and Lebeaux point out, is based on the view that "social welfare institutions should come into play when the normal structures of supply, the family and the market break down."[2]

The institutional concept, on the other hand, is concerned with services that will enhance the social functioning of the population as a whole and that are considered normal, "first line" functions of modern industrial society. This rests on the growing recognition that in a complex society certain basic services must be available to all elements of the population as a matter of right. These "social utilities," as Kahn describes them, are designed for use by all people as needed, as are public schools or parks.[3] Social insurance to deal with retirement or unemployment meets a need that can be experienced by almost anyone. Counseling services are coming to be looked on not as therapy for pathological conditions but as facilitative services to help individuals and families make better use of their own resources and those of their environment.

[2] Harold L. Wilensky and Charles N. Lebeaux, *Industrial Society and Social Welfare*, New York: The Free Press, 1965, p. 138.

[3] Alfred J. Kahn, "The Societal Context of Social Work Practice," *Social Work*, 10, No. 4, October 1965, pp. 145–155. Reprinted in Paul E. Weinberger, Ed., *Perspectives on Social Welfare*, New York: The Macmillan Company, 1969, pp. 33–46.

But even if one accepts the residual view and rejects the notion of "the welfare state," it must be acknowledged that many problems of marginality cannot be solved without more general measures that affect the whole society. This has become increasingly clear recently with respect to the persistent problem of poverty. Efforts to deal with the poor as a marginal group have been inadequate, and attention is now being given to policies that involve redistribution of income and of access to employment, education, and housing.

Whatever one's concept of social welfare, there can be little disagreement with the statement that "development and change—not stability and equilibrium—are dominant features of the social services."[4] The dynamic, evolving nature of social welfare institutions and provisions affects not only what happens within the field, but its boundaries as well. For instance, organizations that are "outside" the system at one time may move "inside" the system later on, as when a group organizes a self-help project that demonstrates a need that has been neglected by established agencies. Such has been the history, for example, of programs established by groups of parents of handicapped children who have been absorbed over a period of time into the existing network of socially supported resources.[5] But changes such as these do not happen automatically. They are the product of deliberate actions of individuals and groups who make value judgments and develop proposals on the basis of such judgments. The field of social welfare is a system of services and benefits that reflect value judgments arrived at through various channels of decision-making in society. Some services are concerned with meeting the needs of marginal or specially disadvantaged people; others are addressed to general needs in the society for which the market does not provide. Titmuss puts the matter succinctly when he observes that the services rendered by the social welfare system "are manifestations, first, of society's will to survive as an organic whole and, secondly, of the expressed wish of all the people to assist the survival of some people."[6]

Throughout the broad field of the human services there are organized structures that have established functions. The tasks of organizing, planning, and problem-solving revolve around the relationship between

[4] David V. Donnison and Valerie Chapman, *Social Policy and Administration*, London: George Allen and Unwin Ltd. (National Institute for Social Work Training Series), 1965, p. 29.

[5] For an analysis of the nature of such groups and their evolution from informal beginnings toward professionalized formal organizations, see Alfred H. Katz, "Self-Help Organizations and Volunteer Participation in Social Welfare," *Social Work*, **15**, No. 1, January 1970, pp. 51–60.

[6] Richard M. Titmuss, *Essays on the Welfare State*, Chapter 2, "The Social Division of Welfare," Boston: Beacon Press, 1969, p. 39.

these structures and the people they are designed to serve as well as the relationships among the agencies themselves. In the previous two chapters we have given attention to the first set of relationships, as seen from the vantage point of a voluntary group trying to deal with an agency. In this chapter and the next we shall examine this from the point of view of the agency. But we shall also be interested in interagency relationships.

SPECIALIZATION

One of the reasons there is a need for deliberate measures of intervention in service systems is that agencies are all *specialized* in some manner, in the sense that they are necessarily limited to specific functions toward which they mobilize and commit their resources. Human needs, on the other hand, do not fall into such orderly compartments. Specialization, which takes place within as well as among agencies, offers advantages of efficiency in the use of scarce resources, speed, and enhancement of skill on the part of service providers. But the rigidities that accompany specialization also create problem situations when agencies are pressed to respond to the changing demands of their environment. How to utilize the benefits of specialization and to avoid its negative consequences is one of the basic issues in the organization of social services.

We begin our exploration of these issues with some suggested ways of classifying the several dimensions along which agencies may be specialized, again using the social welfare field as an example. Wilensky and Lebeaux suggest the following scheme:[7]

Basis of Specialization	Exemplified by Such Specializations as:
Purpose (or program)	Public assistance, corrections, recreation, vocational rehabilitation
Skill (or process)	Social casework, group work, vocational counseling, psychiatry, community organization
Clientele	Children, adults, aged, veterans, non-veterans, religious background, financial ability
Auspices (or sponsorship)	Government (Federal, state, local, state-local), voluntary (sectarian, non-sectarian, jointly-financed)
Geography (or location)	Geographic jurisdictions and boundaries of service

Frequently a condition or problem is the basis for organizing a service, and the number of these is legion—physical ailments or handicaps of

[7] Wilensky and Lebeaux, *op. cit.*, p. 248.

various kinds, crime and delinquency, or the status of being an alien, a veteran, or a victim of a natural disaster. Some notion of the scope of social welfare, taking a broad definition, is provided by this listing of major fields:

Field	Illustrations
Employment-related services	Public employment office.
	Sheltered workshop.
Housing-related services	Relocation program.
	Tenant relations in public housing.
Health	Hospital.
	Visiting nurses.
	Health department.
	Mental health clinic.
Income maintenance	Public assistance.
	Aid to the blind.
	Social insurances.
Family and child welfare	Family-service agencies.
	School social work bureau.
	Medical social work.
Corrections	Probation and parole.
	Juvenile court.
Recreation and informal education	YM's and YW's.
	Public recreation.
	4H Clubs.

In each of these categories interorganizational relationships are both necessitated and complicated by the variety of auspices. In most fields both governmental and voluntary agencies play a part, and the relationships between them involve organizational and planning functions such as promotion, recruitment, standard-setting, study of needs, policy development, and legislative action. Increasingly government agencies account for the major resources and programs, and many voluntary agencies receive public funds for all or part of the services they perform.

Notwithstanding the growth of government programs, very large numbers of voluntary agencies continue to provide services under the sponsorship of different groups. These agencies reflect the heterogeneity and pluralism of American life. They are not merely instruments for performing particular tasks or functions; they represent groups of people with common interests and needs for group affiliation and identification. Typical of these were the organizations formed by immigrant groups to provide mutual support and to increase their collective strength in facing their common problems. Among them are religious, sectarian agencies as well as non-sectarian organizations. Religious organizations frequently fulfill a range of functions, not all of which are necessarily of an intrinsically sectarian character. Some services, like hospitals or neighborhood centers, are open to all members of the community although sponsored by a religious group. Against this background of specialized functions and auspices, we ought now to look more closely at service agencies as organizations.

In accordance with their classification of organizations according to the principle of "who benefits," Blau and Scott point out that the prime beneficiaries of a service agency are its clients.[8] But service to the client group takes place within a system that includes other elements as well. For this reason, Donnison has suggested a useful three-part model consisting of (1) the providers of services, that is, the staff, (2) the determiners of demand—clients, those who refer clients, and those who advocate the "urgency of their needs," and (3) those who control the resources needed to deliver the services.[9] This scheme provides a framework for examining interactions such as congruence or conflict among the interests of the different constituencies affecting the development of services.

The providers of service occupy a particularly important role in creating and modifying the programs of service agencies. The administrators and direct-service staffs, with the support of technicians and clerical and maintenance workers, function *in part* as a formal bureaucracy in the classic Weberian model. Agencies are characterized typically by a differentiation of roles and responsibilities, channels of supervision, some degree of formalization in decision-making processes, rules and regulations, and stated qualifications for different positions. Organizational studies have shown, however, that informal communication and activity often circumvent and even subvert formal structures. Service agencies are no exception. Informal relationships among the staff are frequently more determining of the actual quantity and quality of services provided than written manuals and policies.

[8] Peter M. Blau and W. Richard Scott, *op. cit.*, p. 51.

[9] David V. Donnison and Valerie Chapman, *op. cit.*, pp. 232–236. A similar analysis is made by Warren, who distinguishes between "input" and "output" constituencies, the former referring to supporters of and sponsors of an organization, who have an influence in determining its program, and the latter to the "targets" of the organization's activity. See Roland L. Warren, "The Interaction of Community Decision Organizations: Some Basic Concepts and Needed Research," *Social Service Review*, **41**, No. 3, September 1967; reprinted as "Planning Among the Giants: The Interaction of Community Decision Organizations," in Roland L. Warren, *Truth, Love, and Social Change*, Chicago: Rand McNally and Co., 1971.

The fact that service organizations usually have representatives of professions on their staffs accentuates the tendency of such agencies to deviate from the strictly bureaucratic model. It is one of the characteristics of professionals to claim autonomy in making judgments on matters within their domain and to resist any constraints imposed by "laymen." Professional demands are potentially in conflict with organizational requirements, as Zald notes:

"Where large-scale organizations are typically hierarchical and locality-based, professions are collegial associations that are cross-community in their linkages. In many ways, there is a built-in potential for conflict between professionals and large-scale organizations because professions develop ideal standards of operation while agencies must grapple with their environments and develop operating standards that often depart from those that the professions consider as ideal."[10]

In recent years, challenges to professional hegemony over service agencies in various fields have come from two directions—from sponsoring ("input") constituencies and from representatives or advocates of client ("output") constituencies. New types of sponsors, mostly in the form of governmental funding agencies, have acted as external stimuli toward change in the established modes of practice of agencies. Similarly, representatives and advocates of client groups have demanded and to some extent obtained the opportunity to participate in the determination of agency policies and practices, thus introducing an additional set of considerations, over and above those determined by professional criteria, into the decision-making process.[11]

Professional domination has also been modified by the introduction into service agencies of large numbers of paraprofessionals, as part of the process of modifying and redefining the nature of service functions.

---

[10] Mayer N. Zald, Ed., *op. cit.*, p. 507.

[11] We leave aside from this discussion, at least for the moment, the question of whether these pressures do in fact bring about change. The ability of organizations to resist change is well documented. Our focus in this discussion is on the role of the planner within the agency in responding to the forces within the environment. In accordance with the general value position in favor of social change, which represents our view of all phases of community organization and social planning, these pressures are to be seen as opportunities rather than obstacles. It is nevertheless important to understand the forces that must be dealt with in moving toward change. This chapter attempts to delineate the factors that impinge on change efforts within the context of a service agency and how these are and can be dealt with by people in such settings who are responsible for their community work functions.

The issues that arise in relation to paraprofessionals are presented in dramatic form in the casebook.[12] The administrators see them as a source of manpower, perhaps more suited to some tasks than trained professionals, and as a way of making the agency more acceptable and more fully used by people in the community. Some professionals view paraprofessionals as a threat to their hard-won status. Local people either accept the paraprofessional job as a source of employment for poor people or reject it outright because it may mean "second-rate" service. In any case, the employment of paraprofessionals is growing in the human services, and they are both the source of pressures for change and a reflection of changes that have already taken place in the relationship between service agencies and the communities they serve.

"Of one thing at least we can be certain, when all else is uncertain," Titmuss writes, "the situation in which different kinds of need arise and are recognized as 'needs' has changed and will continue to do so."[13] This is the climate in which the service agency plays its part. It is subject to alterations in the needs and demands of consumers, the skills of its manpower, and the decisions of those who provide financial support and legitimation. The writers cited in Chapter 3 agree that organizations tend toward equilibrium until some external or internal "cramp," as Norton Long calls it, upsets their static condition. In reality, service agencies are vulnerable to an unending stream of external pressures and internal cramps and therefore are seldom in a state of equilibrium.

This sensitivity to changes in the environment is related to the very nature of organizations. Parsons throws light on this when he refers to four problems that all social systems must solve: (1) adaptation of the system to its environment and active transformation of the external situation by the system; (2) defining goals and mobilizing resources to achieve them; (3) integration, that is, organizing relations among the consistent parts of the system so as to coordinate them into a single entity; and (4) maintaining the system's motivational and cultural patterns.[14]

[12] Ecklein and Lauffer, *op. cit.*, Chapter 10, "The Indigenous Sub-Professional: To Employ or Not to Employ."

[13] Richard M. Titmuss, *op. cit.*, p. 40. See also "Social Administration in a Changing Society," Chapter 1 in the same volume.

[14] This summary is from Blau and Scott, *op. cit.*, p. 38 and refers to Talcott Parsons, *Structure and Process in Modern Societies*, Glencoe: The Free Press, 1960, pp. 16–96; and Parsons, *et al.*, *Working Papers in the Theory of Action*, Glencoe: The Free Press, 1953, pp. 183–186.

Thompson, writing on administration, brings us even closer to the processes and issues that are central to our concerns. He speaks of these basic functions:

"The *organization-managing* function is concerned with the sustenance of the organization as a total entity, that is, with acquiring, assigning, and planning for the orderly and coherent utilization of resources, namely finances, personnel, physical facilities and materials, and authority.

". . . 'organization-directing,' in the sense of discovering opportunities for the organization to satisfy needs or demands of the environment, and in the sense of winning environmental support for organizational goals . . . . This function is concerned with what the organization as a total entity is now, is becoming, and should become, and with making sure that the organization continues to fit into the changing scheme of things.

". . . technical and professional actions must interlink with the administrative process, and it is at this point that we find the third major function . . . the *supervisory* function of administration governs the utilization of the resources provided by the organization-managing aspect of administration, and orients their utilization in the way outlined by the organization-directing function of administration."[15]

There are both semantic and conceptual matters to be clarified here. Thompson labels the totality of his three functions "administration." It is clear that the supervisory function is peripheral to our interests in community organization and social planning. But both the "managing" and "directing" functions correspond closely with the kind of practice we are considering.

Sieder has directed her attention specifically to direct-service agencies in social welfare and has described three functions that comprise their "community work": interorganizational relations, mobilization of community supports for the agency, and change of community resources and services on behalf of the agency's clients.[16] We find it useful to think of interorganizational relations as an aspect of the two other functions. Our focus therefore is on two major organizational tasks—*the acquiring of resources vital to the agency's operation* and *the redefinition of goals, functions, and programs* vis-à-vis a changing environment.

---

[15] James D. Thompson, "Common Elements in Administration," in William A. Glaser and David L. Sills, *op. cit.*, pp. 113–114. (Italics ours.)

[16] Violet M. Sieder, "Community Organization in the Direct-Service Agency," *op. cit.*

It is more realistic to think here in terms of functions rather than full-time jobs. The two functions we have just defined may be concentrated or dispersed in an organization depending on its size, its objectives, its sources of support, and other factors. It is likely that much of the community organization and planning work in an agency consisting of only a few workers will be in the hands of the administrator.

In a large bureaucracy the same functions will be carried by workers at several levels. The tremendous increase in the size and complexity of service agencies has made necessary their employment of specialists in community organization and planning. This has forced reconsideration of the community work responsibilities of the administrator and of the staff in various management and professional positions in the agency. Sieder argues that the fulfillment of a direct-service mandate requires the distribution of community work tasks to personnel throughout the agency, but that these tasks must be coordinated by a specialist in community organization.[17]

ACQUIRING RESOURCES

Each agency is highly dependent on its environment for the elements or inputs that are vital to its functioning. What are the factors that are essential to the organization's operation? They can be subsumed in the following categories:

1. A *mandate* or legitimation to perform particular services comes from legislative bodies, public administrators, or voluntary groups, although the latter usually are required also to obtain a public charter or license.
2. It is a truism that service organizations cannot operate without *consumers* or clients to serve. Locating people to use the organization's services is essential lest an agency reveal that it is no longer fulfilling its mandate.
3. Practically no organization can provide services without *material resources* and especially *funds* with which to purchase manpower, physical facilities, and the services of other providers. The giving or withholding of financial support becomes, in practical terms, an important means of endorsing, invalidating, or changing the mandate of a service agency. Maintaining and increasing the flow

[17] Violet M. Sieder, *The Community Organization Responsibility of the Direct-Service Agency*, unpublished dissertation, Heller Graduate School, Brandeis University, 1966.

of funds to an organization is therefore one of the primary tasks involved in planning and organizing.

4. *Personnel*, prepared to perform a range of responsibilities, represents another *sine qua non* for the service agency. Specialized roles include elected, appointed, or volunteer board or committee members; administrators; professional, technical, clerical, and maintenance staff; and volunteers who provide services directly to consumers. Attracting and retaining such personnel are crucial for a service organization.

5. Because supply and demand for most of the factors noted above are in constant flux, *information* on their availability is needed along with the capacity to analyze this information. Without such an intelligence system, agencies cannot be aware of the changes to which they must respond if they are to survive and fulfill their mandates.

The acquisition of these elements is facilitated by what Levine and White call "interorganizational exchange," that is, mutually beneficial trading between agencies. They define an exchange as "any voluntary activity between two organizations which has consequences, actual or anticipated, for the realization of their respective goals or objectives."[18] The elements of exchange include not only clients, staff, funds, and facilities but also influence and support for institutional changes that one party may be seeking. Included under the rubric of exchange are such procedures as interorganizational referrals, agreements on fees and service conditions, reciprocal arrangements for the use of facilities or staff, interagency case conferences, negotiation of policies or joint programs, and cooperation with respect to legislation and public education.

In order to engage in exchange successfully an agency must satisfy some prerequisites. The agency's functions must be specific, understood, and accepted by the agencies with which it interacts. The exchange must be reciprocal, bringing about a mutual sharing of benefits between the parties to the agreement. Reciprocity may not be immediately satisfied, but the parties to the exchange must feel that they are being or will be equally compensated. Finally, an agency staff must be equipped with the necessary authority, knowledge, and skills.

Interorganizational exchange has produced a new role or mechanism, that of "boundary personnel" whose function is to manage these relationships.[19] This calls for the investment of staff time (1) to impart and

---

[18] Levine and White, *op. cit.*

[19] The experience with this role in a multi-service center has been documented in Brian W. H. Wharf, *Boundary Personnel: Exploratory Study of Their Role, Rela-*

gain knowledge about the services of other organizations in regard to the need conditions they satisfy, their quality, availability, and methods of procurement; (2) to identify the particular outside services that can contribute to goal fulfillment of one's own agency and the conditions under which they are available; and (3) to develop the arrangements for referrals, purchase of service contracts, loan of staff or equipment, and the like.

Another view of the processes by which an agency obtains needed resources devotes more attention to power and influence. Thompson and McEwen describe a number of strategies for getting support.[20] In each case they estimate the "cost" to the organization's autonomy.

Competition is defined as rivalry between two or more organizations for resources, with a third party choosing among them. The competing organizations attempt to influence that choice through some "appeal" or offering. The outcome is a vote of support for one of the competing organizations and a denial of support to the others involved. In the case of service agencies, the third party could be legislators deciding on budgets, foundations, individual contributors to philanthropic campaigns, or federations and councils that allocate funds.

Bargaining refers to the negotiation of an agreement for the exchange of goods or services, a concept that corresponds closely to the theory of Levine and White. Bargaining entails compromise. It concedes a greater measure of control over an organization than is the case with competition.

Resources may also be obtained through *co-optation,* "the process of absorbing new elements into the leadership or policy-determining structure of an organization as a means of averting threats to its stability or existence . . . this makes still further inroads on an organization's independence in decision-making."

Finally, coalition or the *combination* of organizations to achieve a common purpose places the most severe limits on an organization's freedom of movement and its ability to obtain support for its own goals and program.

Thompson and McEwen weigh the implications of choosing among these alternatives.

"It is here that the element of rationality appears to become exceedingly

tionship and Interorganizational Behavior, unpublished dissertation, Brandeis University, 1969.

[20] James D. Thompson and William J. McEwen, "Organizational Goals and Environment: Goal-Setting as an Interaction Process," *American Sociological Review,* February 1958, **23**, No. 1, pp. 23–31, reprinted in Zald, *Social Welfare Institutions, op. cit.,* pp. 409–414.

important, for in the order treated above, these relational processes represent increasingly 'costly' methods of gaining support in terms of decision-making power. The organization that adopts a strategy of competition when co-optation is called for may lose all opportunity to realize its goals, or may finally turn to co-optation or coalition at a higher 'cost' than would have been necessary originally. On the other hand, an organization may lose part of its integrity, and therefore some of its potentiality, if it unnecessarily shares power in exchange for support. Hence the establishment *in the appropriate form* of interaction with the many relevant parts of its environment can be a major organizational consideration in a complex society.

"This means, in effect, that the organization must be able to estimate the position of other relevant organizations and their willingness to enter into or alter relationships. Often, too, these matters must be determined or estimated without revealing one's own weaknesses, or even one's ultimate strength. It is necessary or advantageous, in other words, to have the consent or acquiescence of the other party, if a new relationship is to be established or an existing relationship altered. For this purpose organizational administrators often engage in what might be termed a *sounding out process*."[21]

This way of viewing an organization's efforts to secure resources and to solve its problems of adaptation combines the analytic and interactional aspects of problem-solving presented in Chapter 4. The rational calculation of costs and benefits is informed by the "sounding out process," which brings to the agency information on the position and power of other actors.

Against the background of these theoretical approaches to acquiring resources, we can now examine in pragmatic terms how practitioners obtain funds, clients, and the other elements under consideration.

The ways in which practitioners mobilize financial support depend on an agency's traditional patterns and on exploiting opportunities for tapping into new sources. Among these is support by public funds that come as a result of legislative or administrative action. The task here is to maintain close and effective relationships with key legislators and with centrally placed administrators who influence allocation decisions.

Decisions on funding by legislators and administrators are, of course, related to public opinion and the activities of interest or pressure groups. The creation of an informed public is therefore an integral part of

[21] *Ibid.*, p. 416.

practice. It calls, among other things, for the careful selection of which "public" is to be educated in order to build understanding and support for a program. The professional in a service agency may cooperate with or stimulate this kind of educational work by another organization, as was the situation when a social workers' association undertook an ambitious effort on behalf of a public welfare program.[22]

Concerned that influential community leaders were ignorant and misinformed about the workings of the public welfare system and that their lack of understanding would hurt the department's chances of getting adequate funding, the social workers went into action. After touching all the necessary bases for clearance, they arranged for a small group of newspaper editors, clergymen, prominent businessmen, and members of the League of Women Voters to talk with welfare caseworkers and with recipients. This firsthand experience had a powerful impact on those who participated, and while its immediate payoff in terms of appropriations could not be measured, presumably it contributed in the long run to building support for the welfare program.

Another source of public funding, which calls for quite different skills, consists of grants and special project funding for which an agency must submit proposals. The difference between the two methods can be illustrated by the annual but variable appropriations of a state legislature for support of an ongoing program in contrast to the award of a grant by a panel that reviews applications for special projects.

The casebook presents three vignettes on grantsmanship.[23] The first shows a frantic effort to put together a proposal, obtain the necessary legitimation for it, and get some funds fast, a performance that was evaluated as demonstrating neither skill, planfulness, nor integrity. The second case illustrates the careful use of formal and informal lines of communication to shepherd a proposal through state, regional, and Federal offices in a display of political astuteness.

The third case demonstrates the work of a craftsman who tries to write proposals clearly and in operational terms. The planner describes how he begins with a statement of the problem being addressed, the objectives of the proposed program, the conceptual framework undergirding the design, the precise actions and procedures to be carried out, and the evaluation that will be conducted.

Another pattern is that of direct solicitation by an agency among individual contributors. This may be on an annual basis or a one-time

---

[22] Ecklein and Lauffer, *op. cit.*, Chapter 12, "Debriefing for Influentials."
[23] Ecklein and Lauffer, *op. cit.*, Chapter 11, "The Planner as Grantsman."

fund-raising campaign. The task is one of organizing people who will both solicit and themselves contribute to the agency. Some organizations rely heavily on a relatively small number of wealthy contributors whose interest in the service depends on a combination of conviction and family and social ties to the organization itself.

At the opposite extreme are the agencies that direct a broad appeal to many individuals in a community, collecting funds on a house-to-house basis or by mail solicitations.[24] Networks of personal, religious, and other associations are often utilized in organizing a fund-raising campaign, so that support is not always a direct reflection of the degree of public understanding of a particular service or community need, but more a reflection of interpersonal relationships and patterns of influence.

Some agencies obtain part of their support from central fund-raising and allocating organizations, such as United Funds or sectarian federated funds. Gaining support from these organizations calls for the same processes of winning friends in court as is the case with getting appropriations from a legislature. It requires a combination of lobbying, education, and pressure on those who make the allocative decisions. This entails a long-range process, in which each annual presentation of the agency's needs contributes to the building of a base of understanding and support.

In short-range terms, an organization may have to mount a hard-hitting campaign to hold its own or to improve its position in the competitive race for scarce funds. There is a dramatic example of this in the Havilland House case, in which a settlement house literally fights for its life, which hangs on the decisions of a welfare council.[25] The situation concerns a settlement that for many years had been running a limited recreation program while most other settlements had moved into anti-poverty programs, civil rights, and urban renewal. The board of the agency had deteriorated in number and in interest. The welfare council, which supplied the money, had decided to bear down hard on "incompetent" agencies that were out of touch with their communities. The Council conducted a secret study that recommended terminating operations of the settlement in six months.

The settlement staff went into action and interested an ambitious and energetic young businessman in taking over the chairmanship of the board. An agreement was then negotiated between the settlement and

[24] David Sills documents this kind of fund-raising in his study, *The Volunteers: Means and Ends in a National Organization, op. cit.*

[25] Ecklein and Lauffer, *op. cit.,* "Havilland House Fights to Survive," Chapter 9.

the Council to survey neighborhood needs and to see whether the agency's program was relevant to those needs. The consultant hired to do the study confirmed that there were significant things a settlement could do and outlined the steps Havilland House should take to equip itself for this role. The Council, however, turned down a recommendation that the agency's life be extended by another six months. But the new president of Havilland House, who by this time had brought more active people onto the board, went to the press, local politicians, and the mayor and mounted a pressure campaign that won a full year's extension for the settlement.

The Havilland House case illustrates a number of points touched on earlier—the fact that change can be induced by an impact from outside a service agency; that control of financial resources is critical to the existence of such an agency; and that marshalling support is a political process but that appeals to "reason" and to the "facts" play an important role in the process. Not only in a situation such as this but also in the other means of obtaining support, the practitioner needs to be skilled in the writing of promotional literature, speaking to small and large groups, writing reports and proposals, organizing groups of volunteer workers, and using persuasion, lobbying, and pressure.

Among the manpower resources needed by most service organizations are volunteer workers who serve on boards of directors and committees and take part with administrators in the formulation of agency policies.[26] This has always been significant in the operation of voluntary agencies, but increasingly public-service organizations are making use of Citizen Advisory Committees. Traditionally these policy-making groups have been chosen from "community leadership," which has meant principally people from the social and economic elite. As other groups, such as organized labor, made their voices heard in both governmental and private organizations, they have taken their seats at the board tables of service organizations. Recently this has meant the participation of blacks and other minority groups.

More recently there has been a sharp departure from tradition by the placement of consumers and clients of service agencies, such as the recipients of public-welfare assistance, on policy-making boards and committees. This movement to increase the influence of the poor and the disadvantaged is now taking the form of pressure to decentralize au-

[26] Violet M. Seider, "The Historical Origins of the American Volunteer," pp. 4–12, in William A. Glaser and David L. Sills, *op. cit.*

thority and control over certain services, such as education and the police, and to devolve it into district and neighborhood structures.

Whether the volunteer is a banker from an early American family or a recently arrived Puerto Rican manual worker, recruiting and training these people and utilizing their contributions to a service organization constitute an important phase of practice. This requires that agency staff know the communities they serve and the present and emerging leadership and that they recruit people with skills of value to an agency and those who reflect significant parts of the community.

The policy-making process necessitates two-way communication between community representatives and agency staff, but there can be little doubt about the key role of the administrator. The naive assumption that he is simply "executing" the will of the board or that he is a "partner" of the board in policy-making does not reflect reality. "We know," Thompson writes,

"that often the chief executive is the key member of such a group and that when the board or council does effectively discharge organization-directing responsibilities, this fact frequently reflects the chief executive's capacity to energize his board or council."[27]

This tallies with Senor's finding that in many private social work agencies the executive is able to increase his power markedly by controlling the flow of communication to the board of directors as well as by emphasizing the expertise of the staff.[28]

A great amount of volunteer activity consists of a direct contribution to the delivery of services. Students who spend time with patients in mental hospitals, women who volunteer as receptionists and friendly visitors in hospitals, and people who serve as group leaders in recreation and group work agencies, present both a challenge and an opportunity to service organizations. The use of volunteers in services and on policy-making bodies requires that the staff not only orient them initially to the work of the organization, but also carry on a continual educational process to keep them informed of the agency's operations.

Attention has been focused in the recent past on the need for service agencies to engage in community work in order to assure that the services will in fact be used by the people for whom they are intended. That is an issue that had failed to receive attention for a long time, because most agencies, operating with limited resources, tend to fill up the time

[27] James D. Thompson, *op. cit.*, p. 113.
[28] James Senor, "Another Look at the Executive-Board Relationship," in Zald, *op. cit.*, pp. 418–427.

available through their staff without making special efforts to maintain a stream of clients. Minimum publicity, word of mouth, and interprofessional referral channels have generally proved to be adequate. The result, however, was that many services failed to reach disadvantaged people in low-income areas.

As a result of the stimulus of the new programs addressed to such areas, more elaborate methods have been employed to assure a proper connection between the agency and the intended clientele. One way has been to locate the agencies within the area, in order to assure greater visibility and easier access. In addition to ordinary publicity measures, neighborhood-based agencies developed "outreach" staffs of community workers who visited people in their homes and brought information personally concerning the availability of services.

The notion of interorganizational exchange is particularly appropriate to the referral of clients. Referrals from other agencies are contingent on a continued demonstration of ability to perform satisfactorily the functions implied in the agency's proclaimed goals. This calls for a constant assessment on the part of referring agencies. When this assessment is negative, there may be pressures on an agency to change its services, since interorganizational exchange involves both top-level policy decisions as well as day-to-day working relationships between direct-service personnel.

Another of the vital resources required by a service agency is information about its environment, especially because this information is important in obtaining other resources. There is therefore a need for an agency to be linked to significant parts of its environment through a communications or intelligence system to handle what Loomis calls "the process by which information, decisions, and directives are transmitted among actors and the ways in which knowledge, opinions and attitudes are formed or modified by interaction."[29]

The intelligence and communications system operates in both directions, bringing data to the agency as well as disseminating information about the agency's ideology, program, and needs. All elements in the organization play a role in this: the clientele; the board or policy group; the line workers; the administrative and supervisory staff; and, if the agency is large enough, a research and planning department.

The next part of this chapter discusses the intelligence operation as a mechanism that is vital to the agency's adaptation to its changing en-

[29] Charles P. Loomis, *Social Systems: Essays in Their Persistence and Change,* Princeton: D. Nostrand Co., Inc., 1960, p. 30.

vironment. Suffice it to say here that an important community organization and planning task is to ascertain and process information on such matters as trends in services, the presenting problems of clients, the availability of referral resources, and local social conditions.

ADAPTING TO CHANGES

The processes by which a service agency adapts to its changing environment can be viewed in problem-solving terms, because that is how new developments and pressures are experienced by practitioners engaged in community work.[30] The intelligence system, operating as the organization's eyes and ears, detects changes in the circumstances surrounding an agency. This information, when appropriately analyzed, offers clues to emerging problems and indicators of the need for modifying the policies and programs of the agency in question or of other agencies. What are these indicators?

Shifts in the availability of the resources needed by the agency—funds, personnel, and the like—will be significant. Perhaps most important are demographic changes, that is, changes in the characteristics and numbers of users and potential users of the agency's services. For example, the staff may notice that there are requests for which no service is available. Or they may record shifts in the age, sex, ethnicity, or place of residence of people applying for service. This has been the situation in many American cities when a black ghetto has replaced a Jewish population in a relatively short period of time or when middle-income housing goes up in the place of a slum. These situations, which have serious implications for the agencies involved, are sometimes long and slow in coming, sometimes sudden and dramatic in their impact.

Direct-service workers often sound the alert that needs are changing. They are potentially in an excellent position to define problems. But this potential is often not realized because, as Sieder points out, "the usual agency statistical reports of services given relate what was done, not what was impossible to accomplish."[31] In another sense, service providers themselves are a source of change when improvements in technology, such as more effective rehabilitation methods, create new opportunities.

[30] See Chapter 4 for an outline of the problem-solving framework.
[31] Violet M. Sieder, "Community Organization in the Direct-Service Agency," in Ralph M. Kramer and Harry Specht, Eds., *op. cit.*, p. 159.

The stimulus for an agency to adapt to new conditions can come from many points in the network of relationships in which it is embedded. The impetus may originate in the larger system of which the organization is a part. For example, a state department of public welfare must often accommodate to changes in the laws and administrative decisions of the Federal government. Client and consumer groups are now successfully exerting pressure for changes in many fields of service. Or Agency A, which experiences difficulties when it refers clients to Agency B, can initiate discussions of the need for change in the way the latter operates. People whose function it is to review and criticize—the press, academicians, writers, and the like—as well as legislators or citizens serving on committees and commissions frequently point to the need for altering services. Planning organizations that will be discussed in the following chapter can provide a forum in which programs are examined and modifications in services are recommended.

Another situation—and a painful one for the agency concerned—is brought about when the support for a service is diminished or eliminated. It was this kind of crisis, the withdrawal of the welfare council's financial support, that the Havilland House settlement faced in the case cited above. Another settlement house was compelled to reassess its function and program as a result of its sponsor's cancelling support for the maintenance of the agency's building.[32] A reduction in demand for an agency's services can lead to the not-so-rare situation in which the organization's resources exceed the demands being made on them. This is likely to generate pressure for taking on new functions.

In each of these circumstances there is a stimulus for an agency to adapt, but not a guarantee that adaptation will occur. To some extent the outcome will depend on whether there is a free flow of information from one part of an organization to another—from consumers to line workers, from line workers to administrators, and from administrators to policy-makers. If there are blockages in this movement of information, decision-making is impaired and the processes of adjustment may be aborted.

When the information and decision processes function reasonably well, they will produce judgments from time to time that there are disjunctions between an agency's services and the needs that the agency should be meeting. This is so, for example, when it is "discovered" that

---

[32] Ecklein and Lauffer, *op. cit.*, Chapter 10, "A Settlement House Staff Loses Its Building." This case will be discussed later in this chapter.

people receiving Aid to Families with Dependent Children need more cash income than they have been receiving "because" their income is below the level of a modest family budget developed by the Bureau of Labor Statistics.

The problem of a disjunction between programs and needs is intensified by what we pointed to earlier as an outstanding characteristic of service agencies—their high degree of specialization in terms of function and program, geographic coverage, sponsorship, clientele, and skill. To harvest the benefits of specialization, boundaries and limits must be observed. But as they are made clear, these lines of specialization tend to become rigid, with the result that agencies face a changing world with restricted and static programs. As Wilensky and Lebeaux point out, these rigidities lead not only to gaps in service but also to "dividing the client" according to program lines that ignore the interrelatedness of his multiple problems. Specialization can also mean segregating the old, the poor, and the handicapped and further stigmatizing already disadvantaged people.[33]

We noted in Chapter 4 that problem definition is often a decisive step. It is therefore important to understand in what terms emerging conditions are defined as problems by agencies, since the early definitions tend to lead, sometimes imperceptibly, to particular policies. In other words, the direction in which an agency will move to cope with an unmet need will be influenced by the organizing ideas the decision-makers use to think about a problem. The main choices are to interpret a situation in one of the following ways.

1. There has been a quantitative change in demand that therefore requires an expansion (or contraction) of the kind of services currently being offered.
2. A new need has arisen and this calls for a change in the nature of the service itself.
3. The problem is more basic and cannot be met by modifying services; it necessitates an institutional change, a non-service approach.

We consider each of these possibilities in turn. An agency may conclude that it has evidence of an increase in demand for its services. The assessment can be based on a lengthening waiting list or an increase in the general population or in the size of a particular group. If the or-

[33] Wilensky and Lebeaux, *op. cit.,* pp. 250–265.

ganization makes the further judgment that what is needed is "more of the same," that is, an increase in the volume of services it is currently delivering, then several paths of action are open.

Additional resources can be sought to expand the program, perhaps into new geographic areas, or to add personnel in present locations. Obtaining these resources, we saw previously, can require legislative action, a larger allocation from a source of voluntary funds, direct money-raising by the agency itself, borrowing staff, and the like. To move in this way, the organization must calculate its chances of obtaining the necessary resources.

If additional resources are not easily obtainable, the agency will explore alternatives. It can mount an educational or pressure campaign to focus attention on the unmet need and its own need for more funds or staff or buildings. It may try to shift the responsibility to another agency or to a planning organization. A decrease in demand for services might lead to a decision to contract an agency's program, but given the tendency of organizations to maintain themselves, this situation is more likely to energize a search for new functions the agency can take on to absorb its unused resources.

A decision to step up the provision of an existing service may be made by a higher authority. This was the situation that a state department of welfare anticipated.[34] Immediately after the Nixon Administration announced its intentions to reform the public welfare system, the state welfare department, assuming that there would be a doubling of people receiving income assistance, launched its planning. The department estimated the number of people who would qualify for assistance at various income levels in order to project how much money the state would have to contribute in addition to the Federal payments. The department also tried to anticipate the need for child-care centers and to assess the appropriateness of existing building code requirements for such centers. And in order to have an informed citizenry and a receptive state legislature, the staff began planning an educational program on the coming changes in public welfare.

The second problem definition noted above is based on a judgment that a qualitatively different kind of service is required. This entails a choice: should the agency itself develop the new service or should it try to have another organization assume the responsibility? Assuming that

[34] Ecklein and Lauffer, *op. cit.*, Chapter 13, "The New Federalism and Client Analysis."

Agency A adopts the first policy, a number of issues arise. Will this be interpreted by Agency B as an invasion of its territory? Even if Agency B acquiesces, can Agency A obtain from other sources the legitimation to launch a new service? That sanction may have to come from a governmental body or from a voluntary planning federation that adjudicates those domain questions and often exercises its sanction through control of funds. An agency that finds itself blocked from carrying out its desire to mount a new kind of program will be compelled to canvass other strategies.

Sometimes an agency is jolted from the outside in such a way that it is compelled to redefine its purpose and program. This happened when the staff of a settlement house was notified that its sponsor would continue to support services but not the building.

"The settlement house had been operating in this neighborhood for 40 years. The problems had changed and the traditional program which we still conducted seemed a far cry from the community needs. There had been three police-community confrontations within the month and one bombing of a local retail merchant store. The whole area is very tense. The schools are bad. Urban renewal has never considered it a target. For some reason it's become a forgotten area. . . . When the Board met, they told me to do three things: (1) determine the problems in the area; (2) determine those services that were critically needed and suggest how we ought to be involved in meeting those needs; and (3) answer the question about whether or not we needed the building to offer our services."[35]

The settlement director set up a series of meetings in the community. From these emerged the conclusion that people needed (1) recreation and social services; (2) day care and preschool services, and (3) expert help in running organizations and in community organization processes in general. These called for modifications in the program of the settlement house. Once they were accepted as policy, including the finding that the building was not essential, the Board, the staff, and the new people who had become involved through the study process went to work to devise ways and means of reaching the three new program objectives.

It has been assumed thus far that an agency that sees the need for

[35] Ecklein and Lauffer, op. cit., Chapter 10, "A Settlement House Staff Loses Its Building."

quantitative or qualitative changes in services will actively seek to respond. But we must note another possibility: an agency can try to ignore the need for change or it can make ritual gestures of response, such as undertaking studies that are calculated only to buy time. These non-responses may succeed for a while in warding off change, but they may—as was seen frequently in the 1960's—be countered by explosive attempts to sweep away unresponsive agencies or by efforts to take control of them. Attempts by agencies to deny the need for adaptation are consistent with the tendency of organizations to maintain their present equilibrium and to resist change.

There is a counter-tendency for organizations to seek to expand their domain, and this accounts for a widespread phenomenon that is quite the opposite of resisting change. Frequently organizations perceive changes in their environment not as problems to be ignored but as opportunities to be seized. Thus many organizations are alert to changes in legal and administrative regulations, to increased appropriations for particular purposes, and to the changing concerns of foundations. Here again, however, an organization is constrained to weigh the advantages of exploiting these opportunities against the costs that may be incurred in pursuing them.

But organizations can find themselves in a position in which they are unable to respond directly to either problems or opportunities, and their response is to look for someone else to act. For example, a public housing authority can recognize that there is a lack of recreational facilities and activities for its tenants but consider itself ill-equipped to take on the development of a recreational program. It can turn to an organization such as the city's parks-and-recreation department or a settlement house to provide the services. Or it may encourage the tenants' organization to develop a recreation program on a volunteer basis. On the other hand, the housing authority may throw the problem to a planning group or council with the request that someone be found to do what is needed.

The other side of this coin is represented by situations in which a policy decision has been made to assign new functions to an agency, a decision that must be accompanied by the necessary resources if it is to be meaningful. This arises continually in governmental programs and often involves the grant-in-aid and/or the special demonstration mechanism. It can be illustrated by a recent effort of the Social and Rehabilitation Service of HEW "to help selected State agencies hire specialists to promote and establish new services, and to pave the way for incorporating these specialists as permanent staff after completion of the project."[36]

Lack of staff had made it difficult for public welfare agencies to extend and improve their programs. Demonstration funds were therefore offered to help them to hire people with knowledge and skills in legal aid, homemakers' services, group work, the use of volunteers, and other program areas. The Federal grant provided money for salaries, travel, and equipment but not for demonstration of the ideas the specialists developed; these were to be carried out by using local resources. SRS, reviewing the results in one state, reported that it had been so successful that the state was continuing at its own expense to fund the specialist positions and is planning to expand some of the new programs that had been introduced. It is interesting to note the final comment in the report: "All agreed that to be a specialist in a State-administered agency required salesmanship and the ability to work with county departments and the community to show them the value of the service and to provide them with practical ways of making it available."

Another example is provided by the decision of Congress to transfer the responsibility for providing health services to American Indians from the Department of the Interior to the Public Health Service (PHS).[37] This decision was a response to criticism by leaders in the health field who pointed out that Indians were 40 years behind the rest of the population in achieving increased life-expectancy and that a health-oriented agency should be given this responsibility.

In the legislation Congress had requested a comprehensive survey of health conditions on Indian reservations. The PHS survey report recommended new services and asked for double the amount of money the Interior Department had requested. When one asks how the PHS arrived at its recommendations, questions emerge that are typical of a search for the underlying conditions that contribute to a problem. Our interest at this point is in the criteria that are used for analyzing informational inputs and for making decisions or recommendations.

In the analysis of social problems it is rare that a single factor can be considered "the cause" of a phenomenon as complex as the substandard health of Indians. A search for causal factors is more likely to produce a number of possible explanations, and the planner's difficult

---

[36] SRS *Newsletter*, November 27, 1970, Office of Public Affairs, Social and Rehabilitation Service, U. S. Department of Health, Education, and Welfare.

[37] Ecklein and Lauffer, *op. cit.*, Chapter 13, "A Health Study for American Indians."

task is to sort them out, keeping two major criteria in mind. One is to choose the factors that are presumably most powerful in generating and maintaining the problem condition. The other is to select elements that are amenable to change. A theory of causation is not *per se* a prescription for action, since all "causes" are not equally accessible to intervention.

The earlier discussion of voluntary associations pointed out that they must choose between incremental and more far-reaching social-change objectives. The same issue arises for the service agency. The Public Health Service must have considered the relationships between low income, poor diets, substandard housing, and the health conditions of the Indians. But could they take effective action on all these fronts? The question of what to do must be balanced against the criterion of *what can be done.* In this case, the feasibility of a new program will be limited by the authority and resources of the PHS, the willingness of Congress to alter these, the goals and priorities of the Indians, and many other factors.

The choice of a policy for action must take into account the opportunities for change and the resistances that can be anticipated; it needs to be consistent with the causal analysis at the same time that it holds promise of a feasible change. This does not mean that the planner is restricted to proposing programs that can be immediately and easily implemented, if they deal only with peripheral causes of the problem. He might well conclude that adjustments in service programs will have little impact on the problem as he has defined it.

This line of analysis brings us to the third policy choice, namely the judgment that the problem at hand is not amenable to a service approach but requires intervention at a broader and more basic institutional level. Such a decision could call for legislative or legal action, as with campaigns for stricter laws on racial discrimination or efforts to use the courts to enforce the rights of tenants in dealing with landlords. The narcotics program case illustrates this policy.

What had begun as a volunteer effort to help addicts had been turned into a professional service. The director writes:

"About two and a half years after the project started we had done nothing to stem the tide of addiction. We were forced to ask ourselves what we should do. The attempt to assist the addict through an agency was doomed to failure. We had two alternatives, one was to continue as we were doing—assuring salaries to our staff. The other alternative was to close out the agency.

"At this point we called in two top people from the New York Medical Center to advise us. . . . They identified for us how the community was creating addiction. If a great deal of the social fabric is not changed, including the legal structure, you won't get any place with addiction. Even though I'm a community organizer, I had become so involved in directing an agency that I failed to realize that addiction was not a problem of the addict. It was a problem *for* the addict, and *of* society.

"O.K., the experts helped us to see that. But we did not know what to do about it. One possibility was to document the structural and social causes of addiction. If we could do that, at least this community might be able to recognize how it was creating the problem."[38]

The agency mounted research and produced extensive documentation of the thesis that addiction is an adaptation to the environment. From there they moved to the establishment of an education task force that won the attention of the Mayor and his support for a community-wide attack on the problem.

The capacity of most service agencies to engage in this kind of social action is limited by the same factor discussed in the chapter on voluntary associations—constraints on the autonomy of the organization. Service agencies face a similar dilemma. In their struggle to survive and to maintain a viable base from which to deliver their services, they need co-operative relationships with many other organizations, and this inhibits them from putting pressure on them. On the other hand, the responsibility for meeting changing needs as well as the tendency to expand their own boundaries push them into competition with others in the scramble for scarce resources.

Clearly, an agency that is a branch or subdivision of a larger organization on which it is heavily dependent will have to turn to its parent organization for approval of any aggressive strategy. This is more and more true of contemporary organizations, where decision-making is constrained by the vertical form of organization. As part of the "great change" in American communities, Warren sees this growing importance of vertical organization as severely restricting the scope of planning by lower units in the system.[39]

Some organizations, while nominally independent, have significant relationships that affect the ways in which they can respond to problems. Voluntary agencies that are affiliated with welfare councils and receive much of their support from federated fund-raising campaigns will be

[38] Ecklein and Lauffer, *op. cit.*, Chapter 10, "Building It, Killing It, and Making It."

[39] Roland Warren, *The Community in American, op. cit.*, pp. 257–259.

expected to refer most of their planning problems to the council. In-creasingly, public agencies are subject to controls by Human Resources Administrations or the Governor's or Mayor's equivalent of the Office of Management and Budget and the agency that seeks to expand its operations or alternatively have some other organization expand its program may be required to work through such a structure.[40]

It may be both possible and necessary to create an ad hoc planning body in connection with a problem an agency wants to present to other organizations. The problem may be beyond the scope of existing plan-ning bodies or the latter may be unable or unwilling to take it on. An agency may have to convene a task force or committee for joint planning. This calls attention to another phase of the problem-solving process, the *development and use of structure.*

What Thompson and McEwen refer to as "The establishment in the appropriate form of interaction with the many relevant parts of its en-vironment," is a continuing responsibility of those charged with com-munity work in a service agency.[41] Note that there are two issues here. One is to find the "appropriate " form and the other is determining who is "relevant" to the problem at hand. This latter question needs to be further refined because the same actors are not equally relevant at every stage of a problem-solving or planning process. Thus, some will be more useful in defining the problem, others at the point of testing out possibilities for obtaining new resources.

DESIGNING AND EVALUATING PROGRAMS

The choice of a structure for decision-making, together with the selection of a problem definition and of policies for dealing with it, all move toward *implementation,* which involves translating the previous decisions into specific actions. Whether the earlier assessments culminate in a decision to expand a currently operating service or to create a new one, implementation entails the tasks of designing a program and marshalling the resources to carry it out. We can consider these tasks by going back to the point at which the planner was weighing causal factors and feasible interventions. The decisions made then provide the basis for answering these questions:

What are the objectives of the program, that is, what specific changes are sought?

What is the target population in terms of numbers and characteristics?

[40] The next chapter takes up practice and methodology in planning organizations.
[41] Thompson and McEwen, *op. cit.,* p. 416.

What resources will be required to mount the program?

Where will the resources come from?

How will the resources be used, that is, what operating procedures will be required? What coordination will be necessary among elements of the program and in relation to other systems?

What provisions will be made for monitoring the operation and for utilization of feedback?

The answers must be sought, again at this level, by a combination of value judgments and an analysis of the opportunities and constraints in the situation. It may be useful, by way of recapitulating much that has been touched on in this chapter, to offer an example of a planning process from the beginning.

Let us imagine that as a result of mounting concern about high school drop-outs and pressure by minority groups, a superintendent of schools has agreed to develop a new program to cope with the problem. The plan is to be worked out with the participation of a citizens' committee. In the opening discussions these points are made: the current curriculum is geared to college-bound students; no provision is made for the growing number of students who enter the school speaking only Spanish; and the number of dropouts is estimated at 1500 a year, but the school has no information on what happens after a youngster drops out. The legal age at which students can leave the school is 16, and most of the dropping out occurs within 12 months after the students' 16th birthday.

One suggestion is to set up a storefront program and recruit drop-outs off the streets for retraining. Another is to have "success models" come to the school and lecture the older students on the tremendous personal losses they will suffer if they drop out. The first suggestion is rejected as too costly for too little anticipated payoff, the second as naive and ineffective. After several meetings it is agreed to take a preventive approach, since it appears possible to predict which students have the greatest likelihood of dropping out.

With the prospect of being able to obtain funds for a special program, the superintendent assigns one of his staff to draw up a plan. The following is the program plan that was submitted to the committee for discussion and action.

Proposal for a Work-Study Program at Adams High School

This is a preventive program aimed at reducing drop-outs among students whose drop-out potential is recognized and acted on early. The first step will be a review of the records of all male students who have passed their fourteenth birthday. A "drop-out profile" will be administered in order to identify students who show certain characteristics, such as failing marks in English and mathematics and frequent absences from school. The records of students who fit the "drop-out profile" will be sent to guidance counselors, who will consult with students and their parents to determine whether a student will be placed on a voluntary basis in the work-study program.

The program will consist of half a day in the classroom and half a day on a job where the student will receive training. The classroom curriculum will stress reading and mathematics, geared as much as possible to the practical world of work rather than to college-entrance goals. Job placements will be sought in retail stores, business and professional offices, small manufacturers, and medical and social welfare institutions. Wages will be paid for work performed on the job.

For the first year 100 students will be accepted into the program. Each student's progress will be reviewed monthly to determine whether he should be returned to the regular school program or whether there should be some readjustment in his job placement or his classroom work.

Careful records will be kept on all aspects of the program, and research personnel will be assigned from the superintendent's office to evaluate the program at the end of the first year.

The budget for the program is a follows:

Director	$12,000
4 job Coordinators @ $9,000	36,000
Secretary	5,300
Supplies and Equipment	3,000
Telephone, travel, etc.	1,000
Research consultant	3,000
Total	$60,300

In the discussion of the proposal the committee raised questions about "dead-end jobs," what pay the boys would receive, whether the committee would have any control over the program, how and where job opportunities would be found, and who would be responsible for the student during his work hours.

The questions posed by a researcher who reviewed the program plan brings us to another phase of the problem-solving model, *monitoring and feedback*. The research consultant wanted to know concretely what the program was designed to achieve and how he would be able to know whether the program had succeeded or failed. In the research plan that ultimately went with the program proposal to a prospective source of funds, the researcher said that he would attempt to answer these questions:

Has there been any change in the number of students dropping out? If so, to what extent can the change be attributed to the program?

What was the full cost of the results obtained?

Were certain parts of the program more or less effective than others?

What kinds of students benefited most or least from the program?

These questions are typical of the task of assessing effectiveness in services. We spoke earlier of the importance of information by which an agency is made aware of changes in its environment. A parallel flow of information is needed with respect to its own operations, and an expanding technology is available to planners to meet this requirement. The systems analyst in one of the case records talks about how he would design an information system.[42] He first lists typical problems of an inadequate system:

1. Misuse of professional staff time in recording useless data.
2. Loss of information as it moves from worker to worker.
3. Lack of necessary information.
4. No automatic feedback on change or effectiveness of program.
5. No possibility for cost-effectiveness studies because data are unavailable or improperly recorded.
6. No possibility of comparing data from this agency with other agencies.

He notes that partial information can be misleading and makes this observation:

"No underling is going to willfully be the bearer of bad news to his superior. Only good news gets bumped upwards, and because a lot of people can block information at any point in the system, policy-makers never really know what's going on. Now an efficient, open and available data system gives access to information to everyone—including, incidentally, clients. A good information system, therefore, redistributes power. You have to know that, and the people with whom you're con-

---

[42] Ecklein and Lauffer, *op. cit.*, Chapter 13, "Designing an Information System."

sulting have to know that or you may be wasting several months of hard work to set up an ideal system that no one will use."[43]

The information consultant goes on to describe how he would analyze the operations, relationships, and problems of the agency as a basis for redesigning its information system. This becomes a whole new problem to be solved, including the development of policy statements on the goals of the system, decisions about computer hardware, forms and other software components, as well as feedback and evaluation on the feedback-and-evaluation system itself.

Given a set of organizational goals, program planning and budgeting systems (PPBS) can be used to measure performance against the objectives. This system focuses on the achievement of goals with a minimum expenditure of resources. While it cannot determine goals, it helps to reveal when goals are unrealistic or poorly specified. PPBS, which will be discussed in Chapter 9, is generally accompanied by cost-benefit analysis, which seeks to measure the utility and efficiency of a program operation. The following case vignette illustrates both the process and the problems of employing these techniques.[44]

The object of study here was a mobile tuberculosis detection center that covered a whole state. In one year it screened 300,000 people at a cost of $150,000, but only 50 new active cases were found. Was this method, which cost $3000 per case detected, preferable to others, taking into account both direct and indirect costs and benefits? Could this same mobile facility be utilized more efficiently? If so, which areas should it cover?

The study ended with a recommendation that on a trial basis the mobile unit should be kept in the metropolitan area around Detroit. The reasoning behind this conclusion is worth noting because it represents cost-accounting put at the service of humanistic values:

"If in screening 300,000 people, it would now detect 80 new active source cases, then we could make decisions based not only on cost effectiveness, but on the basis of the most humane criteria. True, we might be sacrificing 10 people from outside the metropolitan area; on the other hand we would be finding 40 new people from within Detroit. Should we sacrifice those 40 people?

"There was another question which I could not answer. A man from

[43] *Ibid.*
[44] Ecklein and Lauffer, *op. cit.*, Chapter 13, "Costing-Out A Tuberculosis Screening Program."

the governor's staff asked me: 'How are you going to satisfy the people in Port Huron and Grand Rapids? Their congressmen have to vote for the T. B. detection program, and if that mobile unit isn't traveling around the state, we're not going to find funds for Detroit either.' As I said earlier, benefits-cost analysis doesn't answer every question."[45]

This brings us full circle. The evaluation of a program poses new appeals to value judgments and presents new situations requiring political assessment as well as opportunities to bring research and planning skills to bear. The process of making choices about services, based on informed estimates of the consequences, begins again. Another round of interaction and analysis is called for and another set of decisions and actions will flow from these in the continuing attempt to resolve disjunctions between needs and services.

[45] *Ibid.*

CHAPTER 8

Planning Organizations

CHARACTERISTICS AND TYPES

Planning organizations constitute the third context in which we shall examine the practice of community organization and social planning. If it is the basic task of a voluntary association to express the aspirations of citizen and consumer groups, and the role of a service agency to render a human service effectively, the central function of a planning organization is to improve the effectiveness of a system of programs and services and to create new instrumentalities that will make a greater impact on social problems.

This central task provides the practitioner in the planning organization with a different perspective than those of his fellow practitioners in other settings. In comparing the service agency and the planning organization, it is the difference in perspective that is crucial, since the actual organizing and planning tasks in these settings have many similarities. However, the practitioner in the service agency looks outward from the vantage point of his responsibility for that service toward the environment in which his agency operates; he deals with that environment in such a way as to pursue the purposes to which his agency is committed. In planning organizations, that perspective is reversed.

A planning organization in the human services field is oriented (or should be) toward an examination and discovery of needs in the social environment as the basis for determining how resources can best be mobilized and allocated to meet those needs. Thus, a service agency committed to providing aged people with residential care will seek resources from the community to support that type of service and will, if properly motivated and managed, strive to improve the quality of the service. A planning organization, on the other hand, will try to determine how best to balance alternative forms of residential and non-residential care in order to meet the needs of aged persons most adequately. Or it may be concerned with how best to distribute limited resources among the aged and other groups in the population. This is not to imply that the planning organization is necessarily more "progressive" or broader than a service agency. That depends on many factors that are not intrinsic to the difference in function, such as ideology, quality of leadership, and command over resources. What is intrinsic, however, is the difference in perspective.

A planning organization ordinarily does not engage in the direct provision of services. It pursues its objectives through influencing other organized groups and agencies that do have operating responsibilities to modify their activities in accordance with its proposed policies and plans. However, there is an underlying tension here. The constituent service-oriented organizations in these interorganizational bodies, as we have seen throughout this text, are highly specialized and fragmented as to their purposes and responsibilities. Each is constrained to pursue its own ends as it participates in a planning organization. On the other hand, it is the function of the planning organization to concert the specialized activities and resources of its constituents in order to achieve goals that supersede those of the individual components.

The resulting tension between the planning body and its constituents (as well as among the constituents) is the paramount issue in practice in this area. Practitioners try to resolve the issue by developing the structural or organizational arrangements best suited to concerting power and resources to deal with the problem at hand. Much of the practitioner's attention is given to analysis of the factors that make for cooperation or competition among the parties relevant to an enterprise and to analysis of the strategies that will advance the goals of the planning organization. As we shall see below, when practice is discussed in terms of our general problem-solving model and its five components, considerable emphasis is therefore given to the building of appropriate structures for planning.

Several basic types of structures have been developed for purposes of planning and coordination in the human service fields in order to cope with the diffusion of power and responsibility. Some of these take as their point of departure a specific problem or program field, such as health, manpower, or the needs of the elderly, and planning is addressed to this *sector*. Other mechanisms attempt to coordinate planning *across* a few closely related sectors while still others seek to encompass agencies and organizations with a very broad range of interests and responsibilities. Sectoral planning bodies may operate horizontally at the community, state, or Federal level or they may be vertical, linking similar agencies from one level to another. They include councils of hospitals, associations of settlements or of nursery schools, and federations of special-purpose organizations. While these associations generally do not have directive power over their affiliates, they may exercise functions that are important to the constituent members, as for example, joint financing and budgeting. Typically they provide services to their affiliated units and undertake studies, planning, joint purchasing, or public education for their constituents.

There are a number of structures that try to cut across sectors. In social welfare, as we noted in Chapter 2, many communities and metropolitan areas have health and welfare councils, united funds, and sectarian federations that engage in joint fund-raising and allocating of monies and in coordinating and planning activities usually on behalf of voluntary agencies, with some participation by governmental agencies.

Sectarian federations are geared to the health and welfare activities of a particular segment of the community, although their functions may be broader than a United Fund or Council. For example, the typical Jewish federation includes not only the conventional areas of welfare services, but educational and cultural activities of the Jewish community as well as extensive participation in overseas health, welfare, and educational programs. Sectarian federations are most extensive in the Jewish community but are expanding in other religious groups.

Somewhat similar to the specialized federations are commissions or councils in fields such as intergroup relations or race relations. Some of these are under the auspices of a mayor; some are completely voluntary in nature. They attempt to bring together a very wide spectrum of organizations representing religious and ethnic groupings in the community with a view to facilitating communication among them and having available channels for discussion and negotiation at points of intergroup tension and conflict.

One of the important developments of the 1960's in the field of sectoral planning was the initiation of large-scale social welfare programs that called for a combination of Federal, State and local planning, decision-making, and financing. In particular, the states, following the provisions of Congressional legislation, obtained grants from Federal agencies and engaged in successive waves of planning in such sectors as mental health, rehabilitation, and mental retardation.

Planning in these categorical fields is typically an effort to mobilize resources and to achieve coordination of activities among all the services directly and indirectly involved in dealing with a specific area. It is, in other words, an attempt to be "comprehensive" within a sector by including all kinds of public and voluntary agencies and by involving citizen and consumer groups. This is illustrated in the following case, in which we trace the evolution of the national mental retardation program during the Kennedy Administration.

The case illustrates a number of points. It demonstrates the importance of the "definition of the problem" and it shows the parts played in shaping that definition by an aggressive consumers' association, by the President, the Congress, the Department of Health, Education, and Welfare, and a state department of mental health. The case portrays the impact that each actor's definition had on subsequent decisions.

SECTORAL PLANNING

From medieval times until well into the 19th century, mental retardation was looked on as the work of the devil or as punishment for sinful behavior. Popular fears, later reinforced by theories of genetic determination, have produced a long history of ostracism and inhuman treatment of retarded persons, whether they were hidden in attics or kept out of sight in institutions. Following World War II there was a sharp increase in public interest and support for services to the retarded, generated mostly by local and state groups and a national association formed to advance the interests of the retarded.

These associations had grown out of local self-help efforts of parents to obtain better education and other services for their retarded children. Their small-scale demonstrations were buttressed by new knowledge of the multiple causes and forms of retardation. Most important, evidence was mounting that less-severely retarded children and adults were trainable and educable and could live at home—some independently—and many could be employed. The scattered activities of the parents' groups gave way in the 1950's to intense political activity aimed at getting changes in the policies of state agencies and in having legislatures appropriate more funds.

At issue in all this activity was the underlying question of the definition of retardation. What is it and what causes it? For a long time a medical or clinical frame of reference labeled all retardation as individual pathology, requiring diagnosis and treatment on an individualized basis.[1] An opposing view holds that mental retardation is more frequently a product of a faulty social system—that is, of bad health conditions, lack of prenatal and postnatal care, poor educational programs, and measuring and labeling devices that are themselves distorted by middle-class and professional biases. By 1960 research, some of it sponsored by the National Association for Retarded Children,[2] had called attention to the substantial economic, cultural, and social components in the causation of retardation.

Leading the growing concern, President Kennedy, made more sensitive by the fact that one of his sisters was retarded, used the medium of a nationwide TV address to appoint a panel in 1961 to make a study and recommendations. In his mandate to the panel, Kennedy tried to set the terms and the tone for what was to follow. He defined retardation not as a disease but "as a symptom of a disease, of an injury, of some obscure failure of development, even of inadequate opportunity to learn." He called it a national problem requiring a national solution and he instructed the panel to explore "the possibilities and pathways to prevent and cure mental retardation," to appraise the adequacy of existing programs, to identify gaps, and to recommend the programs that were needed.[3]

The panel's 200-page report emphasized research and prevention and made some 90 recommendations covering clinical and social services, methods and facilities for care, clarification of the legal rights of the retarded, the need for increased manpower, and public education on retardation.[4] The panel urged that the new program thrust should be (1) *comprehensive*, that is, including day care, recreation, residential services, and educational and vocational opportunities; (2) *community centered*, operating close to where the retarded live; and (3) *coordinated* so as to assure a sufficient array or continuum of services to meet different types of needs. The fourth policy recommendation departed from the

---

[1] Thomas P. Holland, "Social Planning Implications of Alternative Views of Mental Retardation," unpublished paper, Brandeis University, 1970.

[2] Richard Masland, Seymour Sarason, and Thomas Gladwin, *Mental Subnormality —Biological, Psychological and Cultural Factors*, New York: Basic Books, 1958.

[3] *Statement by the President Regarding the Need for a National Plan in Mental Retardation*, October 11, 1961. U.S. Government Printing Office, 1961.

[4] *A Proposed Program for National Action to Combat Mental Retardation*, The President's Panel on Mental Retardation, Washington: U.S. Government Printing Office, 1962, pp. 14–15.

President's perception of the national scope of the problem and placed the "principal responsibility" for financing and improving services on the states and local communities, although it suggested Federal aid to the states for planning purposes.

Using the panel's findings and recommendations, the President asked Congress to provide larger appropriations for certain existing programs and for special project grants to be awarded to state agencies "presenting acceptable proposals for this broad interdisciplinary planning activity."[5] The President stressed, as the panel had, the strong link between retardation and socioeconomic deprivation. While some retardation could be traced to biomedical factors, he said, the great bulk of cases for which the cause is not clearly known shows a remarkable correlation between the incidence of mental retardation and the living conditions of families deprived of the basic necessities of life.

It is important to note the shift that was taking place in the approach to the problem. When Congress enacted legislation in 1963, it provided Federal matching funds for perinatal medical care for indigent mothers, support for comprehensive planning by the states, and money for constructing new facilities. This was, in effect, a retreat from the view of retardation as largely a social-structural problem and was a reversion to the individual pathology-service approach.[6] Connery reports that in the Congressional hearings preceding passage of the legislation, the American Medical Association mounted a strong attack on any proposals to change the definition of the problem and opposed the emphasis on the social aspects of causation.[7]

"Major national social programs were avoided in favor of state responsibility. And at the state level, Connery continues, the medical profession continued its opposition to government involvement in programs for the retarded, and then it insisted that any services that were implemented should be attached under the control of existing hospitals and medical programs. . . . Popular American ideology of an open social structure and individual responsibility precluded many from even hearing the idea that the social system itself may be handicapping some individuals' chances for growth and development. At this point the

[5] *Message from the President of the United States Relative to Mental Illness and Mental Retardation,* House of Representatives, 88th Congress, 1st Session, Document No. 58, February 5, 1962, p. 11.

[6] Holland, *op. cit.,* p. 27.

[7] Robert H. Connery, *The Politics of Mental Health,* New York: Columbia University Press, 1968.

popular ideology and the medical perspective on retardation meshed closely to produce strong opposition to any changes which would upset the current social allocation of statuses and resources."[8]

The passage of legislation, however, only indicates the will and intent of the legislators; responsibility then passes to the administrator, to implement their intent through his regulations. In this case it was the Department of Health, Education, and Welfare, which issued its guidelines for planning by the States seven months after the new laws had been enacted.[9] The publication explores the difficulties of achieving interagency coordination and suggests approaching this through improved communication, closer cooperation, and the use of authority. The guidelines list the areas to which attention must be given (for example, prevention, clinical services, records and reporting, and financing) and then suggest these steps for building a structure and taking the first analytical steps in the planning process:

1. Establishing an "executive-level policy group, composed of top personnel" in the agencies concerned with retardation.
2. Setting up a broadly representative advisory committee of State and local public and voluntary agency personnel.
3. Having the planning staff evaluate the retardation situation, making rough estimates of existing resources, needs, and a determination of what additional services, personnel, facilities and other resources are required. This planning should dovetail with the planning of physical facilities and specific goals should be set for services.

After these steps, "the plan can then be developed" to include provision for coordinating mechanisms, case-finding procedures, service components, evaluation, regional organization, the stimulation of greater public awareness, and the drafting of necessary legislation.

Within three months after the appearance of these guidelines, a planning project was activated in Massachusetts, where the State Department of Mental Health contracted with a voluntary health organization to do the planning.[10] The structure followed the Federal guidelines and consisted of a top-level policy board of the heads of

[8] Holland, *op. cit.*, pp. 33–34.

[9] *Mental Retardation Guidelines for State Interagency Planning*, U.S. Department of Health, Education, and Welfare, Public Health Service Publication No. 1192, 1964.

[10] *Massachusetts Plans for Its Retarded*, The Report of the Mental Retardation Planning Project, Boston: The Massachusetts Department of Mental Health, 1966.

relevant state agencies plus the chairmen of nine task forces set up to deal with various aspects of the problem. During the two and one half years before it reported to the Governor, the planning project conducted inventories of facilities and services, held hearings around the state "to feed data into the decision-making machinery and to increase local identification with, and commitment to, comprehensive planning," and designed a special study of the characteristics of potentially employable retardates.

The planning board recommended to the Governor a system of decentralized programs in 37 areas within the state and set forth its own guidelines for the specific services to be developed locally. The existing institutions were to shift to an emphasis on social development of retardates and to an "individual and small group approach and meaningful links with the community." Support of new programs of special education and of preventive work was recommended, and the board urged that, in addition to the $50 million then being spent each year on retardation, $13.7 million would be needed annually by 1968 and $45 million would be needed by 1976.

But the board felt that the major problem was one of coordination. It found that 50 of its specific recommendations reflected the "need for an interdepartmental planning agency." The political problem could be summed up simply: which of the seven state agencies serving the retarded would be designated the coordinator? Moreover, how could this be resolved with all these departments heavily represented on the planning board?

The solution was to create a new agency, an Office of Retardation, which would be responsible directly to the Governor. The new agency, presumably a neutral among the large agencies, would

"develop, and keep current, a state plan to aid retarded persons; establish standards for services; provide liaison with the federal government; and assist all departments and other agencies and organizations to improve their programs and services for the retarded."[11]

Without tracing the process beyond the preparation of these recommendations, this account has indicated something of the nature of planned change. In the four-and-one-half years covered by these events there were some changes in the distribution of resources, power, and functions. This was due in part to the concerting of energy by the parents of retarded children, in part to growing public concern, and in

[11] *Ibid.*, p. 3.

part to Presidential leadership. But the thrust to redefine retardation as primarily a failure of the social system was blunted, and the massive changes that some wanted were denied. This was the result of the opposition of certain political leaders and of some professionals and bureaucrats who were protecting their domains, as well as being the reflection of old but persistent public attitudes toward the retarded.

Running throughout this case illustration has been another theme: the difficulty or at least the undesirability of isolating mental retardation as a social problem and the mentally retarded as people from the rest of society. This fundamental limitation in sectoral planning has given rise over the years to different kinds of planning bodies that strive to cut across service fields and problem areas. Here we concentrate on one such type—the welfare council—and return later in this chapter and the following one to other kinds of cross-sectoral planning organizations.

WELFARE COUNCILS

In social welfare, welfare councils evolved, as we have seen, from the decisions of separate agencies and their financial supporters to form partnerships for common purposes. The Charity Organization Societies that were formed to combine and to regulate the efforts of numerous relief-giving groups were an early form of such coordination. Later, community chests were organized to rationalize voluntary philanthropy.

Today, the most prevalent form of intersectoral coordination at the local community level is the United Fund-Council complex, which is found in more than 2000 communities of the United States and is represented nationally through the United Way. These organizations are direct descendants of the earlier Community Chests and the Councils of Social Agencies. Over the years, their scope has become progressively broader. After World War II, the community chests expanded into United Funds, incorporating the fund-raising campaigns of national agencies as well as local health and welfare services. While originally these were essentially organizations of organizations, this is no longer true, and the trend for some time has been toward a greater degree of control by a leadership group selected not on a delegate basis but because of individual qualifications. In point of fact, many members of such boards have leadership positions in other organizations, reflect the views of various groupings in the community, and exercise influence in a number of overlapping circles.

A central instrument for joint fund-raising, as represented by a Community Chest or United Fund, necessarily becomes involved in the allocation of funds and therefore in some degree in concerted decision-making and the setting of priorities. A planning function is at least implicit in these organizations. In practice this function is often performed at a very rudimentary level, due to some of the built-in characteristics of a joint fund-raising mechanism. At least in the early stages, a fund-raising partnership is formed through agreements concerning the division of funds on some negotiated formula. The formula rests on the relative strength of the parties, as measured by their past ability to raise their own funds. Such agreements were used in the formation of early community chests and were quite common in the agreements reached between community chests and powerful national organizations such as the American Red Cross or the national fund-raising campaigns for specific health programs. It is only as the basis for fund-allocation moves away from the negotiated formula to an examination of community "needs" that the potentialities for planning begin to emerge.

Since the early days of chests and councils, it has been recognized at least in theory that there is a close logical and practical relationship between the allocation of resources and the planning of programs. There has been no consistent pattern, however, in the way these functions have been organized. Allocating funds and planning programs have sometimes been combined, with chests and welfare councils united in a single organization. More frequently, especially in larger cities, the Community Chest or United Fund has been a separate organization that raises philanthropic funds for voluntary agencies, while the welfare council or federation functions separately as an organization committed to a broader planning responsibility, including both voluntary and governmental agencies. The following is a sketch of the different levels of planning that may be found in the course of the development of a United Fund-Council structure.

1. *Setting minimum standards for affiliated agencies.* At the simplest level, a central organization that is responsible for joint fund-raising will establish minimum standards as requirements for agency inclusion and participation. For example, it may require that an agency be a *bona fide* nonprofit organization, properly organized under the laws of the state, that its financial accounts be properly kept and audited, and that it have a duly constituted board of directors and by-laws.

2. *Providing informational and other services.* A central organization may render joint services to affiliated agencies, contributors, and citizens on an informational level. As an adjunct of fund-raising efforts, informa-

tion will deal with the programs and "needs" of the included agencies. Education programs for board members can be addressed more broadly to community-wide issues.

3. *Reviewing budgets and programs.* The beginning steps in assessing the experience of the agencies and their projection of needs for the period ahead are usually taken through the procedure of reviewing budgets. This is a major step in that it superimposes on the separate and independent judgments of the autonomous parties a review procedure. The reviewers are empowered to raise questions and to make comparisons between the different parties. At this point there begin to arise generic and recurring questions as to the composition of the central review body and its powers.

4. *Coordination of services and programs.* Either separate from or combined with budgetary review, a first-level approach to joint planning is to bring programs and services that have some relationship with one another into ongoing contact. The nature of coordination, its limitations, and its relationship to planning will be discussed later.

5. *Organization of new services.* New services may be established either as the result of the activities of an independent group or through the mechanisms of a planning council. When new problems arise there is frequently a choice between addressing them through a modification of the work of existing organizations or forming a new service. In recent years, new programs have been organized as the result of the initiative of welfare councils in fields such as services to the aged, where a more integrated program was needed than had been available through the activities of separate organizations. Sometimes new agencies are established through the merger of several organizations, brought about as the result of studies and recommendations developed in the planning councils.

6. *Determination of priorities.* Another major step, which moves from acceptance and facilitation of all existing programs and services to the process of making *relative* judgments, is the setting of priorities. Welfare councils have from time to time attempted to develop systematic schemes for determining priorities across a large number of agency structures and different fields. A limited amount of progress has been achieved in establishing criteria within a particular field, weighting the importance of programs on the basis of such factors as the number of people reached, the severity of the condition being treated, or the effectiveness of the services being rendered. It has been particularly difficult, however, to establish quantitative criteria for choosing priorities across fields (as, for example, health services as against youth

services) because of the many value judgments and partisan interests involved.

7. *Long-range planning.* Planning councils will frequently attempt to look beyond their normal year-by-year decisions to plan for development of programs and services over a five- or ten-year or longer period. This is an extension of efforts to determine priorities and is subject to similar limitations. Long-range planning usually becomes most meaningful and substantive at the point when councils and funds are involved in decisions about capital expenditures. Decisions on whether or not to construct facilities represent crucial choices concerning the future scope and character of various service programs. Long-range planning exercises, while not always resulting in concrete plans that actually are implemented, serve at times as ways of clarifying agreements and differences over basic objectives.

It is worth pausing here to look in some detail at the ways in which a practitioner carries out a number of the functions noted above. We draw upon a case illustration in which the executive of a welfare council explains his actions in a situation that arose with four small institutions serving delinquent girls in his community.[12]

The institutions, independent of each other, were affiliated with the welfare council. The council provided funds to three of them, two of which the council staff felt were providing services of dubious quality. All three, plus the fourth institution, which had not been receiving funds from the council, came, one by one, to press for more money to employ psychologists, caseworkers, group workers, and other professionals to bolster their treatment capabilities as distinct from their custodial functions. The council could agree in principle but did not have the money that was requested, nor did it seem possible to find the number of professionals required, even if funds were available.

The council staff began looking for ways of putting the agencies together so as to make maximum use of whatever new funds might be found. But two institutions were affiliated with religious groups, one with a sorority, and one with a nonsectarian group. Under these circumstances, amalgamation was not possible. The council planners decided it was best to begin with a study to evaluate existing services and their quality and to determine what new professional services should be added.

A study committee was set up. There were representatives on it from

---

12 Ecklein and Lauffer, *op. cit.*, Chapter 9, "Delinquent Girls Get A New Treatment."

the four institutions, but a majority of the committee members had no affiliation with the institutions. The staff's reason for establishing the committee with this composition was to avoid giving control to the insitutions; they gave the major voice to people representing broader community interests. Meanwhile the executive spoke informally with a judge in the Juvenile Court, the Public Welfare Department, the Board of Education, and other key organizations. These conversations were designed to inform these agencies of what was getting under way and to obtain their views on the matter.

An out-of-town consultant was employed by the council to collect information and prepare recommendations for the study committee. The council staff consulted with the consultant to give him the benefit of their knowledge of local conditions and to indicate what approaches they had in mind. Based on the consultant's work, the study committee endorsed the need for more professionals and proposed to the four institutions that they remain independent but that they form a federation with a central board that would provide for the new professional services on a shared basis. The executive of the welfare council undertook to help "sell" the plan to the boards of the institutions and to his own board. The latter agreed readily, but difficulties arose with the institutions and the executive had to use different incentives (beside the leverage of the council's funds) with each agency.

One board was absorbed in searching for a new executive and had to be reminded that they had promised to examine the recommendations. It took some time to explain the plan to another board, which did not understand its implications. A third agency had already sold its physical plant but went along with the plan because the board wanted to start a similar program. The fourth agency, which had not previously received support from the council, eagerly accepted the proposal because it was the only way they could get funds from the council.

After the plan had been accepted in principle, the council asked the study committee members to participate in appointing a new committee to be responsible for implementing the recommendations. The implementation committee refined the proposal and then selected a board of directors for the federation of girls' institutions. While this formally ended the council's planning role, the executive indicated that he intended to stay close to the situation, particularly the budgeting for the new federation and the setting of standards. He would also try to see that the juvenile court judges followed through on their agreement to place girls in the institutions.

The case depicts a rather typical welfare council project. It is useful, however, to contrast this case with the previous one dealing with mental retardation, in which a sectoral planning organization strives to reach out toward more comprehensive policies and programs in related fields. In the welfare council case, a planning organization that was set up to coordinate on a comprehensive basis, in actuality, facilitated program development in one sector, namely services to delinquent girls. This was so largely because the study committee proceeded from the clear, although unstated, assumption that while services to delinquent girls should be improved, the committee was not authorized to weigh institutional care against other approaches to the problem of delinquency among girls.

The welfare council's definition of the problem as one of improving existing services may well be an inescapable concomitant of the fact that the council would not have the resources in power or finances to plan in preventive terms by addressing issues in the educational field or in housing, let alone questions of adequacy of income among families with a high incidence of female delinquency.

Nevertheless, given these constraints, the council—or more accurately, its executive and staff as planners—used a variety of techniques and incentives to achieve its goal of more effective and coordinated institutional service. The power of the purse strings, although never openly exercised, was also never too far in the background. The use of expertise and the careful orchestration of communication furthered the planners' objectives. The case illustrates especially the differential selection of structures (the study committee, then the implementation committee, and finally the board of directors of the new federation) to provide the kinds of input as well as legitimation required by the planning.

COMMON ISSUES

Above all the case illuminates the central dilemma of planning organizations—how to mobilize the necessary degree of authority, power, and resources to influence the policies and programs of the very organizations on which it is dependent for the implementation of its plans. Differences in structure, while not necessarily determining, can affect the potential of the central organization to achieve such a position.

An analytic distinction has been made in the literature between a "federated" and a "unitary" organization, with the community welfare council standing as the prototype of the federated structure. The classic model of the federation is the Council of Social Agencies or the Community Chest with its board made up entirely of representatives from the constituents, so that decision-making rests entirely on agreement among the parties. This is an "ideal type" description under which there would be no independent authority within the central organization, the functions of which would be severely limited to those required by the constituents for their own independent purposes. This is obviously an exaggeration, but it is one pole of the analytic dimension. At the other extreme would be an authoritative organization whose decisions are mandatory upon the component parts of the system.

Neither of these extremes is likely to be found in a pure state in the real world. In a federated structure that is based theoretically on complete equality and consensus among the parties, there are differentials of power and resources among the constituents that in turn create inequality in their relative influence on the decisions of the central organization. On the other hand, central organizations that presumably have a substantial degree of authority are nevertheless subject to constraints on their ability to reach decisions and to implement them. Although these constraints may be latent for a period of time, they are potential obstacles to what the practitioner is trying to achieve and therefore need to be taken into account in a calculation of strategy. A further complication is that the constraints may be quite different depending on what the specific problem or issue may be.

These considerations again illustrate the underlying contradiction in federated structures. On the one hand, they are partnerships or coalitions of independent agencies or departments on whose goodwill and support they depend, often for their very existence. On the other hand, once established, federations inevitably develop an identity and purposes of their own, and the pursuit of improvements in services, or other goals of the parent body, must at times require changes in the operations of the affiliated agencies.

The location and distribution of authority affects the ability of the central organization to control such resources as money, manpower, and physical facilities. Indeed, it is the extent of control over these that largely determines the limits of the federation's function and purpose. The possibilities include "coordination," "allocation," and "innovation," and it is important for the planner (and others) to understand which of these is applicable to a particular organization.

Both coordination and allocation imply that the present distribution of responsibilities among agencies is accepted and that the task is to improve implementation of programs through improved use of resources and better working relationships. One reason that an organization may be limited to these functions is that it does not have access to additional new resources and therefore cannot engage in the kind of planning that would require uncommitted funds. Given these premises, the purpose of a central body, as we saw in the case illustration concerning delinquent girls' institutions, is to arrange for minor adjustments in line with the limited availability of funding. Innovation, on the other hand, springs from a questioning of existing definitions of problems and interventions and opens up new possibilities for policy and program directions. There is some incompatibility between these two goals, and they may well require different structural arrangements and strategies for their realization.

In the underlying tension that necessarily exists between the perspective of the single organization and that of the planning organization, a wide range of objectives, orientations, and ideologies may be involved on both sides of the relationship. For the "outside" voluntary association representing the needs and demands of disadvantaged or disenfranchised groups fighting their way into the system, the central body frequently represents forces of conservatism, reaction, and resistance. On the other hand, a central body that is concerned with pursuing a new approach to social problems will look on old, established service agencies or voluntary associations that have a stake in older ways of doing things as the forces of conservatism and resistors of change.

It is therefore not valid, in any general view of the practice of community organization and social planning, to assume a necessary or constant relationship between a social change orientation and the particular context of practice or type of organization. The differences among the contexts are related to the differences in their basic functions and tasks. Generalizations about the conservatism of an organization are subject to variation, depending on the place of the sponsoring groups within the society, the objectives that they are pursuing, and their ideological orientation.

It is, however, possible to avoid a completely relativistic situation and to adopt a value stance, as we have done in this volume, which identifies the overall objective of community organization and social planning as the achievement of changes that result in a more equitable distribution of resources to meet social needs. That value position provides a benchmark for examining the effects of various organizing and planning activities. In a given situation, the actors may be placed in relation to their contribution or opposition to this social-change goal. To some extent such an evaluation can be made empirically, although it may have to rest at least in part on ideological judgments not entirely subject to verification. In any event, whatever the evaluation there is no basis for assuming that either a unitary agency or a central body will necessarily turn out to be the proponent of social change.

Another issue related to structure concerns the nature of decision-making powers. One prototype is the traditional council of social agencies or its counterpart in interdepartmental committees of state and national government. The rationale for the traditional model rests primarily on the idea that the parties who have a stake in a program or whose cooperation is required to carry out a project should have a voice in the decisions. This is based on the central notion that involvement is the most basic, necessary mechanism for the achievement of working agreements. A simple implementation of that idea is to call together into an *ad hoc* committee or ongoing interorganizational body all of the groups and agencies that have a potential contribution to make to the solution of a problem or construction of a program. A typical committee to plan a program for the aging, for example, would include representatives of hospitals, nursing homes, homes for the aging, family service agencies, recreational agencies, as well as various citizen groups that have an interest in the problem, including groups of aged themselves.

Such an approach has an apparent common-sense plausibility. It assumes that there is a sharing of interests among the parties in achieving improvements in program and that their participation in a common consideration of needs and alternative solutions will bring about an optimum result. Both analysis and experience indicate, however, that this approach, while possibly appropriate under some conditions, is inadequate as a general guide to the objectives of interorganizational planning. It is an oversimplified model that fails to take sufficient account of a number of dimensions that have a bearing on structure, especially control of resources.

All of the types of structures that have been employed in community organization and social planning have both strengths and weaknesses. The practitioner must therefore make the optimum choice among less-than-ideal alternatives, based on his analysis of each situation. The strength of an inclusive coordinating body, as described above, comes from the participation of the groups that have the resources of money, manpower, and expertise necessary to achieve the goals of a project. But its weakness stems from the inclusion of many other interests, whose varied and often conflicting views frequently make consensus impossible, thereby blocking the possibility of achieving change.

Two other types of structures remain to be reviewed: (1) the outside body, such as a task force or citizens' commission, and (2) a planning mechanism that serves as an arm of central administration. The task-force type of structure brings together a group that is presumably in a position to examine issues on their merits and to render judgments concerning a preferred course of action. It functions at the level of problem identification and policy choice and may extend its work to the making of programmatic recommendations, but it does not have responsibility for the implementation of programs. Its assets lie in the prestige of its membership and the consequent credibility of the judgments reached.

The major problem lies in the hiatus between the work of the task force and the body that in fact has implementing responsibility. The effectiveness of a task force is dependent on the ability and willingness of the latter to act on the recommendations. Analysis of experience with task forces indicates that they may be used as frequently to avoid dealing with a problem as to help in achieving change. That, in fact, turned out to be the history of some recent Presidential commissions established to consider burning questions of social change in the United States.

On the other hand, when a task force is set up to lend impetus to the efforts of a planning agent already committed to a change, it can be an effective instrumentality. Examples of that type are found more in other countries than in the United States. The Royal Commission in England is a type of task-force operation that is usually established by the government to develop recommendations and to lend support to changes in an area where the government has decided to seek change. As a result, Royal Commissions frequently have important effects upon policies.

Increasingly, particularly in the United States, the dilemmas inherent in the relationship between planning and implementation have been leading to a centralization of interorganizational planning within the arm of the executive authority. At the state and local level of government, recent years have witnessed the growth of planning sections within the office of Governor or Mayor. Planning in these structures is closely tied to budgeting, bringing together program development and control over implementing resources. At the level of the Federal government, the growing power of the Office of Management and Budget reflects this trend. States and municipalities have been experimenting with human-resource or human-service administrations to strengthen the executive's knowledge and control of operating departments.

The variations in structure that have been outlined have an immediate effect on the ways in which problems will be identified and objectives established. Summarizing much of the preceding discussion and oversimplifying to some extent, we find that structures in which authority is rather evenly distributed among constituent organizations will tend to focus on the coordination of programs and services. There is a tendency in such operations to define problems in terms that assume the basic premises of the existing programs. In order to achieve innovations of any substantial degree, some change needs to occur that will stimulate a reexamination of existing assumptions and introduce a new frame of reference to guide the planning activities. In one way or another this involves a shift of emphasis from *programs* to *problems*.

In fact, pressures to make this shift are always present and help to account for the periodic reorganizations that occur in the grouping of services and programs. These reorganizations take place in order to bring resources of personnel, finances, and decision-making powers into a more effective attack on newly identified problems. A recent example in the Federal government, which is typical of this approach, is the reorganization of the Department of Housing and Urban Development. From a structure based on large-scale program entities, such as home mortgage loans or public housing, the Department has shifted to divisions based on problem-solving functions such as "community development" or "community planning." The Department of Health, Education, and Welfare has a history of successive attempts to overcome the fragmentation of the many specific programs contained within this huge, heterogeneous complex.

At the local level, an important change took place in the post-World War II period in the structure of many local welfare councils. We noted earlier the expansion of community chests into more inclusive United Funds. That development on the fund-raising side was accompanied at about the same time by reorganizations of planning councils from an agency-based to a problem-oriented type of structure. As against a traditional structure made up of divisions, such as family and children's services, recreation and group service agencies, and health services, new committees were set up to cut across agency lines in order to focus on problem conditions such as juvenile delinquency or the needs of the aging.

It is important to note that this shift in structure reflected not only a change in the focus of the problem that was being identified, but also a change in the power relationships within the organization. The basis for the composition of the divisions in the older structures had been representation from agencies. In the newly reorganized committees, prominent and influential citizens representing business, labor, minority groups, and other *community rather than agency interests* were drawn upon. Moreover, the traditional council of social agencies had been based on a small, upper-class group engaged in philanthropic activities. Later chests and funds were based on large groupings such as industry and organized labor. During the past decade local planning councils have become arenas for the struggles of previously excluded minority groups to gain entry into participation in the planning of projects and the allocation of funds.

All these reorganizations of governmental and voluntary planning structures have been prompted in part by a need to gain more centralized direction over the various components. But a more fundamental reason for these regroupings of planning functions has been to bring about (or respond to) different ways of conceptualizing social problems. It will be recalled that "the definition of the problem" is a key element in the practitioner's problem-solving work. We now turn to an examination of this and other practice elements in planning organizations.

CHAPTER 9

Practice in Planning Organizations

STUDYING NEEDS AND IDENTIFYING PROBLEMS

Different types of structures, we saw in the preceding chapter, represent alternative solutions to an important issue facing planning organizations—how to concert the power and resources of other organizations so as to implement policies generated by the planning body itself. Cutting across differences among these organizations, however, is a common set of tasks performed by practitioners. These components of practice can be seen in terms of the problem-solving framework that was introduced in Chapter 4 and then applied, with appropriate variations, to voluntary associations and service agencies.

In this chapter we shall be "walking through" the planning process, viewing it from the perspective of the practitioner as he moves from the study and formulation of a problem through the choice of goals, the specification of program details, and the evaluation of results. For the most part he does not formally make the decisions on these matters, but he does make recommendations. Before discussing the planning process, we need to inquire into the grounds on which the practitioner makes these recommendations to other actors. In order to reach his own decisions, the practitioner juggles three main considerations: *values*, patterns of *influence* or power, and *rationality* or knowledge of costs and consequences.

An important aspect of the practitioner's responsibility is to understand and make clear to others what each of these factors means in a concrete situation and how they interrelate. All decisions, for example, include value judgments. The very determination to study the need for services to delinquent girls in the case cited earlier rested on a judgment that this group deserved better of society than they were receiving. By the same token, if one had to choose in allocating resources between this group and the elderly living below the poverty line, he would face a difficult value choice.

Value implications extend beyond the initial decision to place a need or problem on the agenda for study and action. They permeate every step and every decision. The desire, for instance, to promote re-integration of the girls in their community is, after all, a value position. It is quite a different one from saying that delinquent girls should be quarantined in a remote place so as not to "contaminate" other young people. It was largely the former stance that led the welfare council staff to reject the notion of building an out-of-town institution.

It is not enough in a planning situation to have value preferences. Their realization will depend in no small measure on the distribution of power and control over resources. The practitioner is called on, therefore, to analyze the positions of various actors who are relevant to a planning project. Especially when the planner and his organization have arrived at their own preference, he must know who are supporters and opponents and who is indifferent—and why—and the degree of influence each grouping can bring to bear on the result. And he must put this knowledge to use.

This was apparent in the case of the girls' institutions in connection with the selection of the study committee. The representatives of those agencies were confined to a minority position on the committee that was looking into their request in order to give more influence to people without those ties and commitments. Nevertheless the institutions had enough "muscle" to block any move to force them into an amalgamated organization, while the welfare council, for its part, had sufficient influence (which it did not have to exercise overtly) to promote a federated type of arrangement.

There would be little need for professional practitioners if planning were simply a matter of the most powerful interests announcing their position at the outset and having it accepted by all concerned. Decisions are based, at least in part, on information and the rational examination of its meaning for the problem at hand. The practitioner is a processor of information—not only on value preferences and influence patterns, but also on the causes and extent of a problem condition and on the implications of alternative solutions or interventions.

Knowledge of the costs and consequences of possible lines of action is vital in planning, and the collection and analysis of such information is a key part of the practitioner's job. To put this another way, he should be able to illuminate the potential impact and cost of a given decision on the goal that has been set. If, for example, the chosen objective is to reduce the cost of hospital care, the planner must be able to marshal information on alternative forms of care and evidence as to their suitability and feasibility as substitutes for hospitalization.

Rationality is again involved in evaluating programs and in assessing whether they have achieved their objectives, at what cost, and with what unanticipated consequences. Here as in all phases of problem-solving, the practitioner is engaged with considerations of values, power, and rationality. One of his responsibilities is to try to separate these elements from one another, even though they are intermingled and generally perceived as inseparable in concrete situations. The purpose of separating them is to avoid making decisions on the basis of unclear or mistaken premises.

Sometimes, as Rein and Miller argue, problems that are defined as technical are in reality based on value differences.[1] In discussing issues related to poverty and how to attack it, they point out that technical analyses of the extent of poverty, as well as measures of the effectiveness of programs in reducing it, are influenced by the way in which poverty is defined—whether as lack of income, or inequality, or lack of skills with which to compete in the market economy. These alternate definitions rest, in turn, on value assumptions as to the nature of poverty, its causes, and what aspects of it are undesirable and in need of correction.

It is equally true that instrumental issues can be defined or sometimes obscured in value terms. The criticisms that have been made recently against professional practice in the human services rest on the contention that particular forms of practice have been allowed to become ends in themselves instead of being examined for their efficacy in achieving the social objectives to which they are officially committed. Another side of this coin is to endow certain strategies of social action with an ideological aura that changes them from means to ends.

To the extent that information can in fact be produced, the practitioner serves as the agent for correcting the domination of the decision-making process by considerations of values alone (without regard to

---

[1] Martin Rein and S. M. Miller, "Poverty, Policy, and Purpose: The Dilemmas of Choice," in Leonard Goodman, Ed. *Economic Progress and Social Welfare,* New York, Columbia University Press, 1966, pp. 20–64.

rational calculations of efficacy, feasibility, and cost) or by the patterns of influence prevailing within the situation. These issues were alluded to earlier in the general discussion of rational and non-rational elements in planning in Chapter 3. The practitioner in a planning organization who is responsible for the conduct of a project increases its rationality primarily by being able to provide information and by maximizing the conditions for its effective use. One of the realistic limitations that practitioners in the human service fields face is that their information is frequently not adequate to the task. There are great gaps in knowledge in virtually all areas related to the etiology of social problems and the efficacy of various forms of intervention.

In the absence of more secure knowledge, decisions tend to be based on preferences that may or may not be well-reasoned, and the operational issue for the practitioner becomes one of "engineering of consent" among the actors whose participation is necessary to the project. The tendency to emphasize consensus that was noted earlier as a characteristic of many types of planning organization is due, in part, to these limitations in knowledge. Skill in practice under these circumstances tends to become equated with the diplomatic art of finding agreement among conflicting parties or, alternatively, of making a value commitment to a given course of action and employing the arts of influence to have it prevail. It is for this reason that "models" of practice have tended to emphasize either the "enabler" or the "advocate."

While the practitioner in a planning organization engages in enabling and advocacy roles, these are not sufficient in themselves to define the nature of his practice. More essentially it is his role to contribute to the process of policy choice and program development the most pertinent knowledge that can be adduced. Since choices of policy and program proceed in a continuous ends-means chain, evaluation of alternatives and consequences can be made at every point, except for the underlying value assumptions that provide the very foundation for the action being undertaken. The practitioner is certainly not being visualized here as a "value-free technician," and it is expected that he will have preferences at every stage in the ends-means chain. However, his preference, if it is only that, makes no special contribution to the process. What is distinctive in his role is the analysis he can bring to bear on the range of choices available and the potential effects of each. How that role can be implemented under the present state of limited knowledge will be described in the following sections.

Launching a Project. It will be recalled that the problem-solving framework was proposed, not as a step-by-step linear model, but as a number of elements that are logically related, although not necessarily in any fixed time sequence. The point of departure in planning settings— conceptually if not always chronologically—is the expression of discontent with some existing condition and the call for a change. This can be initiated in several ways and can come from various sources. It may proceed from a service agency, as we noted in Chapter 7, as a result of population shifts, changes in the availability of funds, pressure from organized client groups, or the brickbats of outside critics. The impetus may come from a segment of the community, perhaps an ethnic or racial group that feels aggrieved by the lack of particular provisions and is forcefully advocating its own cause.

Or the initiative may originate in the planning organization itself. Here the planner may be engaged in the "engineering of discontent," since it is his role not only to identify conditions that require change, but also to activate potential sources of support for change. This may require him to facilitate the expression of discontent on the part of groups that are excluded from the "normal" channels. Or the practitioner may be called on to make known the existence of new needs that have emerged from changes in concepts, values, or methods. To refer again to the case of the girls' institutions, the planner convinced the board of the welfare council to sponsor a study and planning project largely because of the shift in emphasis from custodial care to treatment.

The practitioner, in short, may transmit expressions of discontent from other actors or he may, on the basis of his own identification of a need or problem, "awaken" others to his concern. Whatever the source of pressure for change, one of the planner's tasks is to make explicit this discrepancy between an existing state of affairs and some desired or valued condition. This disparity may be articulated in the form of a goal to be achieved, such as the construction of low-cost housing, or of a "need" to be studied. But whether cast as a goal or a need, an important part of practice requires the documentation and analysis of what provisions exist, what deprivations appear to be present, and what is required to close the gaps.

In the social welfare field the traditional way of approaching problem specification was through a "study of needs." The older types of studies were based primarily on social agency data. Recent research has made it clear that only a fraction of the people who might be eligible for services actually become clients, so that measurements of need based on agency clientele are inevitably an understatement of need even as defined by the agency itself.[2] Because of this, it is necessary to seek

---

[2] For a review of relevant studies, see Robert Morris, "Social Planning," in

broader measures within the population. The techniques of survey research based on samplings of populations can be employed in order to approach greater adequacy in the measurement of need.

However, this is but one—and, in a sense, the simplest—of the issues involved in determining need. The major questions are not technical or procedural, as is the differentiation between need in a population and need as measured by agency clientele. The most difficult problems are conceptual, because there is no single or precise meaning to the term "need." Are needs to be defined by "objective" criteria—that is, by standards external to the motivation or behavior of the "needy" person—or by a person's own view of his condition and requirements?

Another problem is that needs are not static but develop in relation to changes in the environment. Not the least among these is the availability of resources to meet "needs." It has been demonstrated repeatedly that the establishment of a service will bring to light users of the service who were not previously identified as in need because there was no such facility to which they were able to turn. Thus, the creation of services actually defines needs by offering service to certain categories of people and conditions.

Scope of Data Collection. Since information in itself is not useful except insofar as it is directed to the answering of questions, data do not serve as a tool in planning unless these connections are explicated. Such explication leads to selectivity in determining what kind of information will be obtained, among all of the theoretical possibilities. In making decisions on selectivity, one of the first questions is to determine the scope of the data that will be collected.

A planning project, even if small in scale, is frequently part of a large system in that it not only involves a number of different organizations but may very well impinge on a variety of community institutions or population groups not immediately involved in the project itself. Thus, for example, a program designed to provide greater employment opportunities for handicapped persons may develop in such a way as to decrease similar opportunities for out-of-school youth. The problem for monitoring is how widely to cast the net of information-gathering so as to encompass as much of the affected field as possible.

Answers to this question will depend in large part on the specific responsibilities of the individual planner and the scope of operations over which he has some control. A number of proposals have been

Henry S. Maas, Ed., *Five Fields of Social Service: Reviews of Research,* New York: National Association of Social Workers, 1966.

made by planners who take a large view of a total urban community for the development of integrated and computerized information systems that might be constructed in order to provide a framework of current and longitudinal data from which practitioners responsible for much more specific projects could draw. Presumably, such general bodies of data would be specific enough to provide the basis for insights as to problems, needs, and progress in specific conditions of various kinds, and thus facilitate planning on a smaller scale.

One of the most ambitious of such schemes has been projected by Perloff.[3] In his view, this is an "ideal" model that cannot be implemented immediately or completely but would have to be modified on the basis of community variations, feasibility, and degree of community acceptance. The Perloff model leans heavily on the construction of a comprehensive body of data obtained at a number of levels in such a way that connections can be made among different kinds of information.

Information to be obtained at the level of individual households is to be combined into "household welfare indices," which would reveal the existence of social problems and thereby help determine objectives for planning. The indices are based on income, level of self-support, and extent of employment. Estimates are made of those who are potentially self-supporting, and information is obtained concerning the extent and adequacy of existing employment (including measures of underemployment), income, and numbers receiving aid of different types. A suggested long-term measure is an index of lifetime earning power, which would differentiate between temporary periods of low income and the existence of a chronic situation characterized by lack of adequate income or employment.

From the household level we move to a description of the social structure and institutional situation. A system of regional accounts would give a continuous picture of the state of earnings and employment opportunities within the region. An analysis of the social structure would include substantial amounts of information concerning a variety of groups within the population. Information would be differentiated by socioeconomic status and also by age in order to pinpoint the characteristics and needs of different populations at risk. Detailed breakdowns of the regional figures would provide a picture of the concentration of problem situations within particular subsections of the region so that these problems could then be related to information concerning the physical

[3] Harvey S. Perloff, "New Directions in Social Planning." *Journal of American Institute of Planners,* **31**, No. 4, November 1965, pp. 297–304.

environment and other aspects of the community situation. Comprehensive information would also be obtained on all kinds of community services and facilities, including education, health, recreation, and youth and welfare services; and on the physical condition of houses, streets, and other aspects of the physical setting.

Perloff's model visualizes a combination of extensive central data gathering, technical planning, and projection of overall guidelines, together with a diffusion of planning processes through various groups in the community. It calls for an extensive metering and reporting system set up on a regional basis. Such a central service, in addition to maintaining a continuous flow of information, would undertake special research projects in order to analyze problems, suggest alternative solutions, and work with relevant groups in an attempt to improve the attacks on such problems. The central planning unit would also prepare a general community policy plan, including overall capital and operating budgets for the social services and neighborhood improvement programs, and relating a variety of needs to one another and indicating the priority choices that have to be made. This would be done by an interdisciplinary group operating centrally and combining the various skills that are required for technical planning tasks. The group would include physical planners, social scientists, experts in particular fields such as health and education, mental health personnel, social workers, lawyers, and others. The planning process would use a variety of approaches, such as experimental pilot projects, in order to experiment with new approaches for preventing and solving problems.

On the level of broad metropolitan, regional, and national planning to be discussed in the next chapter, events are moving toward the construction of more comprehensive data systems that may have profound impact on planning in the future. For the time being, however, the information that is available on a broad, general basis is not integrated and frequently not suitable to the planner's immediate needs. Decisions are therefore necessary as to how he should use the separate and unintegrated sources of data that are available and also what steps he should take to collect information on his own.

Holleb has provided a useful outline of the sources of economic and social data that are available, summarizing them as falling into the following categories: (1) formal statistical series issued by government agencies in various fields; (2) recurrent fragmentary data available locally; and (3) other social information, not necessarily quantified. The practitioner needs to make a selection among these, but is also faced with problems of inadequacy. Many relationships in which he might be interested, as in the relationship between place of employment and place of residence, for example, may fall between the bodies of information available. The categories may not be those he is seeking. Generally, also, data are not found in consistent series, so that changes over time cannot be determined easily.[4]

While Holleb, like other planners concerned with very large-scale comprehensive urban planning, calls for broad solutions like social indicators and metropolitan data banks, Kaitz and Hyman, describing a specific project in one local program, illustrate the more limited approach that is appropriate to the practitioner who must work with what he has available at a given time.[5] The two planners, who were concerned with developing a program for minority youth employment, found that they needed relatively little information of a general nature, since the overall aspects of the problem were generally known, and they could utilize data collected elsewhere. Their problem was to locate much more specific data on the needs and opportunities in the limited area where they were working, and this they had to find out for themselves by "knocking on doors," projecting trial efforts, and testing out reactions.

Study Processes. Studies of various types are used in planning organizations. One of the most usual is a "process" study in which the emphasis is placed on the participation of people whose opinions and community positions are relevant to the decisions to be made. These are looked on as self-educational efforts leading toward the emergence of a consensus, rather than strictly as problem-solving activities in the analytical sense. A distinction should be made between the two purposes—the development of information and the development of consensus leading to a choice of policy alternatives. Included in a strategy of study geared toward either or both of those ends are a number of lesser issues of strategy, such as the inclusion of outside experts, the timing of their introduction, and the definition of their role.[6]

Self-studies and action research are designed to link factual research with the identification of value choices and expression of preferences. In these methods, an intimate connection is established between the

[4] Doris B. Holleb, *Social and Economic Information for Urban Planning,* Center for Urban Studies of the University of Chicago, 1969, Vol. I, p. 75. Volume I is a general discussion subtitled "Its Selection and Use." Volume II is a "Directory of Data Sources."

[5] Edward M. Kaitz and Herbert Harvey Hyman, *Urban Planning for Social Welfare: A Model Cities Approach,* New York: Praeger Publishers, 1970.

[6] For a useful discussion of the "political" aspects of community studies, see Robert D. Vinter with John E. Tropman, "The Causes and Consequences of Com-

research process and the development of the action project. Those responsible for the action are also the ones who determine what study is to be undertaken and, in the process of conducting such a study, have an opportunity to think through the questions they are trying to answer and the use they will make of the data obtained. It is claimed for self-study approaches that they are useful in educating people concerning problems and in motivating them to become involved actively in contributing to desired objectives. Whether a self-study does in fact have such effects, and whether it is the best method either for those purposes or for obtaining needed data, are matters that need to be evaluated in relation to specific situations.

We saw in the case of the delinquent girls' institutions the way in which a study was used to develop a plan for interagency coordination. Another case in the Ecklein-Lauffer volume is relevant at this point in illustrating the way a study process was able to change the definition of a problem.[7]

Salamanaca, the protagonist in this account, posed a problem frequently encountered by a planning organization. The problem revolves around a prominent citizen, with political influence in the community, who represents a specific cause or interest and is committed to a particular course of action. In this case, the association of which Mr. Salamanaca was president had obtained a foundation grant, and he was determined that it should be spent to add a staff member to his agency to expand its services.

Through a well-organized and far-ranging study, the welfare council brought about a redefinition of the problem and opened up many new alternatives for program development. It became clear in the course of the study that the vast majority of retarded people in the state were not being reached by Mr. Salamanaca's association, but were known to large governmental and other community agencies. The problem was redefined as the lack of understanding on the part of these large institutions of the special needs of the retarded, and the alternative program approach or intervention that was adopted in the end was to conduct activities to influence the policies of these institutions.

Of interest here is the mixture of strategies and tactics that the research director of the council used. His information-gathering activities were

munity Studies" in Fred M. Cox, John L. Erlich, Jack Rothman, and John E. Tropman, Eds., *Strategies of Community Organization, A Book of Readings*, Itaska, Ill.: F. E. Peacock Publishers, 1970, pp. 315–323.

[7] Ecklein and Lauffer, *op. cit.*, Chapter 9, "Salamanaca Buys a Study for the Mentally Retarded: Research and Consultation in Community Planning."

carefully articulated at each step with "interactional" tasks that were designed to achieve the objectives of the planning effort—a new level of attention and allocation of resources to the needs of the retarded. To that end, the practitioner needed to develop a committee that would contain a balance of forces to prevent domination by Mr. Salamanaca's original, limited view of the problem and that would represent enough prestige to influence his attitudes. It was also necessary to deal with protests that arose in the course of the study and to interpret to the chief decision-makers the implications of facts uncovered during the study. And it was important to have available a series of alternative plans, both at the beginning of the project and at crucial points of decision during its life-time, in the event that first-choice recommendations were not accepted.

The research director's summary statement was "It's not so much how many facts you dig up with your research, it's how you use the process." Yet the research was crucial. The facts uncovered may not have been sufficient in themselves to achieve the desired change in orientation, but they revealed information not previously known that was important enough to affect the attitudes of the participants.

This case illustrates how studies of needs and the information obtained can in fact be used to re-focus a problem. The research data compiled revealed that most of the retarded people were not being reached by Salamanaca's organization but that they were known to other agencies. The decision to act on this knowledge and to turn away from Salamanaca's request for staff represented a value choice (between the clients of Salamanaca's organization and the larger number not being served by that agency); however, it was a choice based to some extent on rational consideration of hitherto unknown facts.

But the reformulation of the problem in this case also hinged on the judicious selection of people to serve on the committee with which the research director worked. Committees or commissions such as this, which are given a charge to carry out a particular project, represent a prevalent kind of structure in planning organizations. The establishment of the committee and the determination of its composition are important parts of what we have called "building the structure."

Building A Structure. Creating a mechanism for the development of a planning project poses for the practitioner the question of who is relevant. This can be separated into two parts: which actors are essential for contributing inputs and which for their contributions to the output of a planning operation? The choice of those to be represented at the early stages of exploration and deliberation rests on such considerations as who can bring experiential and expert knowledge of the problem under discussion; who can articulate the ideological positions and the interests of various groups; and who can speak, at least in the preliminary sense, for the organizations that will ultimately be called on to support the proposed program.

On the output side, the recommendations of a planning group need to be legitimated in most instances by respected and powerful figures if they are to carry weight. And they must indicate that persons with command over the required resources have participated in or are in agreement with the decisions. Thus the composition of a planning structure, as was seen in the case of the girls' institutions, may need to be changed several times.

The elements that enter into practice in this regard are touched on in the casebook, where it is noted that the professional must exercise considerable skill in suggesting, if not actually selecting, the membership of a governing body of a planning organization. Although some kind of cross-section of major community groupings is sought along economic, racial, and religious lines, taking into account ideological viewpoints and the interests of neighborhoods or larger geographic units, the actual choices made are a matter of strategy. The dominant decision-makers in the situation will attempt to select the kind of mix that is congenial to their purposes.

Clearly this was so when the Mayor in one of the vignettes asked his staff man to contact 14 people to form a Model Cities board that would (1) convince Washington that the community was involved in planning, but (2) not unduly dilute the Mayor's control of the program or "turn it over to a group of militants."[8] It is instructive to look over the professional's shoulder as he interviews the Mayor's choices and as he gives his own assessment of how the prospective board members will fit in individually and how they will interact.

The selection of people from various groups and interests for participation in a planning project calls for a calculus on the part of the practitioner that weighs several factors. In Chapter 8 we discussed the strategy of broad "involvement," that is, the inclusion of all interests that might possibly have a stake in the planning, and we saw that this cannot serve as a guide for all circumstances. The broader the base, the greater the difficulty of achieving consensus. However, a planning group that consists only of "the Establishment" in a particular field will be unlikely to consider making significant changes. On the other hand, an "anti-Establishment" grouping by itself will probably not have the influence

[8] Ecklein and Lauffer, *op. cit.*, Chapter 12, "Selecting a Model Cities Board, or How Not to Stack the Deck."

and the control of resources required to bring about change. The practitioner's task is to determine in each instance what is the appropriate mix.

One can conjecture, referring to the mental retardation case in the previous chapter, that President Kennedy decided to set up a study panel in order to focus national attention on the mentally retarded; to bring new knowledge to bear on a reconceptualization of retardation; and to support his intention of seeking a national solution to what he considered a national problem. For these purposes he needed a panel that would include the agencies and professions traditionally associated with retardation so as to lend weight and legitimacy to the President's efforts, as well as experts who could challenge established policies and programs.

In the light of these requirements, it is interesting to see how the President balanced the membership of the panel. The chairman was a nationally known social worker and educator with long experience in study and action on social issues. The vice-chairman was a psychiatrist with experience in institutional practice. Five of the panel were physicians, one was a nurse, and one was a clinical psychologist. And there were three people from the field of special education for the handicapped and three administrators of state departments of health and rehabilitation. Thus far, the "mental-retardation establishment" was well represented, although undoubtedly some of these people were ready to think of retardation in untraditional terms.

Perhaps President Kennedy and his staff looked more to others on the panel for innovative thinking. There were six academicians and researchers, some of whom had personal ties to the President. Two members were consumer representatives, one being the president of the National Association for Retarded Children, and there was a judge who not only had a strong interest in this problem but had also rendered some significant decisions on the legal rights of mentally ill and retarded persons. The remaining two people were chosen expressly because they had had no previous connection with the field of retardation.

This description of the President's study panel does not imply that this group constituted the major action system. It was only the first step in a process that went on to include Congress, to whom the President had to turn with the panel's recommendations, as well as the state governments and many other actors. It hardly needs to be pointed out that both formal and informal means of communication were used by all actors throughout to expose people to new knowledge, to explain the intentions of the President, or to express the reservations of the medical association.

In any case, planning often starts with the launching of a study group or committee. Once it is established, attention must be given to its functioning. The choice of a chairman will reflect at least indirectly the interests and influence that are operating in the situation. If the level of actual or potential conflict is low, the chairman may be chosen for his integrity, intelligence, or respectability. In a situation of serious differences, he may be selected by the dominant interests precisely because he is a partisan or, alternatively, it may be considered wiser to have a "neutral" presiding. The balance of authority and responsibility between professionals and laymen in the situation will determine whether the practitioner will have a stronger or weaker voice in making the selection of the chairman.

Ordinarily the practitioner works closely with the chairman of a planning group and is in a position both to help and influence him in making decisions that will have an important impact on the committee. These concern the determination of what goes on the agenda, the kind of material that is introduced for discussion, and the frequency of formal meetings as against informal contacts outside the committee. Usually the practitioner is responsible for the logistics of setting up meetings, sending out notices, and writing minutes and reports. These are not only mechanical tasks that call for efficiency and skill in writing and communication; they also constitute an important medium through which the practitioner carries out the responsibilities of professional leadership that we are discussing.

SETTING GOALS AND POLICIES

Setting a goal or choosing a policy is not an event. It is a process of making a series of decisions. The first decisions establish a broad concern or purpose and the subsequent decisions are more and more specific and operational. It is important to see that the first general goals—which stem directly from value positions—have the effect of setting the direction and the limits for what follows in this ends-and-means chain. This was obvious in the case of the girls' institution: once there was agreement that better professional services were needed, the die was cast, and the subsequent questions revolved around how best to accomplish this.

How broad a goal to propose at the outset and how much it should remain general and flexible is another question to which the practitioner must give thought. There are both advantages and risks in these "preamble" goals. For instance, openness and even ambiguity can be beneficial as a strategy for avoiding closure around the objective of an actor who is narrowly protecting his own interests without knowledge of or regard for wider interests that may be at stake. Certainly Mr. Salamanaca would have been pleased to have had a quick decision to give him an additional staff member to serve his agency's clients. The planners found it advisable to keep the issue open so as to permit an assessment of the needs of the total retarded population.

The danger of maintaining preamble goals too far into a planning process is that some actors will be turned away by the inaction and will seek to advance their ideas and interests in some other way. The basic risk, of course, is that a very general aim, such as "building housing for low-income families," will remain at just that level and not move closer to operational terms and to the possibilities of implementation. It is at this juncture that a choice must be made between attractive rhetoric and realistic examination of possibilities for action, which frequently necessitates some compromise with the hopes of some of the actors and is sometimes rejected as unworthy.

Movement beyond a preamble goal can be fueled by any of the three factors that we discussed at the beginning of this chapter—value judgments, influence, or rational responses to knowledge about the problem —or a combination of these. The President's study panel drew back from proposing a truly "national solution to a national problem" when it insisted that the basic responsibility for serving the retarded belonged to the states. Moreover, while the panel wrote that poverty and poor socio-economic conditions loomed large as a cause of mental retardation, it did not produce a program to upgrade basic services for all low-income people. Their recommendations concentrated more on the delivery of better services to the mentally retarded.

While it is not clear from the record what constraints influenced the panel in the direction of these recommendations, it is known that opposition from the medical professionals surfaced during Congressional consideration of the problem. This opposition was successful in fending off both a stronger Federal role and a heavier emphasis on broad social measures addressed to low-income people. The outcome, as we have seen, was a policy of Federal encouragement and support for state planning, with funds being made available for state plans that met the HEW regulations. One is hard pressed to unravel the professional or rational reasons for these decisions from pure value judgments or from political pressures based on self-interest.

In the movement from preamble to operational goals, the practitioner confronts additional choices that will govern his behavior. If he tries to emphasize the common ground among the participants and to play down their differences, he may hold things together, but at the cost of inaction. If he opts instead to encourage the participants to put all their differences on the table for open debate, he may risk an irrevocable break that destroys the joint effort. But he may find a way of articulating alternatives so they do not threaten the vital interests of the actors as they see them, and thus help them resolve their differences and move on either to a clear-cut choice or to a new synthesis.

At this point we diverge from discussing the process of planning and address our attention to the content and the concrete matters implicated in choices of policies and goals. We shall indicate here a number of substantive issues in the human services field. For purposes of highlighting the issues, they will be presented arbitrarily as polarities, although in practical decision-making they seldom are.

Treatment Versus Prevention. The point at which one seeks to intervene in the cycle of cause and effect is perhaps the most basic policy choice to be made. Many other determinations flow from or are closely related to what we present here as a dilemma facing policy-makers. The last few years have witnessed strong criticism of the human service institutions and professions for "picking up the pieces" of human suffering after the damage has been done by social conditions beyond the control of the individual. The push has been toward interventions that forestall individual breakdown such as joblessness, crime, drug abuse, and the like.

The investment of *all* resources in prevention, however, would raise agonizing value problems. Assuming that the victims of damaging social conditions can be helped through rehabilitation and treatment, or simply by material and emotional support, can their needs and rights be disregarded? Directing resources either to treatment or prevention is not only a question of ideology or of power to force the decision. The limitations of our understanding of social problems also play a part. Preventive strategies of intervention call for making changes in institutions, but it is not by any means clear which institutions should be changed to reduce a specific problem or how they should be changed. The crude state of contemporary knowledge sometimes has the effect of pushing interventions toward the treatment of the symptoms of intractable social problems that are more accessible than the root "causes" of the problems themselves. On the other hand, in a number of fields, claims are made that the services contribute to the prevention of the problem conditions being attacked. Thus community mental health services are sometimes advocated as measures that will prevent the occurrence of mental illness, and some types of youth programs are designed to prevent the occurrence of delinquency.

Before raising the question as to whether such claims can be validated, it must be first asked whether the actual work that is being done is in fact designed to achieve a preventive purpose. Upon examination, it turns out, for example, that community mental health services are most often devoted primarily to dealing with people in some stage of emotional or mental disturbance. The same is true for most of the work of family and children's agencies and others, since they all tend to see people after some problem has already developed.

By far the bulk of social welfare services are related to the easing or treatment of problem conditions rather than to prevention. What is sometimes called prevention tends to be an approach to service that seeks to intervene at as early as possible a stage in the development of problem conditions. Intervention takes many different forms, depending on such factors as the nature of the condition, the state of knowledge concerning treatment, the values of both service providers and service recipients, and many more. Some services are actively rehabilitative, designed to seek a significant change in behavior. Others have more of a sustaining character, designed to help people achieve greater comfort in living with problems even though no significant change may be expected.

Personal Services Versus Group Status Improvement. This is, in effect, another form of the prevention-treatment issue. It involves political considerations, as we saw in the work of Blum and his associates cited in Chapter 6, where they pointed out that, in accordance with the American ethos, there is generally more support for personal services to help people individually than for legal and other changes in the status of whole groups such as the poor and minorities who face systematic discrimination.

Aside from these political considerations, there are serious questions concerning the effectiveness of individualized services. Recent studies, for example, have thrown doubt on the efficacy of certain counseling and casework practices.[9] In actuality, there are great difficulties of both a political and technical nature in making a clear-cut choice between programs that serve individuals and programs that alter the status of a group with common characteristics. Some of the practical problems in achieving one without the other were explored in Chapter 6. To these must be added the fact that there are individual differences in need within any group that may necessitate special provisions. This was illustrated when training and employment programs were launched in

[9] For a recent review of studies, see Richard B. Stuart, "Research in Social Work: Social Casework and Social Group Work," *Encyclopedia of Social Work*, Vol. 16, New York: National Association of Social Workers, 1971, pp. 1106–1122.

the 1960's and were directed specifically at unemployed young black men as a group. It was soon found that many participants in the program could not benefit from training or placement on jobs without individualized services such as medical or dental treatment or basic education.

Another way of posing the policy choice here is to call attention to *universalism* versus *selectivity*. In its broadest form, the question facing policy-makers is whether a program should be made equally available to all persons or only to those in a particular category as defined by age, income, physical condition, or the like. Titmuss has frequently argued for universalism as a policy, pointing out that the programs designed to serve the poor usually turn out to be poor programs.[10] There are moral issues here concerning indignities of the means test as well as value judgments concerning level of "need." For example, how much savings should a family be permitted to retain when they apply for public assistance?

Moral arguments are just as persuasive on the other side. If a government has a certain amount to invest in meeting a need, should it not single out those most in need and tip the scales in their direction by establishing eligibility regulations that screen out those who need the benefit less? Policy analysts have found no general answer to these questions. The answer in each case depends on an *analysis* or prediction of what will be the outcome of each course of action and which, on a *value basis,* is to be preferred.

The policy choices we have mentioned—prevention versus treatment, universalism versus selectivity, and personal versus group-oriented services—are simply examples of the task of choosing *an organizing principle* that will indicate where and how to intervene. The choice rests on whether the problem is conceived of as primarily one of *accessibility, coordination of existing service,* or *adequacy of the amount of service* available.

Accessibility is a problem when services are not physically within reach of consumers, or when the psychological and cultural distances are too great. Physical inaccessibility was exacerbated in the 1940's and 1950's when a number of social agencies pulled back their neighborhood-based offices and placed them downtown in hard-to-reach locations. Cultural inaccessibility of services has been experienced in relationships between middle-class professionals and lower-class consumers, between white providers of service and members of minority groups as clients,

---

[10] For an extensive discussion of this issue, see Kahn, *Theory and Practice of Social Planning, op. cit.,* pp. 201–204, which includes the quotation from Titmuss.

and in the use of intervention techniques that were developed with middle-class clients but that relied on patterns that were strange to working-class and lower-class people.

At least equal in importance to this factor of accessibility is the issue of the adequacy of the service being given. Comprehensiveness of care is a concept designed to overcome the fragmentation and discontinuity that have existed in the past. Many examples have been recorded of both confusion and incompleteness in the services provided by uncoordinated interventions. Thus, families that are beset by a multiplicity of problems are frequently found to be receiving service from a number of different agencies, each with a specialized function related to one aspect of the situation. As a result, a number of professionals may be dealing with the same family, sometimes at cross-purposes, or, in any event, in a manner that is wasteful of resources and confusing to the people involved.

Even more serious is the observation that these fragmented efforts frequently leave untouched some elements that are crucial to a successful resolution of the problem. Thus, services that have been concerned with problems of relationship and adjustment within a family have sometimes ignored such concrete matters as employment, income, and housing, which may have been very crucial to the situation but beyond the competence of the particular agencies dealing with the situation. Another example is that services directed to the needs of one member of a family, as in cases of illness or handicap, have not dealt adequately with the entire range of interactions and interrelated problems within the family as a whole.

Continuity of care refers to the need to assure that there are enough varieties of service available so that an individual does not drop out of the system while intervention is still considered necessary. The major issue in this area that has been highlighted in recent years is continuity between institutional and community care. Community organization and planning activities in fields such as care of the aging and mental health have been directed in large part to the creation of a variety of institutions and community services, as well as systems of referral, that would assure continuity. In the case of mental illness, for example, continuity involves provision for people to live in protected community settings and, should they undergo hospitalization, to obtain service in making their way back into community life. Such efforts have received added impetus from constantly rising costs of institutional care, which have made ever more urgent the need to find alternative forms of service.

Improved accessibility and/or coordination of services may fall short of or entirely miss the target of an intervention if, in fact, there is a basic lack of facilities and services for a designated population or a geographic area. Here the policy will call for obtaining new resources, but this again entails a choice: is there a need for "more of the same" in the sense of purely a quantitative increase in existing programs or is a qualitative change needed in the service itself? If the analysis of the problem indicates the failure of professional techniques and methods, the solution may require experimenting with new methods or new types of facilities.

All of these approaches to program development, whether they center on accessibility, coordination, or creating new resources, are various ways of changing the arrangement of resources and functions. This is the central task of program development. It entails shifts in the allocation of money, manpower, and other resources. And it means finding new arrangements that will come as close as possible to achieving the goals that have been adopted. This in turn means another round of weighing factors of desirability against feasibility.

Since policy choices are usually stated in very broad terms, there is a wide range of options available to the planner in determing how to make them more operational. In the field of health, for example, a policy of improving the health status of a group of people may be operationalized as the addition of resources to hospitals for in-patient and/or out-patient services. Or it may lead to the strengthening of non-hospital health services in the community. A policy strategy that stresses prevention will be likely to emphasize services to individuals in their homes and communities rather than in hospitals or institutions.

The basic program development task of rearranging functions and resources raises a number of instrumental questions. We shall touch on two here to illustrate. One is whether to redistribute resources or responsibilities among existing agencies or to create a new organization to carry out the new mandate. This will hinge very much on judgments as to the capacity and commitment of established organizations to take on the new charge. The usual and understandable response of an organization to the suggestion that it assume new duties is that its resources are fully committed and it cannot handle more demands. Whether it will in fact expand its scope often depends on whether the planning organization can provide it with new funds or new manpower. But the rigidities of bureaucratic organizations also play a part here, and frequently the planners will come to the conclusion that they cannot entrust a new mission to an old organization, but will prefer to set up a new agency that will be fully committed to what needs to be done.

The other issue concerns the level of organization at which new responsibilities are lodged. The pendulum between centralization and decentralization swings back and forth and in part accounts for the periodic reorganizations that take place in the human services field. Implementing new policies may be done most effectively by transferring control to local units, but there is contradictory evidence on this point. Local organizations may take new resources and use them for long-standing needs of their own, in which case the goals of the planners will have been vitiated. A tight centralization of authority, on the other hand, can choke off the kind of initiative and growth that new programs require.

In the mental retardation case, the panel chose not to give the Federal government major responsibility but stressed program development by the states and localities. Within each state there was another problem of centralization and decentralization. The study panel had urged state governments to bring together the three or four departments intimately concerned with the retarded for purposes of cross-sectoral planning. The problem was how to have an effective organization that would coordinate, in the interests of the mentally retarded, powerful agencies, such as departments of health, mental health, and education. On one side, the goal was not to set up services on the basis of a policy of "for retarded people only"; that would have defeated the purpose of integrating them to the maximum extent possible into the general community. At the same time, there had to be a way of moving the departments in new directions. The solution that was decided on in Massachusetts was to establish a new organization, an Office of Retardation, which would be directly responsible to the Governor but would have representation from the relevant departments.

What happens when the desired policy calls for some new arrangement of resources and functions, but no organization can be persuaded or compelled to change in this direction and there are no possibilities at the time of creating a new instrumentality? If services cannot be provided in the form that will carry out the agreed policy, what strategic alternatives are there? One is to abandon the effort and take it up at a more propitious time. Another is to trim the program requirements and try to negotiate their acceptance in modified form. Another is to generate action to overcome the resistances to implementing the desired policy.

In effect, this is what happened in many communities through the community action programs, to which we referred in Chapter 6. The organization of groups for social action—protests, demonstrations, educational campaigns, and the election of new political leaders—represented a strategic answer to a situation in which school systems, public welfare agencies, housing departments, urban renewal authorities, and others would not alter their programs to meet the demands of various groups in the community. Instead of the immediate development of services, these groups had to resort first to changing the distribution of power in order to force changes that could not be brought about by appeals to values or to rationality.

When decisions have been made as to the kind of intervention, the nature of the desired program, and whose responsibility it will be, the details of program design await the planner's attention. These necessitate decisions about the quality and quantity of resources and the costs. At the end of Chapter 7 we illustrated this in some detail with the planning of a school program to counteract the number of dropouts in a high school. The program proposal specified the budget and what it would buy.

The final task that lies between program development and implementation in the typical situation where new funds are needed is determining the source of support. This may come about through the annual budgeting process, in which case new programs are submitted as part of an overall agency request for operating funds. In both public and private agencies, this means that the planners must calculate their chances of obtaining funds in this way. Access to influence is usually part of this strategy. An alternative is to seek support through special grants and contracts negotiated on an *ad hoc* basis.

Since we conceive of the day-to-day operation of a program as an administrative responsibility beyond the scope of the planner, we look now beyond funding and implementation to the evaluation of a program.

MONITORING AND FEEDBACK

The practitioner in a planning organization is concerned with problems of data processing, supervision and control over performance, evaluation of results and costs, and similar matters that are also of concern to the administrator and planner within a service agency. Here again, however, it is the perspective that is different. The practitioner in the planning organization is not responsible immediately for the operation of an agency and its maintenance. His perspective is that of the outside reviewer whose goals are not necessarily contradictory to those of the individual organization but are not identical with them. His questions relate to how the work of the individual organization is fitting into the more comprehensive framework of the concerted efforts for which he is responsible and that encompass the work of several organizations in some pattern of interrelationship.

Another way of making this point would be to say that the practitioner in the individual organization employs monitoring and feedback mechanisms to deal with *all* the work of that organization, but that the practitioner in the planning organization is concerned primarily with the aspects of the organization's work that are germane to the central planning enterprise as defined at a given time. It follows from this distinction that the key to the way in which the practitioner approaches this task is *selectivity*.

Monitoring and feedback systems are an integral part of the entire planning scheme. The objectives of the monitoring systems to be established are set by the decisions made in regard to program and policy objectives. The essential purpose of the system is to determine to what extent these objectives are being achieved; how, where, and why they are not being achieved; and what might be altered in the prior decisions concerning policy and program to achieve a better result. If sufficiently broad, such a system should have the capacity to bring to the attention of planners alterations in the parameters of the problems being addressed in order to help shift the very definition of the problem that underlies the planning project in ways that are appropriate to new conditions.

In this area as in others that we have discussed, the tools available fall considerably short of such large requirements. Up to this point, major reliance has been placed on descriptive data, logical reasoning, and qualitative judgments in order to perform the functions of planning. A beginning is being made today in efforts to employ more complex analytical techniques, borrowed from other fields, in planning and evaluating human services. Major issues, both conceptual and methodological, are still to be resolved before a real technology may be expected to emerge.

We shall review briefly the kinds of questions that a practitioner needs to ask and to answer in considering how to organize procedures for monitoring and feedback, and the methods that are now or may soon be available to accomplish this purpose. In doing this, it will be necessary to go over some of the ground already covered, since the scope of the monitoring operation is determined by prior decisions as to problem identification, policy choice, and program development. In a general sense, the purpose of the monitoring is to evaluate the outcomes of all other steps in the planning process.

Has the problem-issue been conceptualized usefully? Have the policies and programs chosen been the "right" ones—that is, have they achieved their purposes? Is there any way of knowing whether alternative choices might have been more effective? Or—an even earlier question—were the programs decided on actually carried out in the manner that was prescribed and planned? Issues of evaluation must be considered in the very course of the planning itself, at each step in the process, so that the evaluation obtained later on will be relevant to the choice made. The practitioner therefore needs to ask, not only what the potential consequences of a policy or program choice are, but also how he will know at some future time whether the choice was a good one.

Freeman and Sherwood, in a general discussion of the relationship between social research and social policy, have indicated a variety of ways in which formal research activity can be helpful to policy and planning. Of particular relevance at this point is their emphasis on the need for integration of evaluation and planning:

"Evaluation . . . cannot take place when planning and program development have not been thoroughly undertaken. Unless both an impact model and the characteristics of a target population have been explicated, it is impossible to observe to what extent programs are conforming to the expectations of the program's developers."[11]

The authors have also suggested the kinds of data-gathering activities that can be helpful at different steps in the planning process. Thus, the processes of identifying problems ("assessing existing conditions" in their terminology) and setting goals call primarily for descriptive studies of incidence and prevalence of conditions as well as of the values and norms of relevant actors. Program development calls for the use of more predictive and causal types of studies that can be helpful in selecting the target population and in developing an "impact model" that specifies the intervention to be used and the results it is expected to achieve. Evaluation includes description of the program actually carried out as well as causal analysis of the impact of the program.

The planning organization whose program is necessarily implemented through a network of other organizations requires the kind of reporting from the operating level that will reflect the relationship between the work done and the plans made. For this reason, practitioners in planning organizations are concerned with setting up systems of agency reporting that will permit program types of auditing control. Individual organizations do not always have information available in that form, since they are concerned with administrative management to a greater extent than is relevant for the planning organization. Thus, a service agency that is divided into a number of departments may report on the volume of work of each department, whereas a planning organization may be more

[11] Howard E. Freeman and Clarence Sherwood, *op. cit.*, p. 83.

concerned with the volume of total service going to a certain category of people. It is the function of the practitioner to set up uniform methods of recording and reporting across agency lines. The uniformity is necessary so that the different pieces of work done by different agencies that relate to one another in a program plan can be added together. The categorization employed is the one best calculated to reflect the operation of the program plan.

A recent example of this problem became evident in Great Britain, where the local personal social services have been in the process of reorganization, which involved the merger of several departments. The purpose of the merger, growing out of the Seebohm Report,[12] was to overcome the previous fragmentation of the social services into several local departments—health, welfare, and children—and to develop a unified social service department that would try to deal with all the needs of families and with the full gamut of community care that could be provided. In setting up new departments, it was found that the records that each separate department had maintained dealt with volume of service given. This meant that the administrators of the new department could tell how many children were placed in foster homes or in institutions and how many individuals had been helped to readjust to the community after returning from mental hospitals, but they had no way of knowing how many of these cases represented service to the same family. The first step that had to be taken to develop a family-based service was to set up records on a family basis.

It is this need, if planning is to be effective, to view the work of organizations in terms that are meaningful in relation to program that has led to progressive changes in the methods of budget review. In the early days of both governmental and voluntary financing, budgeting was done on a "line" basis in relation to administrative categories such as personnel costs, rent and utilities, supplies, and the like. Budgetary control in such an approach is limited to determining that the agency is living within the amounts prescribed. Rigorous application of such line-by-line controls was gradually relaxed, in many types of planning operations, in order to allow more flexibility to the operating agencies to adjust to changing needs within the total sums made available. More significant, however, has been the recent trend toward performance budgeting, based on programatic rather than administrative categories.

Program planning budgeting systems (PPBS) and cost-benefit analysis

[12] Report of the Committee on Local Authority and Allied Personal Social Services, London: H.M.S.O. Cmnd. 3703, July 1968.

are major current approaches to program planning and evaluation.[13] Although a mystique has grown up around PPBS because of its apparent effectiveness in the work of the Defense Department and its subsequent extension in the Johnson Administration to the rest of the government, at this stage of application to the social sector it is much more of a common-sense approach than a complex technology.

Basically, PPBS is a system for thinking about objectives and means-end relationships in regard to both results (benefits) and costs. It grew out of earlier developments in budgeting procedures ("performance" budgeting) in which costs were presented in relation to outputs (products or services) rather than inputs (costs of capital, labor, and the like). This made it possible to begin to analyze costs in relation to results achieved. PPBS extends this budgeting principle to the planning function. It attempts to use cost analysis not only to evaluate a result but also to help choose a course of action among proposed alternatives. One of its important features is that it cuts across existing administrative structures, such as departments or agencies, in order to bring together for analysis activities that serve related functions.

The following is a schematic view of the major elements in PPBS:

Objectives—specification of what product is being sought, for whom, to serve what need. Simply to state the product (e.g., counseling interviews) is not adequate. An objective would be the purpose of the counseling (e.g., improved earning for specified types of people, or certain types of behavioral changes).

Programs—activities linked to specified objectives. These are not administrative functions (e.g., personnel management) or specific skills (e.g., X-ray examinations). Rather, they are combinations of activities that are related to an overall objective. An example would be a cancer prevention program, which would include X-ray examinations as well as many other activities such as publicity, community organization, other types of examination, research, etc.

Outputs—important products of activities, which are indicators of the achievement of the objective. An output is an end product of a program. The key word here is end product. What is considered end and what means is a matter of definition, but it is precisely this kind of specification which is one of the purposes of PPBS.

Progress measurements—degree of achievement of specified end products, including both amounts and distribution, and their delivery (or distribution) in accordance with plans.

[13] This section is based primarily on the Symposium on PPBS in *Public Administration Review*, **XXVI**, No. 4, December 1966, pp. 243–310.

Inputs—manpower, facilities, equipment, materials, etc., applied to the program. Outputs of one program may represent inputs for another program. When translated into money, inputs are synonymous with costs.[14]

The key to the use of these elements is the concept of "alternatives." The weighing of alternatives occurs at two points. First, there is the problem of choosing among program alternatives where the question is what program is best-suited to achieve the stipulated objective. The second point is in the selection of alternative ways to implement the program, which means choosing the amounts and mixes of inputs that will maximize efficiency in the achievement of output targets. The first issue is at the level of policy, while the second is operational.

Cost-benefit analysis refers to techniques of measurement that assist in the choice of alternatives and in the evaluation of progress. Cost-benefit techniques are applicable both to outputs and inputs, at the point of choosing among alternatives or evaluating results.

Kahn points out that the crucial question in PPBS is the determination of the program unit.

"Identification of programs is a process of delineating major categories so as to capture objectives and goals, doing so in a fashion which makes sense to policy-makers and administrators; utilizing units which lend themselves to consideration of alternatives; while still seeking categories across traditional bureau or unit or departmental lines to sharpen the choices available."[15]

Further, because policy objectives are not always clearly delineated but are subject to progressive clarification, it is desirable to use more than one principle of program categorization. Kahn suggests "the utility of classification by two or three principles in a PPBS undertaking to maximize results."[16] Thus, in social services, programs could be developed by population characteristics (age or socioeconomic groups), program objectives (entrance into labor market, advancement within labor market, maintenance outside labor market, and the like), or type of intervention (income maintenance personal service). Depending on what is seen as the central objective, one of these classifications may be the basis for major categories, with another used for sub-categories (for example, classification by age groups, within each of which there is further sub-categorization in terms of labor-market participation).

---

[14] *Ibid.*
[15] Kahn, *Theory and Practice of Social Planning, op. cit.,* p. 248.
[16] *Ibid.*

Whatever decision is reached, the programming and administration that follow from it need to be consistent. There is a chain from program budgeting to cost-effectiveness analysis, evaluation, and feedback. A whole series of administrative arrangements are required in order to maintain this chain. Both the service-reporting system and the accounting system need to be set up in such a way that information can be obtained in a form that will fit the PPBS categories and make it possible to evaluate the results of the policy and program decisions adopted. There is equal need for communication and decision-making procedures within the administrative process that will facilitate the combinations of activities implied in the program definitions adopted for PPBS purposes.

Thus, for example, if a PPBS projection is based on the objectives of maximizing the upgrading of the economic status of heads of large families, then there has to be some way of coordinating educational, training, and employment-placement activities related to that objective and to that group. If these activities are separated by rigid departmental lines, the central objective may become submerged in the priority concerns of each individual department, which are not necessarily determined by the central program objective but by segmented interests.

The difficulties and limitations of PPBS are both conceptual and technical. Conceptually, it is extremely difficult to formulate objectives in the rigorous manner that PPBS requires. Goal statements in the field of social issues tend to be global value positions and therefore, for the most part, non-operational. The attempt to translate global statements into operational objectives raises a host of problems as to who is to gain and who is to lose what and how much, and whose value choices are to be dominant in any given situation.

At least equally difficult is the task of defining a benefit. This problem is in part an aspect of the first—that is, the difficulty of operationalizing objectives—since benefits are, in effect, objectives achieved. An additional problem is the difficulty of finding a suitable way of measuring benefits so that they can be compared. In order to make comparisons, both benefits and costs are stated in money terms, but translating into monetary terms benefits such as increased participation of poor people in decision-making in neighborhood programs or even the benefits derived from increased tenure in school is not a simple problem. Additional research that establishes relationships among variables in terms of inputs and outputs will help, but the data now available in this form are very limited. Finally, comparison of benefits across different fields—health and education, for example—compounds all of the difficulties of both value choice and measurement.

Because of this, there is wide agreement that the techniques of PPBS and cost-benefit analysis are most applicable, at least for the present, to situations in which there is consensus as to both objectives and the criteria that will be used to evaluate the achievement of those objectives. Under such conditions, PPBS techniques can help to determine a choice among alternative methods for achieving the desired result.[17]

Even so narrow an objective, however, would, if implemented, bring a greater measure of rationality into social planning than exists at the present time.[18] Even more primitively, it would correct one of the major difficulties of the present, which is the lack of adequate service data organized in such a way as to help in the planning process. Elementary information concerning the characteristics of people receiving different types of community services and the factors that account for either their receiving or not receiving service are generally not available under present conditions.

EMERGING TECHNOLOGY

Although the data-collection and analytical tools that are now available for use are generally descriptive, qualitative, and inexact, there is a growing thrust in the human services toward the application of more rigorous and quantitative techniques. Basic to this thrust is the growing utilization of computers. Since these developments are still largely theoretical rather than operational, there is little actual experience on which to draw. We shall, however, comment on two aspects of these developments.

The first issue is a general one that refers to our discussion earlier in this chapter about the relationship of social research to social policy. It seems likely that there will continue to be a great deal of interest in utilizing systematic research for purposes of both problem identification and evaluation. In both cases, it is not sufficient to rely on the data available through the planning operations themselves, even if such planning produces an effective system of organizational reporting and accounting. For problem identification, it is necessary to have a wider framework than is represented by the participants in a planning network. One of the issues, as we have noted, is the need to bring into view possibilities for the definition of the problem that are alternatives to those prevailing at

[17] William Gorham, "Notes of a Practitioner," *The Public Interest*, Summer 1967, No. 8.

[18] See Ecklein and Lauffer, *op. cit.*, "P.P.B.S.—The Politics of Rationality and the Rationalization of Politics," Chapter 13.

any particular time. Similarly, meaningful evaluation generally requires that the results of a planning operation be judged by criteria that are not self-contained within the operation itself, since most planning has the goal not simply of making sure that certain activities take place (like providing service), but that some beneficial end result is achieved in relation to social problems.

The key to such research is to link the data collected from organizations and agencies that are involved in human services with data obtained from the population at large. To take but one simple example: to understand whom a service agency is or is not reaching, one must compare the characteristics of clients with those of the general population in the community. Such a comparison indicates whether the agency is reaching a cross-section of the population or only those who are richer or poorer, older or younger, healthier or sicker than the rest of the population. On the side of evaluation, similar linkages are necessary. For example, if one wants to know what the results of a certain intervention have been, it is necessary to compare those who have been the recipients of the intervention with others in the population who have not been.

Although there is no early prospect that the practitioner will have available a comprehensive system of data such as was visualized by Perloff, the requirements of both problem identification and evaluation lead in that general direction. With the availability of computers as a resource for processing large quantities of information, it becomes possible to think of such comprehensiveness in realistic terms. The practitioner can now build into his plan much more sophisticated proposals for data collection and processing than were possible in the past. The time is fast approaching when the use of systematic research methods will become an integral and necessary part of the practice of planning, rather than a sometime luxury.

Beyond the uses of research for problem identification and the evaluation of outcomes, there looms on the horizon the application of computer technology to the very process of planning itself. Policy science, systems analysis, and simulation are terms that are now appearing with growing regularity in the literature on social policy and planning. They represent attempts to apply methods that have been employed in fields such as space programs and defense programs to the human services field.

These developments are still at a very early stage, and it is uncertain whether the methods of decision-making that have proved effective in the "hard" fields are in truth applicable to the human services. The essential issue is whether the decision-making process in social planning can ever be sufficiently "rational" (in the terms discussed earlier in this volume) to permit the kind of quantification that is implicit in the use of the new type of technology. The case for such application is argued in the following terms by Eicker as he discusses the use of computer simulation in program planning, which "enables us to experimentally introduce new procedures, or eliminate current practices at less expense without enlisting the cooperation of different caretakers, without disturbing the present functioning of current social institutions, and without waiting for months or years to pass for the evaluation of effectiveness."[19]

"The current state of the art of computer simulation affords us the opportunity to build a symbolic model of the day to day reality of the health and welfare operating system. The model is constructed from the collection of data with respect to significant parameters, some of which being: the movement of people through networks, the number and location of decision points in the network, the decisions and transactions which occur, the number and types of personnel involved, the transmittal of information, time and costs associated with all or part of the system's operation. Using quantitative measurements or values of these and other parameters, we obtain a mathematical representation of the real and current operational system. The representational model reflects an accuracy to reality commensurate with our identification of crucial parameters and the reliable values attached to them. . . .

"The essence of simulation then is the study of a complex process over time, and the reduction of that process to a series of logical steps. It is a method of evaluation in which alternative courses of action can be examined in terms of their probable implications for the entire system under study. Its appeal as a research tool lies in its ability to render a descriptive understanding of the present and an analytic forecast of the future."[20]

On the other hand, Dror, an advocate of "policy science," argues that systems analysis is too limited an approach for the human services field because it does not take adequate account of institutional contexts, the political needs of actors to build coalitions and to achieve consensus, and all the "irrational" elements such as values, ideologies, and the charisma of individual personalities. In addition, he points out that systems analysis can deal only with alternatives that are already known and predictable and does not offer a way of bringing new alternatives to expression. Policy science is broader, more qualitative, and deals with the structure

---

[19] William F. Eicker et al. "The Application of Systems Technology to Community Mental Health," Department of Mental Health, Adolf Meyer Zone Center, Decatur, Illinois, February, 1967, pp. 55–56.
[20] *Ibid.*

for policy-making as well as with the content of the decision-making itself. Dror does acknowledge that "policy sciences hardly exists. Therefore, any proposed set of paradigms reflects more the opinions of one author than an established consensus of scholars. Furthermore, if indeed policy sciences does emerge and develop as a significant scientific and professional area—it surely will take forms and shapes which are unpredictable."[21]

In the same volume, which initiated a new periodical on policy sciences, Archibald reviews systems analysis, incrementalism, and what he calls the "clinical approach" to policy-making. Each of the approaches has limitations. Systems analysis and incrementalism are criticized as weak in providing instruments for changing organizations. A more clinical approach would involve building feasibility and acceptability into the analysis. On the other hand, a clinical approach alone gives too little attention to cognitive problem-solving. A combination of the several approaches is therefore indicated.[22]

Although the terminology is somewhat different, such issues should be familiar to the readers of this volume, since they are very similar to those discussed at several earlier points. They refer back to the different approaches to community organization and social planning in which different weights were assigned, respectively, to the cognitive problem-solving elements and to the political or interactional aspects of an organizing and planning process. Both the advocates and critics of the emerging technology recognize that both types of factors must be taken into account, but they have different estimates of the feasibility of accomplishing that purpose through quantitative methods. A severely critical view, from England, is that

". . . far from submitting gracefully to quantitative treatment, social systems are by their very nature so laden with intangible, human variables that concentration on their measurable aspects distorts the problem and confuses the issues."[23]

It would seem to the authors of this volume that there is no need to take a definitive position "for" or "against" the use of such approaches as policy analysis, systems analysis, and simulation. The issue is rather

[21] Yehezkel Dror, "Prolegomena to Policy Sciences," *Policy Sciences*, 1, No. 1, Spring 1970, pp. 135–150.

[22] K. A. Archibald, "Three Views of the Expert's Role in Policymaking: Systems Analysis, Incrementalism, and the Clinical Approach," *Policy Sciences, op. cit.*, pp. 73–86.

[23] Ida R. Hoos, "Systems Analysis in Social Policy: A Critical Review," London: The Institute of Economic Affairs, 1969, p. 25.

to clarify what the proper uses of such technical tools should be. The only ground for controversy would be the exaggerated claims of advocates of quantitative approaches as to the range of problems with which they are able to deal effectively. We have indicated at several points in this volume the need to separate for analytical purposes the various types of factors that are involved in organizing and planning processes—values, patterns of influence, and rational problem-solving methods. The newer technology can be most useful, as Holleb suggests, as a "flexible tool of management to promote organized thinking about complex problems."[24] It can help to measure program inputs, expenditures and costs, performance outputs in relation to stated objectives, and similar quantifiable aspects of planning. It cannot take cognizance of all of the factors that enter into the process, partly because not all of them are quantifiable, and partly because not all of them can be anticipated.

"In the end," writes Paul C. Watt, "the proper use of research and analysis within the context of functional resource allocation is what planning is all about, and until we can get such an approach operational we are only going to be making and talking about plans instead of implementing plans and being a participant in getting things done."[25]

The promise of technology is great, but actual achievements are elusive. "In principle, all these claims sound plausible; in practice, the promised results always seem to loom just over the horizon."[26] The reason, obviously, is the complexity of human decision-making. Yet the search for more systematic approaches is essential if the problem-solving capacity of practitioners in the human services is to be increased.

[24] Holleb, *op. cit.*, Vol. I, p. 68.
[25] Paul C. Watt, "The Value and Limits of Data-Processing," in Ernest Erber, Ed., *Urban Planning in Transition*, New York: Grossman Publishers, 1970, p. 215.
[26] George M. Raymond, "Simulation vs. Reality," in Erber, *op. cit.*, p. 209.

CHAPTER 10

The Search for Comprehensive Planning

One of the great challenges facing the practitioner, as we noted in the previous chapter, is the necessity of coordinating knowledge, influence, and resources on a scale commensurate with the human problems he is addressing. We have seen from the beginning of this text that those problems are interrelated, complex, and resistant to piecemeal efforts. The practitioner is compelled, therefore, to seek interventions that are more comprehensive in several respects.

The search for comprehensiveness in planning is in part a response to the shortcomings of policies shaped according to the specialized functions of agencies, professions, and disciplines. Second, it is an effort to marshal program resources across jurisdictional and organizational lines of responsibility. Perhaps most important, it is an attempt to deal with human problems not in terms of their symptoms but by attacking the conditions and causes from which they spring.

The practice tools that are being used in these expanding efforts at comprehensive planning are in general those we reviewed in Chapter 9. Our interest now is in the substantive matter, the actual stuff of comprehensive planning. In this chapter we shall be concerned with how this is being approached at the interface between social welfare and physical planning at the local level and where this joins with social and economic development at the regional and national levels.

Historically, as we saw in Chapter 2, many of the turn-of-the-century reformers—labor leaders, social workers, lawyers, architects, and journalists—tried to understand and act on the exploding problems of industrialization by seeing the city and its people as a whole. Devine, a social worker, spoke of this approach:

"The modern city has not yet really found itself. Its growth has been so rapid and all its intricate problems are so new that even the ablest municipal statesmen have scarcely grasped their significance, much less the average intelligent citizen. We have specialists in sanitation, in municipal architecture, in finance, in education, in transportation, each group struggling with utmost energy to understand its peculiar tasks as the modern city presents them; but we have few indeed who have even tried to get the general bearings of the manifold life of the great community to form a general idea of the citizenship of the city as it tends to become."[1]

But we also saw that the crusading of men like Devine, Riis, and Veiller tended more and more to become specialized into distinct disciplines, professions, and organizations. In the last 50 years the concern with social needs has been dispersed; this is reflected in the presence of social service coordinators in health and welfare councils, physical planners in the city administration, and social scientists in the universities.

The field of urban planning, as we find it today, has as its overall objective the creation of a more satisfactory environment in urban communities. We shall not attempt here a general description of this field, on which there is a voluminous literature.[2] Our focus is on the practice of community organization and social planning as they relate to urban planning. There is already substantial overlap—social welfare programs and community development projects, for example, are frequently integral parts of an urban planning program.

The theme "Environment for Man" was highlighted by the American Institute of Planners on the occasion of its 50th anniversary. Three volumes resulting from a series of conferences attempted to deal in a comprehensive manner and from many perspectives (philosophy, science, the arts, and the like) with problems of the environment from a long-range point of view.[3] That these are highly tentative and preliminary

[1] Edward T. Devine, *The Spirit of Social Work*, New York: Charities Publication Committee, 1911, p. 36.

[2] See, for example, the bibliography in Henry C. Hightower, "Planning Theory in Contemporary Professional Education," *Journal of the American Institute of Planners,* **XXXV**, September 1969, pp. 326–329.

[3] William R. Ewald, Jr., Ed., *Environment for Man—The Next Fifty Years, 1967; Environment and Change—The Next Fifty Years, 1968;* and *Environment and Policy —The Next Fifty Years, 1968*—all published by the Indiana University Press, Bloomington, Indiana.

efforts is indicated in the introduction to the first volume, in which the editor observes, "Do we know how to define and work toward 'Optimum Environment with Man as the Measure?' To date neither optimum nor environment has been defined, nor have we made an adequate beginning at measuring man." It was the purpose of these proceedings to *"begin the answers to such questions."*[4] (Emphasis in the original.)

Recent planning literature sounds the recurring theme that physical planning in itself is too limited an approach to deal with the needs of contemporary urban communities, but that the physical planners must concern themselves deeply with the social factors that are inherent in their responsibilities. The following are representative statements:

"Having been assigned responsibility for guiding land-use patterns, we seek . . . to induce those patterns that will effectively increase accessibility to the diverse opportunities for productive social intercourse that are latent in an advanced civilization."[5]

"In the long run . . . it seems clear that the future of city planning lies less in the reliance upon land-use plans than in the development of the range of methods that will guarantee the improvement of those aspects of community life that are most in need of improvement."[6]

The retreat from over-specialization and the revival of the historic connection between physical and social planning were a response to the staggering problems of the post-World War II period—the rediscovery of poverty, the acknowledgement that minority groups had been largely excluded from the mainstream of society, and the recognition that our cities were in a crisis compounded of decay and conflict. This raised starkly the question as to whether planning and action along separate lines of physical, social, and economic development could cope with such problems. Experience seemed to indicate not only that fragmented planning was grossly inadequate when addressed to complex and interrelated human issues, but also that one-dimensional actions in fact exacerbated the problems.

We propose in this chapter to explore some of the attempts at multi-

---

[4] William R. Ewald, Jr., Ed., *Environment for Man, op. cit.,* p. 3.

[5] Melvin M. Webber, "Comprehensive Planning and Social Responsibility," *Journal of the American Institute of Planners,* **XXIX,** November 1963, pp. 232–241. Reprinted in Bernard J. Frieden and Robert Morris, Eds., *Urban Planning and Social Policy,* New York: Basic Books, 1968, p. 12.

[6] Herbert J. Gans, "Social and Physical Planning for the Elimination of Urban Poverty," *Washington University Law Quarterly,* No. 1, February 1963, pp. 2–18. Reprinted in Frieden and Morris, *op. cit.,* p. 52.

dimensional planning by focusing on the social component in a number of contexts, beginning with an example from public housing and moving progressively to more complex situations. Several case illustrations will be used for this purpose.

THE COMMUNITY SERVICES APPROACH

One of the most specific and well-defined functions of social planning within a physical planning context involves the development of community services as an integral aspect of new housing facilities. As a case illustration we take the experience of a Community Services Planning Unit in a public housing authority in a major American city.

This unit serves as an arm of the authority's planning function. It comes into play, typically, after a decision has been made to construct a housing project in a certain location, with a certain number of square feet available for community facilities and services. It is then the responsibility of the Community Services Planning Unit to recommend what services shall be offered and to make clear what are the implications for the physical design and location of the community facilities.

The social planners gather whatever information is available on the population in the area and on the availability of community services and facilities. They visit and inspect the area where the new project is to be built and conduct their own limited survey, which will include an effort to ascertain the preferences and desires of the population bordering the new housing site. As tentative decisions are made about the services to be provided, agencies are contacted as potential sponsors and, if they agree to provide a particular service, they are brought into the planning process. These are public or private agencies who offer such services as day care, recreation, health clinics, or family counseling.

Different tasks fall to the planners in connection with housing projects that are already in operation. Here it is important for the planners continually to readjust the social services available to the tenants. One of the resources for facilitating this feedback and modification process is the statistical department, which maintains a flow of current information on the characteristics of tenants. Such information can help to determine, for example, changes in the need for programs for the aged, for mothers with preschool children, or for teenagers. An important tool, whose absence is lamented by the planners, is the capability to carry out evaluative research on programs that have already been implemented. The tenants, from their point of view, tend to distrust the planners as being part of the management apparatus with which they are frequently in conflict. One of the tasks of the planners, then, is to ascertain the desires and preferences of the tenants as an important input in the cycle of planning, monitoring, and readjusting programs to fit changing conditions and needs.

There are a number of questions in terms of planning for the construction of housing projects in the future. It takes several years to move from the earliest stages of planning through construction; the recommendations of the planners may turn out to be inappropriate in view of changes in both the size and characteristics of the population. Here again, a continuing flow of data during the period of planning will help to minimize the effects of poor population projections.

Those responsible for planning the community services must relate to the general planning department of the housing authority and through it to the City Planning Commission. Despite efforts to maintain these lines of communication, the planners find that they do not have sufficient time or staff to coordinate their work with others who are planning for the same neighborhoods, such as the Health Department, the Board of Education, churches, and transportation agencies.

With respect to his position in the housing authority itself, the social planner sees the importance of trying to influence policy at the highest levels in order to achieve "social objectives." But there may be difficulties here too, depending on the planner's status within the organization and the amount of influence he can exert on the decision-makers. For example, the planner may see the importance of revising the authority's eligibility rules, which currently have the effect of excluding many people with special needs and problems. Or he may desire to influence the size and spatial distribution of apartments that influence the character of the tenant population to be housed in a new project. Certain decisions may keep out large families that have great difficulty finding housing in the private market.

The limitations of the "community service approach" are obvious from this description. They lie in the compartmentalization of the "social" factors as specialized services for which provision needs to be made, rather than as integral aspects of the total planning of the environment.

NEW TOWNS APPROACH

An effort to overcome such limitations is found in our second example, which is that of one of the most recent and ambitious new towns now being developed in England.

The decision to develop a city of 250,000 to provide for the growing population of southeast England, especially the overspill from London, was reached in the mid-1960's by a number of local, regional, and national planning bodies. The Corporation that was set up by the government to plan the new city of Milton Keynes decided at the outset that the plan should describe and define the character of life that the new city should provide. The plan would have to take into account social and economic trends that will shape the requirements for the city at the end of this century; it would also have to attempt to meet present realities and needs.

The planners chose to avoid a detailed blueprint and opted instead for a framework of objectives within which the social and economic development of the city would be guided and detailed decisions could be made. The six broad goals adopted early in the planning process were:

1. Opportunity and freedom of choice in education, work, housing, recreation, and other activities and services.
2. Easy movement and access through public and private transportation and good communications.
3. Balance and variety in the age, racial, and socioeconomic groups making up the new community.
4. A city that is attractive to the eye.
5. Public awareness and a high degree of participation in community activities.
6. An efficient and imaginative use of resources.

The Corporation was determined to consider the social aspects of the plan as fully as the physical. This was done in two ways—first by examining all physical proposals for their social implications and, second, by preparing a social development program. Social development in Milton Keynes was seen as the process by which residents would learn to use existing social institutions, services, and agencies and would develop new instrumentalities in areas not provided for.

The nature of the planner's task can be seen in this listing of the components in the social development program:

—Orienting new arrivals to Milton Keynes.
—Community development in the sense of encouraging residents to create their own community life and to find the means of expressing their needs and discontents.
—Promotion of facilities for community activities, especially for recreation and leisure pursuits.

—Identifying the existence and needs of special groups, such as the handicapped or housebound mothers or old people, and developing the services and facilities for them.

—Evaluation and review of the New Town's progress by all interests concerned.

—Public relations and the dissemination of information.

—Cooperation with public authorities providing services and with voluntary groups and churches.

—Close cooperation with housing management to spot indicators of dissatisfaction.

—Use of requests for information and advise as indicators of needs.

—Links with employers, especially to improve the skills and opportunities of the residents.

The planners were particularly concerned about anticipating and providing for two problems—"the New Town blues" and social imbalance. The first refers to the anxieties and dissatisfactions experienced in a new environment, particularly one that lacks in its early stage of development variety and quality in entertainment, shopping, transport, and specialized services. This would call for giving attention to the social processes and structures through which people meet their "less tangible needs, such as those of status, support, affiliation, and crises such as bereavement, unemployment, handicap, etc."

The achievement of "social balance" illustrates particularly well the social component in overall planning. The formulation of the goal itself and then its translation into operational terms truly represent social planning—or the social aspect of comprehensive planning. Thus, avoiding uniformity of the population in terms of age, class, and occupation meant attracting certain kinds of economic enterprise to the community and planning housing types and the rate at which households with different characteristics would be brought to the new town. It also meant "socially conscious" decisions about the location of facilities, like schools, as a means of encouraging people to mix across class and age lines.

THE LESSONS OF URBAN RENEWAL

Although there is some increase in the United States in the establishment of new communities, this has not been the typical way of dealing with urban development. A much more important field to be considered for the lessons that might be derived in regard to comprehensive planning is urban renewal, which was one of a number of Federal programs in the 1950's designed to arrest the process of urban deterioration. One of its main purposes was to eliminate slums, which were thought of largely in physical terms—congested neighborhoods and deteriorated structures —rather than in terms of the needs and problems of the people living there. As the program developed, the social aspects of urban problems became more dramatically visible and the limitations of a strictly physical approach more evident.

It is probably a fair assumption that social objectives were implicit in the urban renewal plans. The line of thinking was based on the long-standing assumptions of city planning that the physical environment determines behavior. As Webber puts it:

"The clearly prescribed therapy for the various social pathologies was improvement of the physical setting. If only well-designed and well-sited houses and playgrounds, and community facilities could be substituted for the crowded and dilapidated housing and neighborhoods of the city's slums, then the incidence of crime, delinquency, narcotics addiction, alcoholism, broken homes, and mental illness would tumble. Acculturation of ethnic, racial, and other minority groups to the American, middle-class, urban ways-of-life but awaited their introduction to the American, middle-class, physical environment."[7]

It is a matter of dispute as to how successful or unsuccessful the program of urban renewal has been in relation to its objectives. Indeed, these differences of opinion involve some dispute as to what the essential objectives actually were. As is typical of many of the post-World War II social reform programs of the United States, there were multiple objectives, which means that different analysts are able to reach different conclusions based on which elements of the program they stress.

Urban renewal, since it involves slum clearance, is necessarily closely related to the problems of housing. It is not, however, a housing program *per se*. It was one of a series of programs related to urban blight. The housing program, dating back to the Housing Act of 1949, is a program in its own right. Some commentators, therefore, take the view that the urban renewal program should not be judged on the basis of its failure to achieve a large volume of new housing for poor people, since this was not its primary objective. Its central purpose was to restore the economic viability of the central city—to make it attractive both to business enterprise and to middle-class residents. Tax revenue would increase as a result, the city would be in a better position to finance its services, and

[7] Frieden and Morris, *op. cit.*, p. 10.

the improved physical environment would help to arrest the growth of concentrated social problems in the slums.

Urban renewal has been severely criticized. The criticisms (and the responses to them) may be summarized as follows:

1. The people who were displaced were not rehoused. It did not help poor people. The inexpensive slum dwellings that were taken down were replaced (because of the land values in the inner-city areas) by very expensive dwellings clearly beyond the economic capacity of the residents. The reply to this criticism is that urban renewal was but a segment of the housing legislation and did not have the responsibility to construct low-income housing.
2. Subsidies were provided for private industry. The response here is that all housing legislation had this effect, since this was the way to get housing built.
3. Urban renewal did not actually create more housing. There is a dispute concerning the figures regarding the number of units taken down and new ones built. It does seem clear, however, that the construction of new housing for slum dwellers fell far short of the number of units destroyed.
4. Urban renewal creates new slums by moving slum dwellers to other blighted areas. Here, too, there is a dispute over the figures, with the government claiming that 80 percent of those displaced did obtain housing that conforms to standards.
5. Some of the slum clearance was unnecessary. Minor rehabilitation could have provided a good deal of adequate housing. Much of it was not in fact substandard. Communities were disrupted, with consequent social and psychological damage.[8]
6. Urban renewal did not take account of the barriers to rehousing in other areas due to discrimination and local resistance. This is part of the general problem that accounts for the inadequacy of low-income housing.
7. Over and beyond these criticisms, urban renewal has revealed the complexity of the problems relating to urban poverty and social deprivation. It has become clear that the problem is not one of

---

[8] Studies of the West End urban renewal project in Boston were a major factor in highlighting such problems. See Marc Fried, "Grieving for a Lost Home: Psychological Costs of Relocation," in Leonard J. Duhl, Ed., *The Urban Condition*, New York: Basic Books, Inc., 1963, Chapter 12. Other articles on relocation will be found in James Q. Wilson, Ed., *Urban Renewal: The Record and The Controversy*, Cambridge: M.I.T. Press, 1966. Wilson's is a comprehensive compilation dealing with all aspects of urban renewal.

housing alone but involves employment, education, and all kinds of special service needs.

Another important aspect of the history of urban renewal is the evolution of community participation as an element in the program. Originally this was conceived in minimal terms, the legislation calling merely for a public hearing before the acquisition of land. In the early period, community participation was used essentially to solicit support for urban renewal proposals. The approach changed fundamentally as militant efforts were launched to resist urban renewal schemes. Eventually, the programs were adjusted to those protests and also to the more general trends, as reflected in anti-poverty programs, toward representing community groups in the policy-making structures of the local agencies.

This brief review of the urban renewal experience provides the background for examining the emergence during the past decade of various approaches to social planning within the urban community context. One direct consequence of the experience is that social factors are increasingly being built into physical planning. Greater sensitivity to the problems of people dwelling in slum areas and their needs in regard to relocation is an example of this. The restraint placed on demolition, the emphasis on the rehabilitation of old housing, and the concern with the retention of old neighborhoods for their possible social values all reflect the learnings of the past that physical plans have social consequences that need to be taken into consideration. One of the most recent innovations, in the form of rent supplements, substitutes money for the provision of housing, enabling some people with inadequate income to secure better housing through ordinary market channels.

DEMONSTRATION PROGRAMS

Approaches to more comprehensive planning were introduced in the United States during the decade that began with the Kennedy administration in 1960. With the largely negative experience of urban renewal programs and the pressure of the civil rights movement in the background, the situation was ripe for experimentation with new programs. At this point, a connection was made between the developments within the physical planning field, which were already moving toward a more social orientation, and ideas about the way in which economic opportunities could be improved in order to attack the problem of poverty.

The notion of a more coordinated and comprehensive attack on urban problems was sparked in no small measure by the approach to juvenile delinquency developed by Ohlin and Cloward, who argued that delinquency represented a response to the blockage of opportunities.[9] A procession of new programs—delinquency control, the "war on poverty," the Model Cities program—was directed especially at deteriorating neighborhoods and sought to employ a battery of interventions. These were based on the premise that there needed to be simultaneous and coordinated improvements in education and job training, health, and housing, as well as organization and action by disadvantaged people to protect and advance their own interests.

Several works have appeared that describe the history of the Federal programs of the 1960's, and others will be forthcoming.[10] A variety of lessons is being derived from the experiences in those programs. Some of the methods of organizing and planning that were developed in the Federal programs were discussed in earlier chapters. At this point, our focus is not on methodology as much as it is on identifying a field of work. The question is, what are the new kinds of structures, programs, services, and activities that have emerged during the past decade and that can be identified as areas for the practice of community organization and social planning? How are these similar to or different from the fields of work that have been described earlier in this text?

The successive waves of demonstration programs directed to low-income neighborhoods have all reached for some degree of comprehensiveness in working on social problems. The programs have differed in the scope and variety of services that they have tried to encompass, with the latest effort—the Model Cities program—being the most ambitious. Two basic limitations were, however, common to all the programs and constrained the degree to which they could achieve their goals of comprehensiveness. One limiting factor was their status as "demonstration" programs rather than ongoing, permanent service structures. The other was their focus on the low-income neighborhood as the planning area.

A demonstration program is, by definition, not permanent. It is designed to provide, in a limited time period, a test of proposed measures. In theory, demonstrations should determine whether proposed programs are desirable. If they are proven to be desirable, it is implied that they should then be transformed from demonstrations to more stable, per-

---

[9] Richard A. Cloward and Lloyd E. Ohlin, *Delinquency and Opportunity*, Glencoe, Ill.: The Free Press, 1960.

[10] A few examples are Marris and Rein, *op. cit.*; Sar A. Levitan, *op. cit.*; Louis A. Ferman, Ed., "Evaluating the War on Poverty," *The Annals*, Vol. 385, September 1969.

manent services or activities and generalized to the population for whose benefit the demonstration was undertaken.

One of the central ambiguities in all of the Federal demonstration programs of the 1960's was the confusion of goals between testing out new approaches to problems and functioning as a channel for the distribution (or redistribution) of resources. The scale of funding involved in these activities, especially under the anti-poverty legislation, was substantial enough to be significant politically. The programs became important factors in the attempt of the Federal government to deal with the problems of deprivation and unrest in the inner cities. In order to serve those functions, it became necessary to distribute funds with some equity or some political astuteness as among different states and communities, quite apart from any of the considerations that were relevant to the testing out of program innovations. What started as a demonstration, therefore, became primarily a channel for the distribution of additional resources to the ghettoes.

The point has been made repeatedly in the commentaries on the anti-poverty and related programs that the criteria for a *bona fide* demonstration were never fulfilled. Since objectives were always diffuse, it was frequently not clear exactly what outcome was being sought and how it would be determined whether the outcome had or had not been achieved. In addition, activities were not limited to the scale compatible with rigorous demonstration criteria but tended to become elaborated on the basis of extraneous factors such as their popularity or political usefulness. In other words, programs were expanded and generalized before their efficacy had been demonstrated.

Perhaps most damaging to the objectives of the demonstration approach was the absence of genuine evaluation of programs. Rigorous evaluation would have required carefully controlled experimental methods, with programs not only limited in scale but also set up in such a way that the variables being tested could be controlled and measured carefully and accurately. The multiplicity of objectives that was built into the programs made it inevitable that the purposes of scientific evaluation would be contradicted by some of the policy and programmatic requirements of administering funds to which various groups in the communities made claims.

On the other hand, the Federal demonstration programs did not take the alternative path of adopting overall national policies for general implementation throughout the country as was done, for example, in the case of the mental health program. Specific service or program entities, such as Head Start or legal services, did in fact become "national programs" in the sense that a general format was developed for them and financial support was provided to local communities to carry them out. These "package" programs were limited to single services. The efforts toward comprehensive planning were treated as demonstrations, subject to local initiative, with funds available not to all who applied but to those proposals that the Federal administrators considered most promising on the basis of the criteria being followed for conducting the demonstration program. The criteria actually used were mixed, as we have indicated.

The second major limitation in all of these programs in addition to their ambiguous status as demonstrations is that they were defined within a *neighborhood* context. It was the purpose of the programs to focus on the needs of the most deprived populations. While such a purpose might have taken the form, for example, of a general national policy on income maintenance, the programs chose instead to focus on the low-income neighborhood as the framework for planning.

In the limited, localized, and avowedly experimental approaches to the attack on social problems that were employed by the United States in the 1960's, "comprehensiveness" seems to have been a combination of elements discussed in previous chapters—community development, social action, and social welfare programs. The most recent of the Federal programs addressed to the urban environment—the Model Cities program—will serve as an example of how these approaches were combined in an attempt to achieve more comprehensive planning.

The Model Cities program has made a bid toward greater comprehensiveness than was achieved by the demonstration programs that preceded it. The program was initiated by the newly created Department of Housing and Urban Development (HUD) and therefore had a physical planning base that was not present in the others. The following sketch, which is based on an actual Model Cities program in a large city, will indicate the scope of these efforts. The organizational structure for conducting the Model City program is known as the "city demonstration agency" (CDA), which is established by the city government. This is a professionally staffed agency. There is also a citizens' governing board that has subdivisions representing different areas within the model neighborhood.

Perhaps a third of the program is related to the "hardware" areas of housing, transportation, and environmental development. The objectives in this respect are quite ambitious and beyond what is actually achievable within the limitations of the program. In our example, the objective is stated as the replacement or reconstruction of 80 percent of the existing housing in the model neighborhood. Such an achievement being beyond reach, specific goals are established for a short-range period of perhaps two years that call for specified numbers of units in each of several categories. The largest number will be new housing units for people with low and moderate incomes. About half as many units are scheduled for rehabilitation and a still smaller number for repair.

The planning responsibility of the Model Cities agency, however, is stated in much broader terms. It is responsible for coordinating the full range of the model neighborhood projects that are financed with Federal HUD funds. But it also has responsibility for somehow relating those programs to projects stemming from local government and/or from other Federal programs that impinge on the model neighborhood area. The agency, as part of city government, is also expected to fit into the general framework of planning that has been laid down by the city planning commission. The image, then, is one of a high-level, centralized planning body that is an integral part of city government and has a general mandate to plan for the model neighborhood in a way that will integrate all facets of the city's planning and program resources in a concerted attack on the problems of that neighborhood.

One may ask what tools or mechanisms the Model City demonstration agency has to fulfill these ambitious functions and how adequate they are to the task. That is not a question that can be answered as yet. However, it is instructive for our purposes to note that some methodology is beginning to develop as the agencies tackle these enlarged responsibilities.

The major "tool" that seems to be emerging is a system for the processing of information, which is then tied into a system for evaluation. This might be called a monitoring system or an intelligence and feedback system. The intention is to have it reach not only the programs financed directly through the demonstration agency but also the programs operating in the Model City area through other sources.

Several additional tools are put into the hands of the Model City agency. It has command over certain resources that put it in a position to implement plans along the lines of physical development. For example, funds are made available to sponsor repair projects and to take up land options. It is thus possible for the planning agency to begin to intervene in the physical development of the model area, taking command over parcels of land or granting funds for repairs. One interesting feature from the point of view of community organization is the authorization to help organize and finance non-profit corporations of an indigenous type, made up of residents in the model neighborhood. Grants can be made for down payments, for rehabilitation, and for purchase or rental of housing. Assistance can also be given to tenant organizations to form cooperatives. The indigenous groups that are emerging as sponsors of projects are given further help through consultation and instruction in how to perform their sponsorship responsibilities.

In short, at least conceptually, there is a comprehensive approach here that starts with a general plan of physical development and carries through to the point of (a) monitoring all developments that impinge on that plan, (b) parceling out the pieces of the plan for implementation by a variety of agents—cooperatives, indigenous non-profit neighborhood corporations, tenants organizations, et al., and (c) using resources directly to help achieve the plans as well as consultation in formulating them.

In all of this, coordinating and planning work in two directions. On the one hand, the agency is in close working communication with indigenous groups in the area. Thus, its neighborhood loan and grant project is administered by a body made up of elected representatives from a number of sub-areas in which the development is to take place. At the same time, the agency is clearly an instrument of local government and is responsible for establishing liaison with the activities of other governmental departments that are relevant to the work of the Model Cities areas and its own projects. It is in effect a bridge between governmental resources and indigenous citizen participation.

One program that exemplifies this kind of amalgam is "physical development," which in our illustration is under the jurisdiction of a new model neighborhood development corporation that was actually formed by the city demonstration agency. This corporation is made up of residents chosen by the overall citizens' governing board from those who live in several sub-areas that are being affected by the redevelopment, together with representatives from the city demonstration agency, the city planning commission, the housing commission, and other official bodies.

The other major areas that are included in the program, in addition to housing and physical development, are manpower (employment and training), education, health, and social service. All of these have been represented to some degree in earlier demonstration programs as well. In what way are they more integrated or "comprehensive" under the Model Cities framework, where they are developed and administered by the same agency that also has responsibility for physical development and housing? It is not yet clear that there is such a difference. As a matter of fact, the preliminary evidence seems to be that the Model Cities are subject to the same difficulties and limitations that have affected the "software" programs in all of the earlier demonstration programs.

Employment and education are the most difficult areas for somewhat different reasons. In the case of employment, it is the general functioning of the economy, determined by forces lying outside the neighborhood, that controls the crucial variable—that is, the availability of jobs. In the case of education, there is continuing frustration due to the general lack of resources and the lack of success of programs that have attempted to raise the levels of achievement in the low-income areas—and the lack of adequate knowledge as to the reasons for these conditions or how they can be overcome.

The planning in our "model" Model Cities neighborhood calls for the creation of several thousand new jobs in the ensuing five years. A "social indicator" type of target is defined. It is to bring down the unemployment rate in the Model Cities neighborhood, which is now much higher than that for the city as a whole, so that it is comparable to the general rate. It is difficult to see, however, just how this goal is to be accomplished. As in earlier demonstration programs, the approach to manpower planning frequently reflects some confusion between two levels—the provision of jobs, and the training of residents to improve their competitive position in the search for jobs by acquiring additional skills. Thus, the program calls for attempts to expand the job opportunities in some respects, particularly in the construction industry through the introduction of residents as apprentices, but mostly to develop more skills through basic education, training programs, and ancillary services like health and day-care provisions. In the end, the greatest expansion of employment opportunities will probably take place through the Model Cities program itself, which creates various positions of a human service character, as did the earlier demonstration programs.

In the model city chosen as a prototype for this review, it is noteworthy that the budget for education was reduced in the second funding year by more than half, reflecting the lack of success in the approaches that had been attempted. The pervasive element in further planning in this field is the search for better solutions. No dramatic new approaches have emerged, but it is apparently proposed to pursue a limited number of available program ideas in a more systematic and controlled manner than previously, in the hope that some further learnings will emerge that can be applied more widely.

A number of task forces on education are being established to consider several areas and hopefully to propose new methods of tackling problems. Emphasis is also being placed on close collaboration among faculty, students, and community. Councils are to be formed whereby these elements may work together. The goals have been scaled down. It is now hoped that programs may help to raise the level of achievement of students by a limited amount each year, rather than seeking more immediate realization of the ultimate goal of bringing all students up to the norms for achievement at grade level.

The health program is another stab at comprehensiveness. In addition to bringing batteries of health and ancillary services together in the form of neighborhood health centers, which had been typical of earlier demonstration programs, the Model Cities program is adding an innovative approach to the *financing* of medical care. Comprehensive service will be tied to a general prepayment medical-care plan that will be administered in a portion of the Model Cities neighborhood for a population of approximately 10,000. This is not full coverage of the population, but it *is* comprehensive coverage for this segment of the population.

Planning in the social services area also goes somewhat beyond the scope of earlier Federal demonstration programs, but does not go fully into the income maintenance area. (Other experiments are under way in an attempt to evaluate the efficacy of certain types of negative income tax and work incentive proposals.) There is, however, some use of money, in the form of loans and grants for special purposes that are not covered by public assistance.

More generally, the Model Cities agency sponsors a public benefits office, which is a type of information and referral service whose purpose is to inform residents of the area concerning the financial assistance that is available through the government and the procedures required to qualify for such aid. The agency is also playing another kind of role in helping to form a larger consortium of the voluntary agencies, so that better coordination of services can be achieved and the resources of the voluntary sector integrated into the plans of the CDA (city demonstration agency).

The breakdown of the budget indicates the emerging emphases and character of the Model Cities program. The largest outlay of funds was for physical development and housing, representing about 30 percent of the total. About one fourth of the total budget was spent for central administration, planning, and community development (for example, the service provided the citizens' governing board, a youth council, and the like). Roughly similar sums were spent, respectively, on economic and social service type programs—about 12 to 13 percent on each. Economic programs included both employment and retraining and business grants and loans; social services included crime and delinquency and recreation and cultural services as well as the usual information, referral, and counseling functions. Health services accounted for about 10 percent and education for the smallest share of all, 8 percent.

There are three levels to the program-financing structure. The CDA does the planning and budgeting, administering some programs itself and contracting others out to other agencies, non-profit neighborhood corporations, and indigenous groups. To perform these functions, the CDA obtains funds from HUD—these are known as Model City Supplemental Funds. The local government makes a large contribution to the administrative budget of the CDA. Second, program funds are obtained from other Federal agencies, such as the Labor Department or the National Institute of Mental Health, in relation to plans made by the CDA. These are channeled through the CDA mechanism.

The third level, and the most problematic one, is the integration into the planning for the model neighborhood of programs that are under the jurisdiction of other agencies and are neither funded nor administered by the CDA. Here there is no clear leverage on the part of the CDA that would enable it to establish some control over the planning and implementation of programs. It is dependent on powers of negotiation and persuasion to achieve the voluntary cooperation that may be necessary for the coordination of programs. Attempts to achieve change in the planning and operations of other agencies call for somewhat different procedures and rest on different preconditions than those attempted in areas where the CDA has operational responsibilities and the resources to implement them.

METROPOLITAN AND REGIONAL PLANNING

Many of the same elements found in planning for neighborhoods and communities persist as one moves to the broader canvas of metropolitan areas or regions, although in somewhat altered forms and proportions. Geographic and time scales increase, and there is some tendency to be more concerned with general guiding policies than with immediate programs. This is illustrated in the recommendations for planning in the

Boston metropolitan area, which speak of a "10-year area-wide comprehensive plan and program . . . related to a more general and longer-range transportation and regional development plan."[11]

Several aspects of planning at this level are of interest to us. First is the strong pull toward *comprehensiveness*. In his useful text drawn primarily from experience in Asia, Africa, and Europe, Gillie argues that the essence of regional planning is that it deals with a number of factors and their interrelationships "in the actual tangle" in which they exist.[12]

The Boston document calls for an effort that would encompass studies of housing needs; economic development; and public services —that is, sewer and water facilities, health and education, secondary roads, and airports. The planning would need to take into account the fact that "changing technology, rising incomes, and rapid suburbanization of both families and businesses have transformed the physical landscape and substantially altered the social and economic character of the metropolis"—factors that are certainly in a "tangle"!

There is another sense in which this planning is pulled toward comprehensiveness. Boston with its 600,000 people and the adjacent 75 cities and towns with some two million people are an integral part of the economy and transportation system of New England. Goals and policies for the larger area inevitably affect and are affected by decisions and actions in and around Boston. In the same way, Gillie speaks of regional planning as part of national planning, "the new modern movement to manage the affairs of nations in a more constructive, considered and far-sighted manner."[13]

Our second observation, which touches also on the comprehensive nature of planning for large populations and geographic areas, centers on the increasing emphasis given to *social considerations*. "Human affairs" predominate in the work of a regional planner, and one of his major concerns, Gillie writes, must be changes in the size, location, and characteristics of the people and their social organization. In the Boston illustration this meant, for example, disparities in income and housing opportunities for minorities and the struggle of suburban governments to keep pace with their population growth.

[11] *Planning Metropolitan Boston*, Cambridge: The Joint Center for Urban Studies of the Massachusetts Institute of Technology and Harvard University, 1967, pp. 1–16.

[12] F. B. Gillie, *Basic Thinking in Regional Planning*, The Hague: Mouton & Co., 1967, p. 13.

[13] *Ibid.*, p. 11.

Gillie devotes considerable attention to social problems, which he defines, positively and negatively, as "those which can be affected by the way in which development is managed or which have to be dealt with if development is not to be hindered."[14] He places poverty first in importance and urges the planner to study its causes and to judge which economic measures will reduce it and which will leave wealthy islands within a sea of poverty. Second priority goes to education, partly because it is a "key to the solution of other problems." Housing is third, followed by ill health, which Gillie notes may require not modern hospitals but undramatic things like improvements in diet, sanitation, and social habits.

It is instructive to look at what Gillie calls the existence of unsound and obsolete institutions. He suggests a line of analysis based on the notion that "unless one knows why the old system went wrong, the new system may all too easily go the same way too." The planner needs to answer these questions: What exactly is the trouble and how are people being affected by the problem? Why did the offending institution come into being and what purposes does it still serve? If it is to be abolished, what can be put in its place?

The final point has to do with the form and purpose of "the plan," which is presumably the outcome of planning. On the one hand, it "has little in common with an architect's plan, which seeks to achieve a single executive result in precise detail."[15] On the other hand, the traditional "master plan," often elegant but unnoticed, is giving ground to more realistic policy and programs guides. The Boston report urges a general planning strategy based on a balance between "today's needs and tomorrow's aspirations,"[16] and advocates a product that tempers the concern for the conventional master plan with an equal interest in short-term planning. The explanation points to the "incremental, fragmented, and short-term character of the vast majority of current public decisions," which can make exclusively long-range planning unreal, risky, and frequently not worth the costs.

NATIONAL POLICY DEVELOPMENT

Several terms are used to indicate the next higher level of comprehensive planning: "national policy development," "national planning,"

---

[14] *Ibid.*, p. 78.
[15] *Ibid.*, p. 11.
[16] *Planning Metropolitan Boston, op. cit.*, p. 13.

or what the United Nations refers to as "social development," which is applied to both developing and highly industrialized countries. The frame of reference now shifts from the physical environment, which is most important at the local level, to the economic structure of society.

The social planner's responsibilities at the national level center on policies governing the social services, but increasingly extend beyond to the social aspects of economic or development planning. We saw much the same thing in the extension of the social planner's role in new town development. At the national level he participates with others in formulating objectives and priorities with respect to production goals, the rate of economic growth, and desired types and levels of employment. To a considerable extent social services are then planned so as to make a maximum contribution toward achieving those goals. In this context "social services" is usually used to include education, health, and housing as well as the traditional personal services.

Perhaps it is easier to see the outlines of planning at the national level not by looking first at the United States but by turning to experiences in other countries.[17] From its perspective the United Nations sees the importance of balancing and integrating economic and social development in these terms: (1) the need to deal with the *social consequences* of economic development, (2) the necessity for overcoming *social obstacles* to economic growth, and (3) the *positive role* of social factors in furthering economic development.[18] A UN report states the position succinctly:

"Instead of treating social policy as a handmaid whose function is to tidy up human suffering and insecurity left in the wake of economic development, social objectives should be built on an equal footing with economic objectives into comprehensive social and economic planning."[19]

There is a hiatus, however, between these grand aims and the practical means of operationalizing them. The UN report makes it clear that there are no "quantitative criteria" for determining which aspect of social development should receive how much investment, and the report calls for empirical studies to build knowledge of this type. What are

17 See, for example, Albert Waterston, *Development Planning: Lessons of Experience,* Baltimore: The Johns Hopkins Press, 1965.

18 *Report on the World Social Situation,* New York: United Nations, 1961.

19 *Report on a Co-ordinated Policy Regarding Family Levels of Living,* United Nations Publication Sales No. 57, Iv. 7, p. 18. Quoted in *Report on the World Social Situation, op. cit.,* p. 23.

available are much more general guidelines and broad policy statements. These are taken from the same UN document:

1. Some social goals represent self-sufficient value commitments that
cannot be justified on the basis of economic benefits, such as adequate care of people incapacitated by chronic diseases. This, however, does not relieve planners of the obligation to calculate the
economic costs of such programs.
2. It is essential to identify and as far as feasible measure the social
costs and consequences of economic measures, such as the rapid
mechanization of agriculture.
3. Although the absolute and relative amounts of money spent on
social purposes tend to rise as the national income increases, social
and economic development do not necessarily proceed at the same
rate. Differences and imbalances crop up. Not enough is known
about this to provide reliable guides. Planning decisions are therefore based on past experience, political priorities, and limited,
special studies. Some programs, however, appear to be strategic
points of intervention for either fostering economic progress or
resolving urgent social problems and should receive priority attention.

The decisions on social development are reached, of course, through
political processes and channels. Differences in political orientation and
tradition will determine the extent and form of citizen participation in
policy-making. They will also affect the balance between centralization
of decision-making and decentralization. The tendency in the period
since World War II has been for highly centralized governments, including some in Communist countries, to decentralize some of their decision-
making and program operations.[20] Discussions are now going on in the
United States and Britain about the centralization of some functions
and the simultaneous diffusion of responsibility for other functions to
regional and local levels. The current move toward revenue-sharing
between Washington and the states is on the side of decentralization.

Even when social planners take part in overall planning of development, their specific responsibilities have to do with the social "sector"
and the social services. Typically they are even more specialized and
deal with only one sector within the social sphere, defined either around

[20] *International Survey of Programmes of Social Development,* New York: United
Nations, 1959, pp. 122–125.

a particular problem (e.g., juvenile delinquency or illiteracy) or a specific field of service, such as elementary schools, prisons, or hospitals. In large and economically developed countries, this kind of specialization at the national level results in a vast network of organizations. It is this network—or rather its components—that is most familiar in the United States.

The most visible aspect of social planning at the national level in this country is the "national program," which extends from the executive and legislative branches of government in Washington down through the state capitals to local constituencies. These vertical programs seek to maintain horizontal relationships with other programs in the human resources system at every level.

Another example of national program development, closely allied with the mental retardation program discussed in Chapter 9, has been in the field of mental health. As the outcome of an ambitious national study, followed by Federal legislation and appropriations and the issuance of administrative guidelines or "regs," a program of comprehensive mental health services has been launched throughout the country. Federal monies are made available to states and through them to localities, which present plans for comprehensive services in line with the regulations adopted in Washington. For instance, one important expectation was that a local comprehensive program should include emergency, inpatient, outpatient and partial hospitalization services, and provision for consultation and education in the community.[21]

Substantial national resources have been available in the past in the field of mental health, and national policies have been more influential than in some other areas. However, considerable latitude remains for local and state organizations to make decisions on the nature of the program they consider necessary in view of the needs and problems as they see them. Thus, for example, one community may emphasize treatment programs for drug addicts or alcoholics; another, psychiatric services to families; and another, improving its preventive work through consultation to local schools, police, and other institutions.

When a social need is clearly recognized and a mode of intervention widely accepted, as in the case of social insurance against physical disabilities, a national program provides a universal benefit or service available to the whole population. Here the concern is coverage and equal

---

[21] *The Comprehensive Community Mental Health Center,* National Institute of Mental Health, Public Health Service Publication No. 1137, April 1964, Washington, D.C.: U.S. Government Printing Office, p. 21.

treatment of those being served. By contrast, there are no clear-cut approaches to many of our contemporary problems and hence no commitment to a broad, well-supported program. This has led to the strategy of pilot and experimental programs, in which the national input is addressed to stimulating innovations in the search for better answers. This has often been compromised by political pressures, inadequate evaluation, or the rapid proliferation of experimental programs as substitutes for really comprehensive programs.[22]

National social planning or social development brings back into our view an issue we considered in the discussion of community development.[23] This concerns the relationship of grass-roots activities and neighborhood projects to intervention at the national level. We concluded from that survey that community development efforts by themselves, without adequate national policies and resources, are of limited effectiveness in dealing with large-scale social problems in contemporary societies. To put this more positively, locally based programs and organizations can be linked to national efforts in such a way as "to enable them to contribute fully to national progress."[24] We noted in that discussion that the recent community action programs in the United States suffered from the lack of such a national policy framework and support.[25]

Some of the policy choices involved in national planning of social programs include the recurring issues of cash versus services; the use of governmental, non-profit, or market resources for the rendering of services; and what population group is to be reached. The planning process is essentially the same as that described in Chapter 9, with more emphasis given in this setting to legislation, administrative regulations, and budgetary planning.[26]

Interdepartmental and intersectoral planning at the national scale has given rise to many types of structures. There have been standing committees and commissions, formed either of professionals or representatives

---

[22] Martin Rein and S. M. Miller, "The Demonstration Project as a Strategy of Change," in Mayer N. Zald, Ed., *Organizing for Community Welfare*, Chicago: Quadrangle Books, 1967.

[23] See Chapter 6.

[24] *Report on Concepts and Principles of Community Development*, Annex 2, New York: United Nations, 1956.

[25] Louis A. Ferman, Ed., *op. cit.*

[26] Charles I. Schottland, "Administrative Decisions and Fund Allocation in Social Welfare," in Leonard H. Goodman, Ed., *Economic Progress and Social Welfare*, New York: Columbia University Press, 1966.

of interested groups and "the public," or both. There have been *ad hoc* groupings or task forces established for a specific purpose.[27] One of the professional's functions is to recommend and implement the form of organization most suited to the goals and strategies that are givens in a specific situation.

Social Indicators. A policy tool that may assume increased importance in national planning is found in "social indicators." There is growing interest in the development of these as quantitative measures of the "social health" of the nation, parallel to indicators of economic conditions. An expanding literature attests to the difficulties of developing such indicators, but reaffirms the desirability of pursuing the search.[28]

Two qualities of social indicators that make them attractive for planning purposes are that (1) they can measure accurately a problem or condition that is presumably amenable to intervention and (2) they can be used to isolate components of the problem so that interventions can be directed to the most appropriate targets. Furthermore, measurements can be taken at different times so that it becomes possible to assess whether a problem is growing or not.

A difficulty that is inherent in this enterprise is that of specifying the social values that are to be measured, in other words, what components constitute "the good life." It is probably more feasible to rely on a series of measurements extending over several dimensions or fields, on the assumption that there is some agreement as to the meaning and usefulness of a particular measure, than on a single measure of social progress. A report by a group working on this problem suggests these possibilities in a few fields:[29]

Health—healthy life is defined as life expectancy free of bed disability or institutionalization; also measures of use of preventive and curative medical care.

Social mobility—intergenerational differences in occupational status (related to education).

Physical environment—measures of air and water pollution; housing adequacy measured by structural soundness and degree of crowding.

---

[27] U.S. Department of Health, Education, and Welfare, *Services for People*, 1968.

[28] See, for example, Raymond E. Bauer, Ed., *Social Indicators*, Cambridge: The Massachusetts Institute of Technology Press, 1966; and E. B. Sheldon and W. E. Moore, Eds., *Indicators of Social Change: Concepts and Measurements*, New York: Russell Sage Foundation, 1968.

[29] U.S. Department of Health, Education, and Welfare, *Toward A Social Report*, Washington, D.C.: U.S. Government Printing Office, January 1969.

Income and poverty—measures of both absolute income and income distribution.

Public order and safety—measures volume of crime and victims of crimes by age, sex, race, and income.

Learning, science, and art—achievement test scores, amount of education, volume of activity, and resources expended on science and arts.

Participation and alienation—the report says that in regard to the functioning of social institutions, the authors can do little more than to ask the right questions. Measures are needed of intergroup tolerance, civil rights, family functioning, participation in neighborhood and community life, and the like.

Summarizing the state of affairs concerning the availability of the kind of information needed for decision-making, the report states:

"Only a small fraction of the existing statistics tell us anything about social conditions, and those that do often point in different directions. Sometimes they do not add up to any meaningful conclusion and thus are not very useful either to the policy-maker or the concerned citizen. The Government normally does not publish statistics on whether or not children are learning more than they used to, or on whether social mobility is increasing or decreasing. It does publish statistics on life expectancy and the incidence of disability due to ill health, but some diseases are becoming more common and others less common, and no summary measure indicating whether we could expect more healthy life has been available."[30]

One of the problems in constructing social indicators is the difficulty of finding a common measure that could unify the diverse components of social life into a meaningful aggregation. This is the function performed by monetary prices as the common measure for aggregating very diverse economic activities into national income and product accounts. A system of accounts requires both aggregation and disaggregation so that the sources of change or lack of change may be identified.

In the field of social indicators, aggregation can be achieved in specific and limited areas only, of which the above are illustrative. Further work is indicated, with complex problems to be solved in regard to the weighing of different social phenomena so that they can be compared (for example, the amount of crime in relation to the seriousness of each

[30] *Ibid.*, p. 95.

type; or the amount of voluntary activity in relation to degree of satisfaction obtained). Many of the crucial questions are quantifiable only as aggregations of people's judgments. Therefore, the use of diverse research approaches is necessary, including techniques such as survey research that will tap people's opinions and attitudes.

The other major problem is that the indicators, even if available, do not in themselves point to either the causes of the condition that they measure or to the results of efforts undertaken to correct undesirable conditions. The report concludes:

"Though an impressive set of social indicators could be developed at modest cost in the near-term future, a complete set of policy accounts is a utopian goal at present. This does not mean that work on a more integrative set of statistics should be postponed. These accounts will never be available unless we start thinking about the statistics we need for rational decision making now, even if this only entails marginal changes in the statistics we already have. . . . Only a systematic approach based on the informational requirements of public policy will do."[31]

Review and Appraisal. Looking back over this chapter and the one that precedes it, we have seen that a very limited definition of "comprehensive" planning calls for the coordination of agencies that may be serving similar groups and performing similar functions. The concept is broadened when attempts are made to bring together within one service field a variety of professional specializations and a battery of different kinds of services. Thus, in mental health, a wider range of treatment modalities within the community become substitutes and supplements for the treatment of acute conditions within the hospital.

Much more than this, however, is inherent in the idea of comprehensive planning. The essence of the argument for comprehensiveness is that it will lead to innovations making for greater effectiveness in dealing with social problems by enlarging the perspective and understanding of the problems. The drive toward comprehensiveness has come about because of evidence that the terms on which interventions have been undertaken by separate intervenors have not been adequate.

The additional benefits that are to be expected may take several forms. For one, bringing together a number of institutions with different responsibilities and perspectives should lead to the generation of additional data—or to the combination of existing data in new forms that can illuminate conditions being studied. A typical example is that

[31] *Ibid.,* p. 101.

the combination of records of a number of service agencies in a community makes it possible to determine the extent to which certain segments of the population use various services. If statistics on the use of services by individuals or families are kept separately, the only measure that can be used is the volume of services rendered rather than the number of families being served by two or more agencies.

To take the matter a step further, if comprehensive planning involves, as it should, the use of the entire population base as a framework for planning for special groups, then it becomes relevant to relate the records of specialized services to data concerning the entire population of an area. It then becomes possible to develop a data base for planning that is not limited, as so much of social welfare planning has been, to the users of particular services. The framework is broadened to embrace the potential needs within the total population.

Fundamentally, the rationale for comprehensive planning is that it extends the options and alternatives that are available in dealing with problems. If both physical and social planning are encompassed in a single process, it becomes possible to determine, presumably, what combinations of physical and social interventions are required to achieve the desired results. Again, the need to bring the two together has emerged because experience indicated that each proceeding separately was not achieving the desired goals. It is not yet clear, however, that merely bringing them together will necessarily solve this deficiency; but it does make it possible to experiment more broadly with interventions that use whatever may be beneficial in the interaction of the two elements.

Thus, it may be true, as some argue, that improvements in the physical environment can be effective only when accompanied by social measures—for example, to increase economic opportunities, to help people gain a sense of participation in their own affairs and power over their destiny, and consequently to develop self-esteem that will in turn help them to achieve more of the benefits that can be derived or wrested from the society. Having access to all of these modes of intervention is essential to testing out such suppositions.

But there have been difficulties in implementing this approach. Demonstration programs, which have characterized much of our experimentation in physical-social planning in this country, have not been given the time or the resources to test the combination of interventions, much less the wherewithal to evaluate the outcomes systematically. Equally significant is the difficulty of attaining meaningful changes in problems that are regional or national in scope by cranking in "social programs" that are limited to the neighborhood or county. Perhaps most important, as we saw in the case of urban renewal, is that basic decisions are often made about the use of resources for economic activity, housing, and transportation without really probing their social implications. The result is that the social component may then consist of "picking up the pieces" and cushioning the social fallout rather than playing a farsighted and preventive role in influencing decisions early in the process toward the accomplishment of what are fundamentally social ends.

The argument for comprehensiveness, to recapitulate, is that the total is greater than the sum of its parts and that coordinated planning can produce more effective results than are achieved by each component operating separately. If we are to look on comprehensiveness this way, then it must be said that it is less a "field" than an idea. The concepts are well established and have been espoused in many quarters for a long time. They are reflected widely in the rhetoric of governmental and voluntary programs in many fields. The major social programs of the 1960's were closely tied to these notions. Yet the reality, as we have seen, falls considerably short of the rhetoric. Comprehensiveness is being achieved primarily within service fields, while coordination of a relatively limited nature continues to dominate in the relationships between fields.

One of the reasons for this disappointing result is that the resources that have been made available for social programs, while considerable, are not yet adequate to a truly comprehensive approach. The theory has been that more coordinated approaches would increase the effectiveness of funds already being used so that their combined impact would be greater. The Model Cities programs are based on this assumption. By making funds available to support central planning staffs in the chosen cities, the administration hopes to provide the leverage that will make it possible for the much larger funds already coming into the community to yield more definitive results.

Experience indicates that central planning staffs are not very effective in changing the use of existing funds, since they do not control them. They can control only the limited additional resources—"the new money" —that are in their own hands. They therefore end up making marginal additions to existing patterns in magnitudes that are not adequate to effect any fundamental changes. The large magnitudes continue relatively untouched.

It is not clear, however, whether it is control or additional resources that are at the heart of the issue. If the central planners were to have control over *existing* resources, could they redirect them, through reexamination of priorities and reallocation of resources, so as to achieve better results—without additional resources? This is a difficult proposition to put to the test because of the tendency, within a given magnitude of resources, to cover the commitments already made. That tends to be true even when reorganization takes place. Organizations are notoriously resilient in their ability to maintain their domains and scope of operations despite changes in organizational structures.

It would seem that both resources and authority are necessary for more basic change to take place rather than marginal adjustments in boundary relationships among agencies. Additional resources without changes in the locus of planning tend to result simply in expanding existing ways of dealing with problems, that is, in "business as usual," and do not necessarily bring improvements.

But authority without resources can be equally frustrating. It seems reasonable to speculate that planners seeking a more comprehensive approach would be able to pursue their ends more forcefully if they could introduce much more substantial resources, both as carrot and stick. Without such basic resources as adequate income, job opportunities, and housing, any planner must be diffident as to what can be expected from new approaches, no matter how comprehensive. The additional resources would give a better basis for hope that the proposed solutions would be superior to those attempted in the past.

The location of power over resources is in continual flux, with tendencies toward both centralization and decentralization in this country and many others. There are pressures to give greater control to national governments in order to mount measures that are proportionate to the serious problems that are most often national in scope. But at the same time there is the pull of forces at work for decentralization. It is interesting in connection with central state planning in the socialist countries to note the experiments in decentralizing certain decision-making to regions, communities, and even individual factories. In the United Kingdom, plans are now under consideration both for creating larger regional planning areas and for giving more administrative control to local units of government that are smaller than the present ones.

The division of authority in this country between cities, counties, states, and the Federal government continues to change almost in see-saw fashion. The trend for many years seemed to be in the direction of a greater degree of centralization; recently there are indications of the delegation of control over certain matters downwards to regions, states, and localities. The current talk of "returning power to the people" obviously has different meanings to a conservative states-rights advocate and a black militant advocating community control of the school system.

The degree of comprehensiveness and centralization in planning raises issues of practicability and desirability, and both empirical and ideological factors are involved in making choices. The question can be posed both ways: is centralized power, in the sense of the ability to control substantial resources, more effective in coping with social needs than decentralized control? Is it compatible with democratic values? We do not pursue the issue in these terms in this book. We have made the observation repeatedly that there exists in the United States a pluralistic society in which competing claims are pitted against each other, so that the outcomes represent the results of these forces rather than the decisions of monolithic authority. In the search for more comprehensive interventions in social problems, planners will undoubtedly continue to find themselves steering an uncertain course between the need for greater control over resources and the centrifugal forces exerted by the countless groups that constitute our society.

CHAPTER 11

The Future of Practice

The causes and effects of human problems, we have seen, are entwined in a tangle of social, economic, and physical factors. As the recognition of this has grown, interventions tend more and more to cut across the traditional fields of activity and across the professions concerned with social problem-solving and development. These tendencies raise a number of questions, some of which were posed in the first chapter of this book.

Is a new discipline emerging from the developments we have been reviewing? If so, what defines this discipline? Is it a common base of methods and skills applicable to many fields and settings? Is it a body of knowledge about social forces and processes—the nature of organizations, the meaning of power, and the workings of the political process? Or is practice always closely related to a particular setting or problem, such as housing, mental health, and poverty, in which there are unique purposes, constraints, and resources that are the real determinants of practice? Or is a discipline evolving that must somehow encompass all these elements—a methodology, scientific understanding, and substantive knowledge?

Historically, planning and community organization originated in specific fields, most notably in social welfare and physical planning, and were directly tied to working on concrete problems. But within each field, specialization has produced generalist "planners." Speaking from his background in physical planning, Fagin sees this as a desirable shift

269

from the practitioner's primary concern with physical elements to expertise in planning as such.[1]

The planner of the future, in Fagin's view, will be one of many persons engaged in a collaborative process with specialists in specific functions as well as other specialists in planning. Fagin sees this as an extension of what had been true in the past since, he argues, the physical planner was never an expert in all aspects of physical development, but one of several specialists along with engineers, architects, and others. Nor was he necessarily the leader, anymore than he will be in the future working as a member of a team. He will merely contribute his "planning expertise."

Fagin distinguishes between the "profession" or practice of planning and the "discipline" or body of knowledge it utilizes. The roles he ascribes to the professional are analyst, synthesizer, collaborator, educator, mediator, advocate, and administrator. In regard to the discipline of the planner, he argues that he should understand the origins of the values held by various groups and the relationship between values and action.

In Fagin's view, the planner must be able to make the bridge from values to the design of options not only for the physical layout of a community but "for social and economic aspects of community change as well." This requires a comprehension of the larger societal context in which planning takes place and that provides both opportunities and constraints. This comprehension lays the basis for the planner's predictions. His creation of options leads to decisions, and decisions to action, although the discipline is concerned mostly with pre-action and post-action, that is, evaluation of performance against predictions.

There is sharp disagreement with Fagin's view of planning as a generic profession or discipline. Lewis challenges it as too sweeping a mandate and questions how such inclusive planning could operate in the real world and how anyone could be trained for it.[2] More fundamentally, considering the scope of the function Fagin describes, Lewis doubts whether there is "a profession" involved. As a solution, Lewis suggests renewed emphasis on "functional" rather than "comprehensive" planning, that is, planning within specific program areas such as recreation, welfare, or transportation. He proposes that within city government, for example, staff people should be experts in these fields, and their expertise as planners should be a secondary consideration.

---

[1] Henry Fagin, "Advancing the 'State of the Art'," in Ernest Erber, Ed., *op. cit.*, pp. 126–141.

[2] Peter A. Lewis, "The Uncertain Future of the Planning Profession," in Erber, *op. cit.*, pp. 142–146.

Instead of comprehensive planning in the sense of some supposedly scientific way of evaluating alternatives across specialized activities, Lewis suggests a "policy advisor" to the chief executive. His role would be to identify and quantify problems, to urge specialized planners to propose solutions, and to measure progress. This is more of a problem-based, present-time-oriented approach as against long-range planning based on systems analysis, for example. We have already noted the acceptance of this type of policy advisor in the planning offices of chief executives, ranging from the President to the mayors of many cities.

We have taken a stance in this book that recognizes the need for both Lewis' planner, who addresses immediate problems, and Fagin's expert in broad-gauge policy development. Roughly, these parallel the distinction we have made between practice in a service agency and practice in an organization set up for the purpose of planning. The necessity for solving the problems of operating agencies, that is, for improving the services they are responsible for providing, is no less important than generating long-range policies to meet emerging needs or, for that matter, undergirding voluntary associations with plans and proposals to further their objectives.

On the issue of specialization by field of activity, we see the importance of having planners who can grasp the connections between transportation and employment opportunities, between income and health, and between housing conditions and the needs of the elderly. The indivisibility and complexity of human problems, as was demonstrated in the previous chapter, require that at least some planners be equipped to function in this way, although there will still be a need for specialized planners both as advocates of groups and as program developers in service agencies.

But we would argue that there are commonalities in terms of both ends and means that link practitioners in these various contexts. These common features provide the groundwork for a new discipline. Despite the fact that neither the "field" nor the "practice" of this discipline is yet well defined, there seems to be a convergence from many diverse orientations around certain common problems to be solved and tasks to be performed. Without minimizing the diversity, we shall attempt in these concluding pages to recapitulate some common themes and shall look to them for indications of future directions in this field.

The activities touched on in this book, however much they may differ in specifics, are expressions of a broad value commitment to solve problems of inequality and social and cultural deprivation. The insistence that these are social responsibilities and demand social action is a moral judgment, but advances in knowledge in the social sciences have strengthened the position that these scourges of mankind are *social* rather than *individual* problems. Notwithstanding the commitment to social change and the contributions of the social sciences, the most basic observation that emerges from our review is the failure thus far of the measures adopted to overcome serious human problems in all countries. We have noted several universal limitations.

First, the lack of broad national social policies backed up by sufficient resources is characteristic of interventions both in the United States and in many recently independent nations. Inadequacies in the provision of income and the failure to achieve full employment, among other shortcomings, have led to anomalies in programs charged with eliminating poverty. No small part of the confusion of goals in community organization and planning projects stems from the false notion that limited, locally-based activities can take the place of adequate income, jobs, and housing. On the one hand the revolt against the social services is due at least in part to the mistaken attempt to use services in place of basic resources. On the other hand, the deficits in community development programs are often attributable to the expectation that self-help and "participation" can substitute for basic social provisions.

Secondly, the commitment to social change does not in itself specify the means or the mechanisms for achieving it. Nor does it automatically point out the targets to which change efforts should be directed. Here again we have found that ideological considerations enter, since the choice of strategies is often as much a matter of value judgments as is the selection of goals. For the most part, the practice of community organization and social planning is rooted in the tradition of social reform. This means seeking change through a combination of voluntary and governmental action within the democratic political process. The products of these efforts during the past century are to be found in the economic policies and social benefits and services of the modern welfare state.

Today's travail in this country stems in part from the difficulties of making the mechanisms of the welfare state work effectively. But our high level of social conflict also represents a challenge to the adequacy of "reform" as a strategy for social change. We have therefore included in our review some elements of a more radical approach. There is no basis for drawing sharp boundary lines between reformist and radical approaches to practice, except on ideological grounds.

We must note, however, that there is often a disparity between the goals of radical social action and its accomplishments. There are many instances of specific actions that have achieved concrete, although limited, results. But there are few indications of how such results can be institutionalized and transformed into a basically different distribution of power or resources. This observation does not imply that reformist efforts have been singularly effective. While organizations operating in the reform tradition have achieved some changes, their accomplishments have also been limited by the scope of the resources available to them and the restricted power they have been able to mobilize.

The limited achievements of both radical and reformist strategies lead us to re-examine the goals that have been set. For the most part, these have been broad *desiderata* based largely on ideological convictions and hopes—the rapid elimination of poverty, the development of satisfying communities, and the building of healthy relationships among groups. One reason for the lack of success is apparent: these goals are so vast and ill-defined that it would be difficult to measure success. But to the extent that there are operational definitions of such goals, it is extremely doubtful that we now have at hand the knowledge or technology for their realization.

What is equally significant is the fact that the means for achieving social-change objectives, even limited and reachable ones, have often been specified according to ideological positions. Thus, the "proper" methods have been tied to such values as self-determination, local control, or "rational" decision-making by experts. One or another strategy—confrontation, negotiation, advocacy, self-help, action-research and the like—has been advanced, apparently with the expectation that, regardless of the specific objective and the surrounding circumstances, the preferred approach is most desirable and will be most effective.

It is now important, in our view, to separate value issues from instrumental questions if progress is to be made in developing a more effective practice. This is not to deny the central place that values occupy in the setting of goals for social change. Indeed, conflicts over values will always be an integral part of a practice that is committed to social change. But these value commitments will continue to be frustrating unless operational goals and strategies can be brought into realistic alignment. In other words, effectiveness in achieving objectives must become the object of analysis and research, rather than a matter of faith and conviction.

In fact, as of this writing, the state of the art in community organization and social planning—or whatever this emerging practice will be called—is primitive. As this book amply demonstrates, the field is barely emerging from a time of cataloging bits and pieces of practice. It has distilled little practice wisdom and has barely begun to develop theory.

On the optimistic side we must note that more researchers, teachers, and practitioners are taking up the challenge of building knowledge that will make practice more effective. They are doing this in ways that are characteristic of knowledge-building, by describing practice more carefully and by differentiating practice in accordance with theoretical constructs and/or observed differences. This book is part of this effort at description and analysis.

We have attempted in the preceding chapters to describe a field of practice with the focus on the practitioner in various organizational situations. We have placed great stress on the organizational context as the major determinant of the characteristics of practice. The perspective of this book has been that of the practitioner within an organization, engaging in organizing and planning activities that are directed toward the improvement of human services and the amelioration of social problems.

Practice activities are carried out through a complex set of interactions in which the practitioner engages with other actors within the organization that provides the context for his work, as well as with other actors in the environment of that organization. Since these actors represent a variety of interests, values, and objectives, much of the practice of community organization and social planning necessarily deals with the management, in some fashion, of interpersonal, intra-organizational, and inter-organizational relationships, as well as with the processing and interpretation of information.

Attempts to conceptualize this practice are beset, as we have seen, with semantic, ideological, and technical difficulties. One of the greatest problems has been the difficulty of separating the three elements which enter into practice: (a) the value premises and choices that are fundamental to the actions being taken or not taken; (b) the technical knowledge on which action can or should be based; and (c) the patterns of influence that affect decision-making. While these elements are somewhat separable logically, they are closely interrelated in the actual arenas where efforts are being made to change organizational behavior, to improve human services, and to deal with social problems. In moving from the present unsystematic body of knowledge that is available to the practitioner toward something comparable to a "science" of intervention, it will be necessary to deal with these interrelationships.

That is not to say, however, that every practitioner needs to be or can be concerned with every aspect of the total scope of practice. On the contrary, we have indicated in this volume the wide spread of practice in many different substantive fields, community and organizational contexts, and programs based on widely differing value premises. While we have argued that "analytical" and "interactional" tasks are always present, their relative weights vary with the organizational context and with the nature of the action being undertaken and may change at different phases of the action.

We have argued that despite these variations there is an underlying coherence to practice based on some combination of knowledge, skill, and purpose. But would it foster the development of practice if its scope were narrowed? A case can be made that community organization and social planning would more usefully be conceptualized as two fields: one concerned with organizing voluntary groups, usually at the grassroots level, and the other concerned with policy planning and program development. In part this is a matter of scale. A serious differentiation can be made between practice at the micro level of face-to-face activities involving participants and the professional as against practice at the macro level, where the policy planner is involved in larger, more impersonal functions touching on broad economic and social forces.

Another distinction, along ideological lines, has been suggested by those who look on the advocacy role with disadvantaged groups as fundamentally different in content and method from serving as a bureaucrat in an established agency. These proponents insist, for example, that preparing people for the bureaucratic role means a trained incapacity to raise fundamental questions about existing social conditions or to attack them vigorously. Those who support advocacy as the primary function of the practitioner do not always make clear whether his contribution and expertness rest on his choice of the purposes to be pursued or whether his competence consists of his ability to help a group implement the goals *they* have chosen.

Perhaps specializations such as these will and should develop. But a strong case can also be made that, however crude our knowledge and techniques are at the moment, the problems and tasks are similar across many settings and kinds of organizations. The critical issue is *the search for greater effectiveness in coping with social problems.* This quest leads in two directions—broadening the scope of interventions in order to have significant impact and developing a more sophisticated practice based on more precise techniques of intervention.

The first of these is now being widely recognized, and the recent attempts at more comprehensive planning, which we saw in the preceding chapter, attest to the serious search for interventions that match the broad scope of most social problems. The second, moving toward more useful practice techniques, requires the knowledge-building to which we referred earlier.

In part, practitioners in this field must look to the social scientists to expose the causes of social conditions that are considered, on a value-basis, undesirable and therefore targets for change. The practitioner may contribute to the understanding of the etiology of these problems out of his own experience, however, and might well bear in mind the point quoted in the previous chapter. Gillie suggested there that the analyst of a social problem should first try to understand it as a solution to other problems. With some knowledge of individual, organizational, and institutional behavior as a background, the practitioner is often in a position to discover the processes that generate problems and the reasons for their persistence. For the most part, however, practitioners must depend on the rapidly growing body of research into social problems to inform their work.

The improvement of methods of intervention will not be achieved with great speed. There is not available, as our review has demonstrated repeatedly, either a grand unified theory on which practice can base itself or a systematic body of knowledge that can tell practitioners what methods are more or less effective. The newer technologies, which promise much in the way of systematic data processing, quantification, and measurability, have yet to demonstrate their usefulness in making manageable the complex interactions that characterize the processes of organization and planning.

The road toward progress would seem to lie, in the immediate future, primarily in relatively modest, limited, well-controlled and well-thought-out studies that attempt to determine the specific relationships between problems and methods of intervention. It is hoped that the framework of organizational contexts and problems that has been developed in this volume can make a contribution to the formulation of investigations that will test out the efficacy of different components of practice. As the volume of such studies increases, the observations that have been made in this book and in other discussions of community organization and social planning can be transformed into sets of principles and methods that will come closer to defining the discipline that is struggling to emerge in the human services fields.

It is difficult to make peace with the slow pace of knowledge-building in the face of the agonizing social problems of our times. The sense of urgency about those problems, which gives the practitioner his underlying motivation and moral justification, makes him properly impatient with his inability to provide useful answers. Here, too, there is need for modesty. The solutions to social problems are not the exclusive domain of the practitioner. They are the concern and the responsibility of all of the participants in the society, contending with one another on the basis of their needs, interests, convictions, and ideologies, and their views of what the problems are, how they are to be overcome, and how the society is to be improved. They cannot wait for the practitioner to supply them with tidy answers, nor should the practitioner presume to replace these political processes with technical answers. He is a participant in these grand processes and can make a useful contribution to them to the extent that he can improve his knowledge and his craft. In the long run this is the only way in which practitioners in community organization and social planning can contribute to the larger goals of social justice and individual fulfillment.

Appendix

Below are the contents of the companion volume, *Community Organizers and Social Planners: A Casebook,* by Joan Levin Ecklein and Armand Lauffer. An asterisk indicates material from which we have quoted. The page numbers indicate pages of the present volume on which the material is mentioned.
